THE FUTURES OF FEMINISM

MANCHESTER
1824

Manchester University Press

The futures of feminism

Valerie Bryson

Manchester University Press

Copyright © Valerie Bryson 2021

The right of Valerie Bryson to be identified as the author of this work has been asserted by them in accordance with the Copyright, Designs and Patents Act 1988.

Published by Manchester University Press
Altrincham Street, Manchester M1 7JA

www.manchesteruniversitypress.co.uk

British Library Cataloguing-in-Publication Data
A catalogue record for this book is available from the British Library

ISBN 978 1 5261 5375 3 hardback
ISBN 978 1 5261 3851 4 paperback

First published 2021

The publisher has no responsibility for the persistence or accuracy of URLs for any external or third-party internet websites referred to in this book, and does not guarantee that any content on such websites is, or will remain, accurate or appropriate.

Typeset by
Servis Filmsetting Ltd, Stockport, Cheshire

To Sofia, Samuel, Benjamin and Joshua – with hope for the future

Contents

Acknowledgements

THANK YOU TO Emma Brennan at Manchester University Press for suggesting that I might have another book in me (although at times I have been cursing her); to Tony Mason, then also at MUP, for his positive response to my initial proposal; and to the rest of the MUP editorial team. Special thanks to the copy-editor, John Banks, for his thoughtful and thought-provoking suggestions. I would also like to thank the reviewers of this book for their constructive and encouraging comments on my proposal and the first draft of the book.

As always, my friends have provided invaluable support. Particular thanks to Penny Noel for providing me with information, ideas and stimulating discussion, particularly on trans issues, and for providing feedback on two draft chapters (although we agree to differ on some points).

Enormous thanks to my daughter, Lucy Bryson, for her intelligent and constructive commentary on various drafts, as well as for proof-reading and preparing the index.

And thank you, Alan Pearson, for helpful feedback on the first draft as well as for everything else.

Introduction

I WAS PARTLY inspired (or, more accurately, provoked) to write this book by Theresa May, the first prime minister of the UK to identify publicly as a feminist. Thinking about this apparent success story for feminism left me angry and dismayed. Angry that the description had been appropriated by someone whose party's policies have done so much damage to so many women. And dismayed that once again feminism was being reduced to its narrowest, tamest, most establishment-friendly version: a version that too often prioritises the needs of the most privileged women and promotes a simplistic version of gender equality that ignores its broader context and risks bringing feminism as a whole into disrepute. Yes, such feminism may endorse campaigns against sexual harassment, domestic violence or online misogyny, and it supports greater political and workplace equality; it may even call for men to play a greater role in family life. However, it readily steps back if campaigners seem in danger of going 'too far', and it fails to make connections between these issues, let alone directing resources to their solution. All too often, it acts as a safety valve rather than a route to meaningful change.

May will now probably be remembered as the prime minister who failed to deliver Brexit, not for her claim to be a feminist. However, the taming of feminism seemed to be confirmed in 2019, when all but one of the six candidates (all male) to replace her as leader of the Conservative Party, including Boris Johnson, declared that they, too, were feminists (Mason, 2019).

Despite these introductory comments, my intention in this book is not to attack those with whom I disagree or to try to establish some form of 'true' or 'real' feminism. Such an intention would be pointless, for feminism has never been a united movement or body of thought; indeed it has always been fiercely argumentative, often self-contradictory and riven by both ideological and personal conflicts (a bit like men's politics, perhaps, but with much less bloodshed). Instead, my aim is to step back and see contemporary issues in a wider perspective, drawing on the long heritage of feminist ideas and political engagement to recover understandings that have been lost; I also hope to move debates forward by identifying points of agreement as well as dispute, and showing the logical implications of particular feminist positions.

This task has become especially urgent, given the increasingly virulent nature of some public feminist disagreements, which are exaggerated and encouraged by both mainstream and social media. Disputes are often also presented as if they reflect the conflicting claims, needs and perspectives of different groups of women, setting old against young, black against white, rich against poor, and trans women against cis women (the term 'cis women', discussed in Chapter 4, refers to women who were legally registered as female at birth). Such simplistic classifications ignore commonalities, complexities and cross-cutting identities, and they shut down attempts at dialogue and reconciliation. In contrast, I hope to disentangle genuine, deep-seated disagreements and/or conflicts of interest from questions of priority or style, to look beyond easy certainties, soundbites and rallying cries, and to identify sources of unity rather than division (in this spirit, I concede that I do not oppose *everything* that Theresa May has said or done). I am not saying that feminists should never be angry (indeed they should, for there is much in the world to be angry about), but that anger should be constructive rather than destructive, and that it should not be diverted onto easy targets or allowed to degenerate into the kind of abuse that, far from winning arguments or support, deters potential allies. What we need is not some ideologically pure feminism, but a feminism that is open, generous and inclusive.

As a feminist, I would like there to be no need for feminism, for feminism is premised on the ongoing existence of patterns of exploitation, inequality, injustice or oppression that particularly harm women but also damage society as a whole. In this Introduction, I set the scene for later discussion by providing a brief, generalised overview of these patterns, before introducing the different feminist perspectives that underpin competing claims about how we can understand our world and develop effective strategies for change. I then outline some of the ways that feminist activism has developed in the twenty-first century. These sections are necessarily largely descriptive, but I conclude by identifying my key arguments through an overview of the book's themes.

Our gendered world

The focus of this book is on the UK and other western democracies. This limited scope reflects my own areas of competence, and I am in no way implying that western countries are somehow more important than the rest of the world. At the same time, western experiences need to be understood in their wider context. This section therefore begins with a brief overview of well documented global inequalities; here it is important to note that these statistics cannot capture either the less tangible and measurable aspects of our gendered world or the complicated ways in which gender interacts with other structural inequalities; they also obscure the experiences of trans people. At this stage, I am provisionally using the term 'gender' to discuss differences between 'women' and 'men'. However, these terms are all contested, and I will discuss them in Chapters 1 and 4.

The global picture

If an alien were to land on Earth, it would probably notice two basic patterns in all human societies: women and men usually play different roles, and the roles associated with men are generally better rewarded. It might well sum up these differences in terms of two rough rules: the more powerful, highly paid and prestigious a position or occupation, the more likely it is to be held by a man, while the lower its status and the greater its association with poverty, the greater the concentration of women. In observing these general patterns, the visiting alien might puzzle as to why financial speculation and the production of material and cultural goods are treated as so much more important than giving birth and nurturing the next generation. It would probably also observe that all forms of violence, from domestic abuse through online intimidation and gang fighting to organised warfare, are disproportionately employed by men, that women are often its target and that many women are denied the right to decide who can have sexual access to their bodies and whether they should bear children. If the alien were on a return visit, it would find that some of these patterns have been modified, in some parts of the world, for some groups of women, but that any changes have been decidedly erratic and uneven, and that the gains of some women often involve the exploitation of others.

Until quite recently, these features of human societies went largely unremarked by (male-dominated) official bodies. However, they have become increasingly recognised and documented, with a wide range of international and national organisations tracking ongoing patterns and providing a basis for comparisons. This monitoring is bound up with an official assumption that greater gender equality is desirable, that discrimination on the grounds of gender is wrong and that women should be able to act independently, make their own reproductive and sexual decisions and compete with men on a level playing field. This marks a major, global shift in dominant assumptions since the mid-twentieth century, and in some ways it is a sign of progress and feminist success. However, it treats women as an undifferentiated group, ignoring the vast socio-economic, political and cultural differences that often divide them. It also reflects a belief that women represent an untapped resource that can be used to produce economic growth and development, and it represents a narrow form of feminism that does not question the exploitative logic of the underlying economic system or the sexual division of labour.

With these caveats in mind, the patterns are clear. Since 2006, the World Economic Forum (WEF) has tracked gender-based inequalities around the world in relation to 'economic participation and opportunity', education, health and politics, and found that these have all been gradually reducing. However, the rate of change is uneven and increasingly slow: at the end of 2019 it reported that if current trends continued it would take, on average, nearly a hundred years to close the overall global gender gap, and 257 years to close the gap in 'economic participation and opportunity' (World Economic Forum, 2019:6). In 2020, ongoing inequalities in all these four areas meant that the impact of the COVID-19 pandemic was highly gendered, with policy decisions in most countries made largely by men, and the specific needs of women often overlooked.

The most significant progress has been made in education, although the gap remains high in some developing countries, and women are generally less likely than men to have the skills needed for professional success. Many countries actively encourage women into the paid workforce, and many support them through maternity or family leave provision and by state-subsidised or state-provided childcare. Despite this, women throughout the world remain less likely than men to be in paid work, to work in well paid sectors of the economy or to be in senior positions. It is therefore unsurprising that women's average earnings in all countries are significantly lower than men's and that women everywhere are more likely than men to live in poverty. In many countries, women have also been disproportionately affected by the austerity policies that have been adopted in response to global financial crises, with the poorest women suffering most. Further economic problems are faced by those women who are international migrants or refugees (nearly fifty per cent of international migrants and about half of all refugees are women: UN Women, 2018).

The lack of women in top jobs extends to their under-representation in the management of large multinational corporations and in the most powerful international political and financial organisations (the appointments of Christine Lagarde and then Kristalina Georgieva as Managing Director of the International Monetary Fund in 2011 and 2019 are notable exceptions). Major gaps in positions of political power remain, particularly at the highest levels; women are also under-represented at senior levels in the judiciary, the executive branch of government and the news media.

Meanwhile, we are seeing what António Guterres, Secretary General of the United Nations, describes as a 'global pandemic' of violence against women (UN News, 2018), and in 2017 the World Health Organization reported that around one in three women in the world experience physical and/or sexual violence at some time in their life, often from an intimate partner. By April 2020 this figure had risen sharply as a result of the COVID-19 lockdowns, and Guterres called on governments around the world to make addressing the problem a key part of their response to the crisis (Neuman, 2020). As new forms of religious and ethnic conflict have emerged or got worse, women and children are often deliberately targeted, and sexual violence has become an increasingly visible weapon of war. Violence can also take the form of female genital mutilation and the trafficking of women into the sex industry, while developments in digital technology are enabling new forms of global pornography and new ways of controlling intimate partners.

Women's reproductive choices are often restricted or under threat. Many women have no access to contraception or abortion, many others are on the receiving end of population control policies that have a decidedly 'coercive edge' (Watkins, 2018:52), and around 830 women and adolescent girls die every day from preventable causes related to pregnancy and childbirth (UN Population Fund, 2018).

Changes have been highly variable and uneven both between and within countries and, in general, the most privileged groups of white, western women have gained the most. The WEF's annual reports rank countries according to how gender equal or unequal they are. At the end of 2019, it found that Iceland, Norway, Finland and Sweden were the most equal countries and Syria, Pakistan, Iraq and Yemen were the most unequal out of the 153 countries for which it had adequate data. Perhaps more surprisingly, Nicaragua and Rwanda were in fifth and ninth place respectively, well ahead of the UK, which came at twenty-first, and the US at fifty-third. These results reflect the relatively low number of women in the US Congress, which at just under 25 per cent overall compared badly with the 61 per cent of female parliamentarians in Rwanda (the highest in the world) and nearly 46 per cent in Nicaragua. While these figures remind us that western countries do not necessarily lead the way in progress, it is also important to note that greater gender equality in poorer countries may mean only equality in deprivation, and that parliamentary representation does not necessarily translate into meaningful political power.

Developments in the UK

In relation to other western nations, the UK is often seen as a hybrid or mid-way point between Scandinavian social democracy and American liberalism or neo-liberalism in terms of its economic system, welfare provision and political culture (for the classic statement of this view, see Esping-Anderson, 1990). As the WEF's ranking indicates, the UK also occupies an intermediate position among western nations in terms of measurable progress towards gender equality. This makes it a useful starting-point for discussing western feminism, and it is the focus for much discussion in this book.

The last half century has seen enormous changes in the legal and political situation of women in the UK. In 1970, average hourly wages for full-time women workers were at least a third lower than for men, with the gap rising to nearly fifty per cent for women working part-time. Before 1975 it was perfectly legal to pay a woman less than a man doing exactly the same work as a man, or to refuse to employ a woman simply because she was a woman. It was also legal to sack a woman if she became pregnant; if she were allowed to continue at work she had no legal entitlement to maternity leave; and it was up to her to sort out and pay for her own childcare arrangements. Rape in marriage was not recognised as a crime in England and Wales until 1991. When Margaret Thatcher became Prime Minister in 1979, 97 per cent of MPs were men. And the idea that one woman could marry another or that people could change their legal gender identity was not on the mainstream political agenda until late in the twentieth century.

The most blatant forms of discrimination and inequality are now generally a thing of the past. However, obvious and measurable inequalities and problems remain, including the gender gap in employment opportunities and pay, and widespread sexual violence.

In 2019, the Office for National Statistics (ONS) found that, for full-time workers, the average gap between the hourly pay of women and men was slightly under 9 per cent, and for those aged under forty it was approaching zero. However, largely because of their family responsibilities, women were more likely to be in part-time employment, where pay and conditions are generally worse; this produced an overall gender gap of more than 17 per cent in average hourly pay. Women are also less likely to work overtime, and their employment is concentrated in low-paying sectors, especially health, social care and leisure (ONS, 2019). These patterns meant that from early 2020, when the COVID-19 crisis took hold in the UK, women were particularly likely to experience acute economic hardship and to be working in jobs that put them at high risk of catching the virus (Women's Budget Group, 2020a; 2020b; Booth, 2020).

Since 2018, it has been possible to see what is happening to the gender pay gap within large organisations, which are now legally required to submit annual figures. Although published figures have shown women earning almost as much or even more than men in a few organisations, 80 per cent of large companies and public sector organisations pay men more than women, with a gap of over forty per cent in some cases (Topping, 2018). This generally reflects the lack of women in well paid senior positions and their over-representation at lower levels, and much attention has focused on the so-called 'glass ceiling': the invisible barrier compounded of discrimination, old-fashioned sexism and unthinkingly male-centred assumptions around 'merit' that seems to stop so many women from reaching the very top of their career ladder. Even those women who reach high positions may face unequal treatment, and TUC research has found that the gender pay gap is highest amongst the very well paid, reaching 54.9 per cent amongst the top 2 per cent of earners (TUC, 2015).

Meanwhile, the economic situation of women who are badly paid or not in paid employment has become increasingly dire, and 'while a small number of extremely privileged women worry about the glass ceiling, the cellar is filling up with water' (Penny, 2014:6). Since 2010, when a

Conservative-led coalition headed by David Cameron took office, inequality between rich and poor has increased, accompanied by a steep rise in poverty. This poverty is concentrated amongst women and their children, who have borne the brunt of austerity measures and regressive changes to the tax and benefits system: figures from the House of Commons library show that, by 2020, over eighty per cent of the cumulative negative impact of tax changes and cuts in social security spending will have fallen on women, who have also been disproportionately affected by cuts to public services and the introduction of Universal Credit. The increase in poverty includes many women in employment; it is particularly acute amongst black and minority ethnic women (Women's Budget Group, 2016; Women's Budget Group and the Runnymede Trust, 2017). Again, these patterns meant that the COVID-19 crisis had a disproportionately damaging economic effect on the poorest women (Women's Budget Group, 2020).

In theory, women in the UK have legal protection against domestic and/or sexual violence. In practice, violence against women remains endemic. On average, two women a week are killed by their partner or ex-partner. Using figures for England and Wales, an estimated 1.3 million women experienced some form of domestic abuse in the year ending March 2018, one in five women over the age of 16 has at some time been sexually assaulted, and 26 per cent of women have experienced some form of domestic abuse. The vast majority of sexual offences are not reported to the police. Of the rapes reported to the police, fewer than 4 per cent result in a conviction. Surveys consistently suggest that sexual harassment in the workplace has been experienced by at least forty per cent of women, and there is evidence that harassment and violence against girls are widespread in schools (TUC, 2016; Women and Equalities Select Committee, 2016; ONS, 2018a, 2018b). Since 2012, Laura Bates's online 'Everyday Sexism' project has documented the constant barrage of unpleasant incidents and remarks experienced by many women that can appear trivial in isolation, but which build up into a generally threatening environment (https://everydaysexism.com; Bates, 2014). Politicians and authorities routinely condemn all forms of violence against women; however, the resources that might help address it have not been forthcoming; indeed in many cases they have been reduced, often because central government funding to local authorities has been drastically cut since 2010. For many women, the situation became dramatically worse in the spring of 2020, when the lockdown imposed by the government to combat the COVID-19 virus meant that they were effectively incarcerated with their abusers. Although Priti Patel, the Home Secretary, said that women could leave home to escape their abusers or seek help (Oppenheim, 2020), support services were already overstretched and many women were already being turned away from refuges (Reis, 2018): help was simply not there on the scale required.

Meanwhile, the internet makes it easier than ever before to access pornography, including very violent and disturbing material; even mild forms of online pornography generally show women in subordinate roles and it is, increasingly, the primary source of sex education for many children (Laws, 2013). New forms of extreme abuse and intimidation are now widespread across social media, with threats of rape or murder used as a way of deterring women from speaking out in public; digital technology is also facilitating increased 'surveillance abuse', whereby men can watch and control every move their partner makes (Krotoski, 2020).

Underlying problems

The evidence I have provided in this section is intended only as an indicative overview of the more measurable aspects of our gendered world, and it is important to remember that women are not a uniform group, that their experiences and interests are not only highly diverse but also at times conflicting, and that they may sometimes have more in common with men in their own community, group or society than with other women. Other critically important but less tangible issues also lurk below the surface of official reports. In particular, the newly dominant global agreement that women should be able to compete equally with men forgets that equality is being granted on terms that men have already set; these terms simply assume that the rewards attracted to male patterns of behaviour are justified. From this perspective, women's entry into the paid workforce is seen as a sign of progress that will benefit both individual women and the economy as a whole, but the ways in which the gains of some women involve the direct and/or indirect exploitation of others are ignored, along with the big questions of who will do domestic and caring work if women are no longer available and why this work is so undervalued. These questions became particularly acute in 2020, as the global pandemic revealed the strategic social and economic importance of badly paid, often migrant, health and social care workers who were magically transformed into valuable (but still badly rewarded) 'key workers' (Norman, 2020).

A more radical approach would extend the idea of 'progress' to include recognising and rewarding the qualities and roles traditionally associated with women. It would also challenge the underlying logic of a competitive and highly unequal system in which only a few people, men or women, can win. These are complex issues, which I will discuss throughout the book.

Theories, politics, themes and chapters

There are no easy or definitive answers to why women throughout the world continue to face discrimination and ill-treatment and what, if anything, we can do about it. However, good feminist theory can shed some light by joining the dots to make sense of wider patterns, identifying potential causal relationships and helping to develop effective political strategies. Good theory should also help us to think more clearly about our own ideas, and to recognise and address inconsistencies in our thinking. And it can help unpack arguments amongst feminists, disentangling transitory issues, differences in emphasis and clashes of style or personality from more fundamental disagreements. Such theory is inevitably sometimes difficult, but it should not be needlessly so. Its aim should be not to create a cosy club of people who have mastered philosophical jargon but to help us understand our world in the hope of changing it for the better.

A brief outline of competing feminist theories

Feminist theory has a long history in the west. This history is not one of steady progress and cumulative insights, for feminist ideas are rooted in a range of competing and sometimes conflicting ideological traditions, while women have always struggled to get their voices heard and their writing published. Even when they have been successful in their lifetime, women have often been written out of the history books and their work largely forgotten, leaving successive generations to start from scratch rather than learning from their feminist foremothers. This is particularly true of working-class women and women of colour, whose history of ideas and activism has often been sidelined in favour of more educated, middle-class white women, who have found it easier to get a public voice. The chronological account that I provide here and in the opening chapters traces developments in the historically dominant forms of white feminist theory, before turning to the development of the black feminist theory that has become central to feminist analysis today. I draw on these ideas throughout this book to help cast light on contemporary issues and debates (I provide a much more detailed discussion of feminist theories and their history in Bryson, 2016).

Much public discussion of inequalities between the sexes remains framed by the liberal language of equal rights that developed in Europe from the seventeenth and eighteenth centuries. Early feminist writers, such as Mary Wollstonecraft, insisted that women were as capable of rational thought as men, and that they should therefore have the same rights. This argument provided the basis for campaigns for women's right to education, employment, property ownership and the vote. During the twentieth century, campaigns were extended to claim equal treatment in the workplace and to bodily integrity. Once radical and fiercely opposed, these ideas have become widely accepted as 'common sense': you no longer need to label yourself a feminist to say that women should be able to vote or go to university, or that they should be paid the same as men if they do the same work, or that they have a right to refuse sex.

Liberal, equal-rights feminism has clearly provided an effective force for progressive change. Today, it sends a message to women and girls that they should cast off outdated expectations around female submissiveness or appropriate career choice and simply 'go for it', and that they should complain – loudly – if their views are dismissed or men behave inappropriately towards them. Such a sense of entitlement can be highly empowering. At the same time, this kind of feminism is in many respects profoundly inadequate as a way of improving the lives of most women in the world. It tends to stress women's rights as individuals within existing societies, rather than asking society as a whole to change. It wants women to be able to compete on an equal basis with men, but it does not question either the man-made rules that regulate competition or the highly unequal distribution of rewards in a system in which most people can only be losers. It is often elite-oriented, treating the concerns of the most privileged women as central issues: for example, it seems to be more interested in the sexual harassment of Hollywood stars or the lower bonuses awarded to very well paid women than in the sexual and economic exploitation of those who are most vulnerable. And it is bound up with liberal and neoliberal economic theories that, as I hope to show in later chapters, are unable to see women's needs and contributions or to allow for the kind of state intervention that is needed to mitigate inequalities and ensure general social welfare.

Although liberal and neoliberal theories reflect the particular perspectives of privileged men, they are presented as if they were universal truths, and they are so dominant that it is difficult for anyone, including feminist women, to avoid getting sucked into terms of debate that they would not otherwise choose. Identifying and challenging such partiality is important, and for many feminists it requires a shift to more women-centred thinking, as advocated by the so-called 'radical feminism' that developed from the 1970s. Some of radical feminism's ideas may now seem dated, simplistic or rooted in white, middle-class privilege. However, its central arguments – that men should not be treated as the automatic standard against which all people are measured, and that gendered power relations extend beyond the public worlds of politics and employment and into the private domain of the family and personal relationships – provide systematically articulated insights that earlier feminists had generally been aware of only patchily. Such feminism also introduced the key concept of 'patriarchy' (discussed in Chapter 2) into feminist vocabulary.

Many feminists have also drawn on socialist ideas to argue that equality within highly unequal societies is of little relevance to most women, and that meaningful change requires a fundamental shift from a society based on individualism, exploitation and the pursuit of profit to one in which both work and rewards are much more equally shared. This critique shifts the focus of analysis from the behaviour and ambitions of individual women towards more inclusive thinking that acknowledges the needs of other people and of society as a whole. It also refocuses the ideas of socialist men, who have tended to treat 'women's issues' as something that can be properly addressed only after more 'important' problems have been resolved. I further argue in later chapters that, while Karl Marx was certainly not a feminist, his methods can help analyse the interconnections between capitalism and patriarchy.

Feminist ideas have always spilled over national boundaries: even in medieval times there were European-wide debates around the status and situation of women, and by the time of the American and French revolutions in the late eighteenth century there was an intercontinental exchange of ideas. During the nineteenth century, some African American women were developing their own perspective, and some working-class women, black and white, were gradually able to gain a voice through socialist parties or trade unions. However, the most widely heard feminist views in the west have always been those of educated white women who have at times expressed direct class and race prejudice and, more often, simply assumed the centrality and universality of their own, particularly situated, interests and needs. When such feminism has addressed the situation of women in non-western societies, it has tended to assume that they are victims of 'backward' or even 'barbaric' cultures from which western feminists can rescue them.

Since the late twentieth century, such assumptions have been systematically challenged by black and postcolonial feminist writers, who have exposed the unreflective and ignorant arrogance of much white feminism, and its failure to understand that many women are exploited by their more privileged 'sisters'. Although public debates around feminist issues often continue to prioritise the views of the most privileged women, there has been some shift towards more inclusive debate and a sense that the west has no monopoly on 'progressive' ideas. In particular, the black feminist concept of 'intersectionality' (the focus of Chapter 3), which highlights the extent to which people are differently privileged or oppressed on multiple dimensions of structural inequality, has become increasingly central to much white feminist analysis. My arguments in later chapters are underpinned by an intersectional approach.

Black feminist perspectives were largely derived from women's own experiences. However, their theoretical articulation has sometimes drawn on post-structuralist and postmodernist ideas about the provisional and situated nature of ostensibly objective knowledge and the malleable and fluid nature of any identity, including gender identity. This perspective rejects both the view that we can generalise about 'women' and 'men' and the binary either/or thinking that underpins such generalisation and that is built into modern western thought. Postmodernism also addresses the ways in which meaning and identity are created and linked to power, and suggests ways in which dominant understandings can be contested. While this may sound very abstract, the impact of postmodernism has trickled down into public debate, and some of its ideas have taken an increasingly visible and tangible form in arguments around the growing transgender movement, discussed in Chapter 4.

The ideas identified in this brief run-through of feminist theoretical approaches will be developed and clarified throughout the book. Its chapters will also investigate the complex and sometimes contradictory relationships between feminist theories and the different kinds of feminist politics outlined in the following subsection.

Feminist politics in the twenty-first century

An extraordinarily wide range of feminist activism emerged, erupted or developed in the first two decades of the twenty-first century (for global overviews, see Enloe, 2017; Arruzza, Bhattacharya and Fraser, 2018; Mlambo-Ngcuka, 2018; Watkins, 2018). Some of this has been local, small-scale and informal, often based on a single issue such as police failure to investigate a sexual assault, and often short-lived. However, some such protests have developed into national movements which in turn have fed into and drawn strength from campaigns in other countries; here the most obvious example is the way that apparently separate protests against sexual violence in Argentina, India and elsewhere have become linked into the #MeToo movement that began in the US. Developments in social media have of course provided unprecedented opportunities for making connections and giving a voice to a much wider range of women than in the past (although it should be remembered that many women in poor countries lack internet access: Dreyfus, 2018); these developments also mean that much feminist activism is taking place online as well as in the 'real world'.

In many countries, feminists have campaigned against austerity measures and the damage these have done to many women's lives. In the UK, this campaigning includes both 'respectable' groups such as the Women's Budget Group, through which feminist economists are analysing and publicising the damaging impact of economic policies on women, and more radical, direct-action groups such as Feminist Fightback and Sisters Uncut, which link austerity to wider issues of power, class, race, violence and misogyny. Feminist demonstrations such as 'reclaim the night' marches have been revived in many countries, sometimes taking new forms such as 'slut walks' (see Chapter 2), while feminist rallies against Donald Trump's inauguration as US president took place from Antarctica to Fiji, Tel Aviv to Tokyo, and London to Nairobi (Enloe, 2017).

Feminists often work through trade unions, which, thanks to the work of women in the past, are often far more feminist-friendly than they used to be; some low-paid and predominantly migrant women workers are gaining a voice through a new union, United Voices of the World, which is specifically aimed at the most vulnerable and precariously situated workers and is encouraging the active participation of women. There has also been a new international feminist strike movement, which began in Poland in 2016, when women staged walkouts and protests against a ban on abortion, followed later in the year by Argentina, where women were protesting against sexual violence. The idea of a women's strike rapidly spread to other South American countries, to some European countries and to the US; it became a truly transnational movement the following year when strikes were organised in many countries on 8 March (International Women's Day), with women withholding not only their paid labour but also 'housework, sex and smiles' (Arruzza, Bhattacharya and Fraser, 2018; 2019:8; https://womensglobalstrike.com).

As in earlier periods, many new feminist groups are deliberately non-hierarchical, and some are self-consciously intersectional (see Chapter 3), taking the most disadvantaged women as the starting point for their campaigns (Bassel and Emejula, 2017, 2019). Such feminism rejects the assumption that a few well-placed women (usually white, western and relatively well-off) can speak for the whole of their sex, and it insists on the need to address differences amongst women. Some are also drawing on the idea of 'prefiguration', which has been used in some feminist circles since the 1960s. This says that the means used to pursue social change cannot be separated from its goals, and that making changes in the here and now, both in our personal lives and in our political activities, is an important part of making changes in the future (Wainwright, 2015; Ishkanian and Saavedra, 2019). In practical terms, this means that socialist men cannot say they will deal with gender issues 'after the revolution' while expecting women to take care of their domestic needs until then; likewise, educated and/or relatively well-off women need to address their own role in excluding or exploiting 'other' women (including by outsourcing domestic work to them for little pay, or by the overuse of alienating feminist 'jargon', such as 'intersectionality' or 'prefiguration').

In addition to collective activism, a number of individual high-profile women have been able to use their position to promote feminism in various ways. For example, the best-selling Nigerian novelist Chimamanda Ngozi Adichie frequently speaks out as a feminist to condemn the gender stereotyping that damages the lives of boys as well as girls. Her book *We Should All Be Feminists* (2014) is aimed at men as well as women, and it has been distributed to all 16-year-olds in Sweden. The actor Emma Watson, appointed UN Goodwill ambassador for women in 2014, helped launch the UN Women campaign 'HeForShe' in the same year, and she has actively campaigned on issues around sexual violence against women. And Facebook's Sheryl Sandberg (see Chapter 6) has set up the Lean In Foundation, which acts to support ambitious women from all walks of life. By early 2020, this had established 'lean-in circles' in over 170 countries; these self-help groups meet monthly, and the foundation campaigns to improve workplace opportunities for women in ways that range from paid family leave to combating sexual harassment (https://leanin.org). Many 'ordinary' individual feminists are also taking small-scale action in their daily lives, from challenging sexist comments in everyday conversation and encouraging other women in their workplace to trying to raise their children in gender-neutral ways. And by 2019 one teenage girl, Greta Thunberg, was both inspiring new forms of climate activism and calling the world's leaders to account for their failure to address the climate emergency.

While many feminists prefer to campaign mainly with other women, many also work with men in anti-racist movements such as Black Lives Matter, anti-poverty activism, LGBTQ+ groups, peace and environmental organisations, and left-leaning think tanks and pressure groups, such as the Runnymede Trust, Compass and the New Economics Foundation in the UK. Others work through conventional political parties, pushing for what they see as 'women's interests' across all policy areas. Many also actively campaign for women to be better represented, both in elected positions and at all levels of their party's organisation. Action here can be highly visible, as with the Conservative Party's Women2Win group (see Chapter 6), but it can also be very low-key – for example rearranging the chairs into a circle at a local party meeting, so that all those present can be part of the discussion. Many other feminists are networking across nations to lobby international organisations including the EU and the UN, and working in NGOs to monitor whether national commitments on women's rights and gender equality are being met (Enloe, 2017).

In the twenty-first century, feminist women are no longer simply political outsiders. Increasing numbers have at least a foothold in national and international decision-making bodies, and many successful female politicians have close links with feminist groups and organisations. In 2020, this meant that, when policy-makers in the UK initially failed to take women's gender-specific needs into account when responding to the COVID-19 pandemic, feminists were in a position to take them to task, and to produce evidence-based arguments to support their demands: in particular, they could show the extent to which badly paid women workers were risking their health in hospitals, care homes and supermarkets, and to highlight the urgent need to address the often catastrophic financial impact of the lockdown on the poorest women, the predictable rise in domestic abuse and the increased stress on mothers and other unpaid carers. As a joint call to the government by an extensive and diverse range of UK feminist organisations concluded:

> hundreds of billions of pounds of taxpayers' money is being spent without considering the specific challenges women are facing. Women and girls in all their diversity must be seen, have their voices heard and their needs met. (Fawcett, 2020)

Nevertheless, governments in many countries were slow to respond to feminist pressure, and although some problems, such as the rise in domestic violence, have been recognised, the resources needed to address them have in general been inadequate.

Chapters and themes

Throughout the book, I develop a number of overarching arguments around the themes of interconnection and complexity, the inability of man-made theories and concepts to provide an adequate understanding of the world, the need to recognise differences amongst women, the incompatibility between the values of free-market capitalism and the pursuit of feminist goals, and the consequent need for feminist politics to develop in a socialist direction.

In the first two chapters, I provide a critical exploration of some key terms and concepts that western feminists have introduced since the late 1960s. Focusing on arguments around the sex/gender distinction, the changing language around sexual violence, the identification of 'sexism' and the concept of patriarchy, I argue that these all contributed to new ways of seeing and understanding the world that had not been available before and that remain important today. However, these understandings also tended to reflect the inequalities of white-dominated western societies, expressing the experiences of relatively privileged white women, and paying insufficient attention to the diversity of women's experiences. I therefore argue in Chapter 3 that feminist analysis should also be based in the wider understanding provided by the newer concept of 'intersectionality', initially introduced into feminist vocabulary by black US-based feminists in the late 1980s. I argue that it is essential to retain intersectionality as a radical political concept that addresses collective, structural issues rather than simply individual experiences, and that it must include the analysis of class.

In Chapter 4, I turn to what has become perhaps the most fiercely contested issue in feminist politics today: between those trans women and their supporters who say that trans women simply 'are women' and should be treated as such, and those feminists who say that someone born with a male body should not be able to define themselves as a woman or enter 'women-only' spaces. I draw on feminist critiques of binary, oppositional thinking to explore some of the complexities of trans politics and to identify the commonalities as well as the differences between apparently opposing groups. I argue that both 'sides' have interests and problems in common and that feminists, cis and trans, should focus their energies on these. I end the chapter with a suggestion for moving beyond the current impasse over the legal status of trans women.

My arguments in early chapters indicate that the analysis of gender cannot be isolated from that of class or race, that patriarchy is entangled with capitalism and that the needs of women (including trans women) will not be met in an economy based on the pursuit of profit. I address these issues in more detail in Chapter 5, which focuses on the capitalist economic system and the liberal and neoliberal theories that support it. I show how women-centred feminist perspectives can both challenge the assumptions and limitations of conventional, male-stream economic theory and expose the often exploitative nature of corporate initiatives that promise new opportunities for women and girls in the global south.

These arguments feed into discussion in Chapter 6, in which I look at feminist politics in the west today. Here I assess some feminists' claims that neoliberal ideology is taking over feminism and using it to legitimise new forms of exploitation. I find that, although 'neoliberal feminism' is influential, feminist activities and ideas are much more diverse than this claim suggests. I also argue that neoliberal feminism is full of contradictions, and that this helps explain why Theresa May failed to deliver on her feminist promises to women. In contrast, Chapter 7 asks whether feminists today can find any answers in Marxist theory. I argue that this has been limited by its male-stream assumptions, but that recent feminist work on 'social reproduction' provides some important insights into women's economic contributions that can help reframe key issues, challenge neoliberal assumptions and expose a looming capitalist crisis as the needs of the 'productive' and 'reproductive' economies are increasingly in conflict.

In different ways, the arguments developed in Chapters 1–7 all seem to point to socialist rather than free-market solutions to gender inequalities and injustices. This is the focus of Chapter 8, in which I explore the affinities between feminism and socialism, and provide a brief history of their relationship before assessing the practical implications for feminist politics and policies today. Here my starting-point is a pragmatic, minimalist approach that sees socialism as a form of society closer to the Nordic social democracies than to the more market-driven economy of the United States, while also acknowledging that there is no 'Nordic nirvana' for feminists, and that serious problems remain in all countries. In this context, I suggest a range of policy options that western feminists might explore.

I conclude that there is clearly no single or simple solution to the complex and interconnected problems that any form of inclusive feminism or socialism will want to address. This need not be a cause for pessimism, for these interconnections also indicate that progress in one area can have knock-on effects on others, while diverse forms of progressive political and economic engagement can help reinforce each other. This means that, although our individual priorities and political choices will, inevitably, often reflect our particular situation, they can feed into a wider movement for change. At the same time, however, the need to address the man-made climate crisis is becoming increasingly urgent, while the COVID-19 pandemic has thrown the limitations of male-stream thinking into sharp relief. Neither crisis can be solved without co-operation, regulation and attention to values other than the pursuit of profit – ideas that seem beyond the ken of most conventional economic theory, but which are central to much socialist feminist thought today.

1

The sex/gender distinction and the language of sexual violence

MY FIRST THREE chapters are underpinned by three linked beliefs: that the language we use and the concepts available to us can be of profound political importance; that man-made language and concepts cannot adequately express women's experiences and needs; and that these experiences and needs are not the same for all groups of women. I begin with a brief general discussion of the political importance of concepts and vocabulary and how these relate to knowledge and power. I then discuss some developments in feminist terminology since the 1960s, arguing that these can help bring overlooked aspects of society into sharper focus and help us to see, analyse and challenge injustices. I also identify potential problems with a number of terms, and warn against their casual or simplistic use. In particular, readers should note that many of the ideas discussed in the first two chapters are part of what is effectively white feminist theory, reflecting the marginalisation of 'other' feminist voices in white-dominated class societies.

It is of course impossible to address everything at once, but many ideas and concepts that at first seem straightforward rapidly spiral into complexity when examined in detail or applied to new situations. These opening chapters therefore raise more questions than answers, and I have postponed full discussion of some important issues until later in the book.

Knowledge, power and feminist 'naming'

As a number of social and political theorists argue, our understanding of the world around us is not direct, but mediated by the language, concepts and ideas available to us. These do not simply describe 'reality' but help construct our picture of it by drawing our attention to some things and ignoring or concealing others, affecting both what we see and how we see it. They can be used to illuminate, but they can also be used to manipulate or mislead, and if we have no way of expressing a perception, an experience or an activity, it is difficult or impossible to recognise it. For example, if we have no word to describe what a woman looking after small children is doing all day, we may see her as economically unproductive and expect her to look for paid employment; if 'rape' is always understood to mean a violent attack by a stranger, a woman whose husband forces her to have sex has no way of articulating what he has done; if jokes that sexualise or denigrate women are seen as 'harmless banter', it is difficult for a woman to object without being portrayed as a puritanical killjoy; and how we see a cluster of cells may become very different if it is described as 'an embryo', rather than 'an unborn child'. Even when we think we have an adequate vocabulary, meanings are often shifting, slippery and context-dependent, so that perfect communication is never really possible. And all of this is often bound up with power, with the perspectives, interests and ideas of dominant groups reflected in the mainstream of politics, culture and education, while less privileged viewpoints are marginalised or actively repressed.

The examples that I give above reflect issues around childcare, sexual violence and pregnancy that reflect many women's interests and experience, but that have not attracted the attention of the male theorists who have dominated the analysis of ideology, knowledge, language and power. To take perhaps the most notable and influential of these theorists: in 1845 Marx famously claimed that in any society the ruling ideas are those of the ruling class; nearly a century later, the Italian communist Antonio Gramsci expanded on this to analyse the ways in which the capitalist state 'manufactures consent' through ideology, so that the 'battle of ideas' can be a crucial aspect of class struggle and resistance; and from the late 1960s the French writer Michel Foucault was writing about the relationship between knowledge and power, arguing that knowledge and culture form patterns or 'discourses' that organise our understanding of society, with dominant discourses reflecting the perspective of the most powerful groups.

By the twenty-first century, many feminists were drawing on and developing these analyses, and there is also a long and separate history of women seeking both to expose the partiality of man-made knowledge and to develop new forms of knowledge based on their own experience and perspectives. As Mary Astell wrote in the late seventeenth century, we already know how men see the world and their place in it: 'Histories are writ by them, they recount each others great Exploits and have always done so' (quoted in Perry, 1986:3). In contrast women's perspectives have not generally been allowed public expression, and when they have attempted to express their views women have often been trivialised, ignored, silenced or forgotten. As the classicist Mary Beard argues, 'When it comes to silencing women, Western culture has had thousands of years of practice', and she traces a direct line between ancient examples and the online abuse and violent threats received by female politicians and other women, including herself, who speak out today (2017:xii).

In the context of the ongoing silencing and/or marginalisation of women's experiences, developing a vocabulary and concepts to name and understand them is not simply an academic exercise but a critical part of feminist politics. As Cynthia Enloe has argued, 'Concepts are not merely abstractions. They have consequences. They can galvanize' (2017:142; see also Krook, 2019). Political 'naming' was therefore an important part of the feminist activism that erupted in many western nations from the 1960s, and this period 'is full of accounts of revelations about oppressions that were not previously named or described and of the joy in recognizing even oppression: diagnosis is the first step toward cure and recovery' (Solnit, 2017:56).

For one group of apparently privileged women in the US, this revelation occurred when Betty Friedan's best-selling book *The Feminine*

Mystique, first published in 1963, identified 'the problem that has no name': that is, the unhappiness and depression experienced by a generation of housewives who had been taught that their fulfilment lay solely in domesticity, and that if they yearned for something else they had failed in their role as women (1963/1986:17). These women had no words to describe their situation, and many said that their lives were changed by reading Friedan's book. One wrote to her saying that, after reading it, she wanted to rush into the streets and cry 'To arms, sisters! You have nothing to lose but your vacuum cleaners!' (quoted in Horowitz, 1998:203); *The Feminine Mystique* is widely credited with kick-starting an important strand of mainstream, equal-rights feminism in this period.

Meanwhile, other women were developing new concepts and a language to *analyse* what Friedan only described, and to push her concerns in more radical directions. By the early 1970s, one important starting-point seemed to be the distinction between sex and gender.

Gender and the sex/gender distinction

In 1949, the pioneering feminist French philosopher Simone de Beauvoir famously wrote that 'One is not born but rather becomes a woman' (1949/1972:297). She argued that there is nothing natural about femininity, and identified the ways in which this was manufactured in her society. By the late 1960s, many feminists were formalising and extending this position to make a distinction between our biological sex (male or female) and the gender (masculine or feminine) that is ascribed to us by society. According to this analysis, we need to expose and challenge the artificial, hierarchical and damaging nature of the gender roles and attributes that restrict and damage our lives, and that are widely seen as 'natural'. This sex/gender distinction has since been complicated by some developments in feminist theory and by wider awareness of the experiences of trans people. Today, 'sex' and 'gender' are often used loosely and interchangeably both in everyday and official use and by some feminist writers. This section traces these developments; I conclude that, although the distinction may not be as straightforward as it once seemed, it remains politically important to retain it.

The sex/gender distinction and feminist analysis

The idea that sex is about our bodies and gender is about our social roles and behaviour did not originate with feminists, but with medical researchers in the US who were investigating and treating intersex conditions in the 1950s. These 'experts' argued that in cases when a baby's sex was unclear, their adult gender identity would depend on whether they were raised as a girl or a boy. They therefore argued that, if a baby were born with a micro penis, 'corrective' surgery should be used to give them a female anatomy; this would be supplemented by hormonal treatment when they reached puberty, and they could successfully be raised as a girl. In other words, a child's biological sex could be changed, and their learned gender would be central to their identity (Davis, 2015).

Such medical interventions are widely condemned today, and the evidence on which they were made was decidedly weak. However, many western feminists developed the idea that gender is an artificial product of society rather than a 'natural' outcome of female biology, and used this to reject restrictive assumptions around 'appropriate' female behaviour. Feminist writers also drew on anthropological findings to show that the attributes, social roles and patterns of behaviour associated with women and men are widely variable – for example, in some societies it is men rather than women who are preoccupied with their appearance and self-adornment; here Ann Oakley's 1972 book *Sex, Gender and Society* was particularly influential. From this new feminist perspective, there was nothing natural or inevitable about how gender was organised and experienced in the west; this could therefore be challenged and changed.

Gender, as many feminists understood it in the 1970s, was not just about men and women playing different social roles, it was also about men's power over women (although Oakley now says that her own book failed to explore this adequately: 2016:10). This means that gender is about much more than individual characteristics, opportunities or identities; rather, it is a basic principle of social organisation through which men, collectively, constitute a dominant group that is privileged in all areas of life. Making the distinction between sex and gender enables us to see that this domination is not inevitable, and that there is no biological reason why men should monopolise positions of power and influence while women take care of the home. From this perspective, women's ability to give birth is a natural outcome of their biological sex, but their ability to change a nappy is learned gender behaviour – or as the novelist Chimamanda Ngozi Adichie (2018) put it: 'I don't think I'm more inherently likely to do domestic work, or childcare … It doesn't come pre-programmed in your vagina, right?'

The sex/gender distinction enables us to see and challenge the gender stereotypes that surround young children from the earliest age, because it sees these as a way of teaching children what they should like and how they should behave, rather than reflecting their innate preferences (here it is worth pointing out that pink used to be seen as a boy's colour, derived from military red, while blue was seen as a softer, girl's colour, associated with the blue of the Virgin Mary's robes in western religious paintings). Feminists have long argued that gendered assumptions limit children's potential, and some have attempted to bring up their own children in more gender-neutral ways, and/or to campaign for schools to develop more gender-inclusive policies and for retailers to stop marketing toys as suitable for 'girls' or 'boys' rather than 'children'. Such campaigns have had only limited success. Indeed, although the concept of gender-neutral toys now exists, a casual visit to the toy area of any big store suggests that this has spectacularly failed to deliver, as the dolls, pretend cookers and pink princess outfits on one side of the aisle face the dinosaurs, construction kits and metallic spaceships on the other. Today in the UK, some new groups such as Let Toys Be Toys and Pink Stinks are challenging retailers to end such segregation (http://lettoysbetoys.org.uk/about; www.pinkstinks.co.uk), and in 2019 the Fawcett Society (a long-established feminist campaigning group) set up a 'Smash Stereotypes' campaign and an expert commission to examine the evidence on the effects of gender stereotyping in early childhood. Its initial literature review found that stereotypes are indeed powerful from an early age, that they are linked to educational achievement, occupational segregation and the pay gap between women and men, and that young men who believe in particularly rigid gender stereotypes are more likely to act violently towards their partner (Culhane and Bazeley, 2019).

Men and masculinity

Most of the early feminist work on gender focused on how artificial notions of 'femininity' restrict women, leaving maleness and masculinity as the unquestioned standard of what it is to be human. From this perspective, 'gender research' was often interpreted as 'research on women', 'gender studies' were a rebranded version of 'women's studies' and 'breaking down statistics by gender' means seeing how women compare with men. However, by the end of the twentieth century there was a significant body of work on men and masculinities that explored the complex ways that masculinity is constructed and the diverse meanings that can be attached to it. This work generally found that, like women, men were constrained by artificial notions of gender and, at a popular level, there was widespread discussion of a 'crisis of masculinity', with many commentators in western societies concerned about the failure of boys to match the educational achievements of girls, high rates of male unemployment, the involvement of young men in crime and drug abuse, the increase in the number of families with no live-in father and the rise in male suicide.

Some more academic writers linked such concerns with ideas around 'hegemonic masculinity', that is, the dominant model of masculinity in the west. This portrays the ideal man as the high-earning, strong, confident, sexually experienced and heterosexual head of a household whose gender gives him natural authority over women. Such a model, some argued, is highly damaging to men as well as women, because many men will never be able to achieve it, and some will compensate for their failures with an exaggerated assertion of the aggressiveness associated with 'normal' masculinity. More recently, with the ascendancy of Putin and Trump, the apparently unstoppable spread of increasingly violent and extreme material on the internet and the #MeToo revelations, there has been much talk of 'toxic masculinity' and its damaging effects on individuals, societies, international relations and the very future of the planet. Here, it seems useful to retain the sex/gender distinction as a way of reminding ourselves that such behaviour is socially produced rather than inherent in all male bodies.

Problems with the sex/gender distinction

While it has been highly influential, the sex/gender distinction has also been heavily criticised by feminists for a range of sometimes conflicting reasons. In the 1970s and 1980s, it ran counter to the claims of a vocal minority of radical feminists who held more essentialist views: at their simplest, these seemed to say that women are naturally good and oppressed, men are naturally bad and oppressive, and that women should therefore reject all association with men, whether this be social, sexual or political. From this perspective, men were the enemy and gender differences were simply the natural reflection of biological reality. Such an essentialist position has obvious flaws (for a critical discussion, see Segal, 1987); it is not one that I argue from in this book.

A more legitimate criticism arises from the way that many mainstream feminists have unthinkingly equated their own experiences of artificially manufactured femininity with those of all women in their society. In doing this, relatively affluent white western women have unthinkingly excluded or marginalised women who are not like them. For example, when earlier generations of white American feminists insisted that, contrary to the dominant view of acceptable womanhood, they were not pure, weak and innocent creatures in need of protection from men, they failed to see that very different qualities were attributed to black women, who were widely seen as physically strong and sexually promiscuous. Moreover, because colonialism in general and slavery in particular involved equating subordinated black people with animals as a way of justifying their ill-treatment, black people were often effectively *de-gendered* (Lugones, 2010; Nash, 2019).

As discussed in later chapters, much feminist analysis today has moved on from treating women as a unitary group, and it is more open to analysing the complex ways in which gender intersects and varies with other dimensions of structural inequalities. However, there is still a tendency for women who are highly placed in terms of class-based and race-based inequalities to be more readily heard and to treat their own experiences as central. This does not mean that we should stop looking at how gender is manufactured, but we need to recognise that this happens in multiple ways within as well as between societies.

A further set of practical and philosophical problems arises from the whole idea that sex provides a stable basis for the creation of gender. While the sex/gender distinction has generally assumed that biological sex differences are straightforward, so that we always know who is a girl or a boy, a woman or a man, Oakley pointed out that even biological sex differences take the form of a continuum rather than any absolute division, for we all have a fluctuating mix of hormones and many of our bodily characteristics, including whether we can give birth, our strength and even where our hair grows, change with age. By the twenty-first century, there was much greater awareness of the extent of intersex conditions, not all of which are visible. The Intersex Society of North America (undated) estimates that one in a hundred people have some kind of variation, many of which, such as chromosomes that do not 'match' an individual's genitals, are not apparent at birth. Some more recent research suggests that if genes are fully taken into account the differences between men and women become even more blurred (Ainsworth, 2015).

The sex/gender distinction also leaves wide open the related question of which of the observable average differences between men and women (such as men's greater competitiveness or propensity to violence) are based in biology, which are socially produced and which represent a combination of the two. The evidence here is fiercely contested, but it seems increasingly clear that popular assumptions about differences between women and men's brains and the effects of different levels of hormones have been exaggerated, and that physical differences often have environmental causes. For example, Gina Rippon, a professor of cognitive neuroimagining, finds that new brain-imaging technology does not show, as she had initially expected, that there are clear, sex-based differences between the brains of men and women; rather, it reveals the 'plasticity' of the human brain, which is not simply fixed at birth but moulded by our experiences throughout our lives. She therefore called her book on the subject *The Gendered Brain*, to indicate that, when we find observable differences between the brains of women and men, we are looking not at biology but at 'the brain-changing effects of social processes' (2019:xxi). In *Testosterone Rex* (2017), Cordelia Fine has drawn on a wide range of studies to similarly debunk common beliefs about the impact of hormones, and she showed that hormonal differences between men and women can be partly a product rather than a source of sex-stereotypical behaviour (high levels of testosterone amongst men on the stock exchange seem to be the result of a highly charged atmosphere rather than its cause, while, if men spend time physically caring for small children, their testosterone levels are reduced). Other observable average differences between the sexes, such as men's greater strength or their higher death rate during the COVID-19 pandemic, may also often be at least partly the product of environmental factors: men in western societies are often encouraged to develop muscles and women to be as slim as possible, while lifestyle factors, such as their higher rates of smoking and alcohol consumption exacerbate the effects of men's naturally weaker immune systems – here, both women's hormones and their double X chromosomes seem to confer an advantage (Ball, 2020; Moalem, 2020).

The language we use around the sex/gender distinction is of course further complicated by the growing voices of trans and gender-fluid or non-binary people, and related recent changes in how women and men are legally defined and recognised in many nations. For some trans people, their gender (which the law sees as their 'acquired gender') is the core of their identity, and it is stable; and some trans people change their body through surgery or hormone treatment to bring it into line with who they believe themselves to be. This effectively reverses feminist analysis of the malleability of gender and the stability of biological sex, but it coincides with the medical views outlined at the beginning of this section.

Most public discussion of trans identity also ignores feminist analysis of the structural power relationships that gender involves: however, as the Australian sociologist Raewyn Connell, herself a trans woman, says (2012), we need to understand that gender is not just symbolic, but is also about economic, political and social power. I discuss these issues in more detail in Chapter 4.

A new level of complexity has also emerged from feminist engagements with post-structuralist and postmodernist theory. Some draw on the linguistic theory of Jacques Derrida to argue that masculinity and femininity are primarily constructed through language and discourse and that, like all apparent dichotomies, they have meaning only in relation to one another. This means that 'masculine' is understood as 'not feminine', rather than being defined with reference to stable, external criteria. Other writers argue that sex itself is a product of society, rather than fixed by nature, because biological differences acquire social meaning only if they are identified and labelled. From this perspective, 'sex' becomes a 'category of meaning' in societies that attach great importance to certain features of our anatomy, rather than a naturally given 'fact' (much as the colour of our skin is given significance in many societies, although it has no inherent meaning). Here the work of the US theorist Judith Butler has been particularly influential, and she has argued that sex as well as gender is socially created from the moment that someone announces 'It's a girl!' after a glance at a newborn baby's genitals, so that 'Sex, by definition, will be shown to have been gender all along' (1990:8).

Butler also argues that gender is always precarious, something that has to be confirmed by what a society sees as gender-appropriate behaviour (involving, for example, how we dress, what work we do or with whom we have sexual relationships). In other words, gender is not something that one *is*, but something that one *does* (albeit something that most people do without thinking about it); gender is, in fact, a kind of 'performance'. This idea of 'doing gender' means that gender is not simply imposed on people, but that they necessarily participate in its constant reproduction by 'performing' in appropriate ways; it also means that gender can be contested or subverted by transgressive behaviour. Here Butler attached particular importance to the subversive potential of drag and other 'parodic' practices that, by disrupting the link between body and behaviour, reveal the fictitious nature of femininity and masculinity and can help people choose which gender to perform.

Other writers have linked the idea of 'doing gender' to the way that heterosexual couples divide their household chores, whereby 'her doing the laundry and his fixing the light not only produces clean clothes and a lit room, they also produce a reaffirmation of gender roles' (Blumberg, 1991:20). Here some also argue that if, as some evidence suggests, unemployed men do less housework than those who are in work, this is not because they are lazy, but because they need to reassert a masculine identity that is threatened if they cannot provide for their family; conversely, a woman who earns more than her husband will often 'invoke significant hyper-feminine displays aimed at neutralizing gender role deviance' (Bittman, 2004:165). However, if gender can be done it can also be 'undone' by those who reject the domestic roles and behaviours traditionally attached to their gender; for a man to take on the main responsibility for childcare and housework in his family may be less dramatic than parading through the streets in drag, but it may have a more disruptive effect on the gender order in the long term.

'Gender' in everyday and official use

While feminists continue to dispute the meaning of sex and gender, the terms are often used loosely and interchangeably in everyday speech. Some people also seem to see gender as a more 'polite' term than sex, perhaps because it is less easily confused with physical sexual activity (when I was a student, I sometimes worked for a market research company, and had to be careful when going through the tick boxes for 'age?', 'occupation?' etcetera, because 'sex?' risked eliciting the response 'Yes, please!').

The use of 'gender' to refer to purely physical features is particularly clear in the increasingly popular 'gender reveal parties', at which expectant parents disclose whether the scan shows that their baby will be a girl or a boy. As discussed above, many feminists would say that a scan can only reveal a baby's sex, as they argue that it does not have a gender until it has lived and developed in a gendered society; from this perspective, it might be more accurate to describe the event as a 'genital reveal party' (thanks to Alan Pearson for this formulation). And of course the baby may grow up and decide that they want to transition to another gender.

In many official documents, reports and surveys, 'gender' has gradually replaced 'sex' over the last few decades, partly in an attempt to meet the needs of trans people. This has become standard practice in public discussion of differences between women and men; for example, when I googled 'sex gap in pay' I was immediately directed to sites on the 'gender pay gap'. However, use of the terms remains at times inconsistent, sloppy and confusing. In particular, UK birth certificates and passports continue to classify individuals by *sex*, which the government consultation on reforming the 2004 Gender Recognition Act says is 'based on physical characteristics'. However, this recorded sex can be changed if an individual provides evidence (most usually a 'Gender Recognition Certificate') that they have changed their *gender*, which the consultation says 'refers to socially constructed characteristics'. Quite how changing something that is socially constructed means that something that is physical has also changed is unclear to me. Meanwhile, the 2010 Equality Act outlaws '*sex* discrimination' between men and women and there is an All Party Parliamentary Group on '*sex* equality', but a recent report from the Equalities and Human Rights Commission is subtitled 'women's rights and *gender* equality in 2018' (EHRC, 2019). Confused? So, it seems, are many policy-makers and officials.

Feminism, sex and gender today

Feminists too can seem confused and self-contradictory, and today many seem to have abandoned the sex/gender distinction, often following officialdom in using 'gender' where 'sex' would earlier have been employed. Many now also agree that the 'common sense' notion that an individual's biological sex is always obvious and stable, so that we can classify everyone from birth in binary terms as unequivocally male or female, does not stand up in practice. It is also clear that there is no one way of being masculine or feminine in a society, as gender interacts with a range of other social variables at both an individual and a society-wide level to produce what might better be described as a 'multiplicity of genders' than an either/or divide (Carver, 1996).

Nevertheless, when we know a baby's sex, we can make certain predictions. In particular, if the baby has female genitals, they are likely to be able to have babies; so long as they keep their uterus, this may remain possible even if they later identify as male and have the hormonal treatment and top surgery that enables them to pass as a man. We can also predict that, in comparison with a similarly situated baby with a penis, they will earn less, be more likely to be sexually assaulted, and do more housework and childcare. Unlike the first prediction, which is the direct outcome of a baby's biological sex, these predictions also reflect the gendered expectations and treatment that they will encounter from the moment they are born, and the organisation of society that systematically rewards the biological and social qualities associated with men. This means that if, for example, we want to look at the pay gap between women and men, we are talking about something that is the product of both sex and gender.

I believe that it is analytically and politically important for feminists to retain elements of the sex/gender distinction, as a way of contesting claims about the 'naturalness' of existing gender roles and highlighting the power relationships involved. Even though biological sex takes the form of a continuum and its significance may be socially created, the clustering of physical characteristics into two main groups remains a constant, the ground on to which gender in all its complicated manifestations is mapped. Sex may not be entirely adequate as a category, but neither is it arbitrary; and gender may be artificial, but its effects are very real. From this feminist perspective, gender is not simply a matter of personal identity or self-expression, it is about patterns of power and ascribed roles; it is also often about *collective* experiences of oppression, discrimination and exploitation.

Unless otherwise stated, I therefore use the term 'gender' in this book to refer to existing social, economic, political and cultural differences between the lives of women and men, as a shorthand way of indicating that these are not the inevitable outcome of average differences between differently sexed bodies. At the same time, I recognise that the experience of gender is mediated by other dimensions of power and inequality, and that, while the sex/gender distinction is useful, it represents a beginning and not the end of a complex story. These complexities are discussed further in later chapters.

Feminism and the language of sexual violence

One of the ways in which gender manifests itself around the world is in men's greater propensity to use violence both inside and outside the home. Women are often on the receiving end of this violence and of men's predatory sexual behaviour, but until recently they have had no readily accessible language to articulate their bad experiences or discover how widely they are shared. However, since the 1970s, a specifically feminist vocabulary has developed to expose, label, analyse and oppose the widespread sexual abuse of women by men. In this chapter, I focus on feminist redefinitions of 'rape' and on the newer term 'sexual harassment', before looking at the #MeToo movement and international campaigns opposing violence against women in politics.

Rape

The term 'rape' is of course not new, nor is its definition as a serious crime. Until recently, it was widely seen as an extremely rare act, a violent assault on an innocent woman by an abnormal and depraved stranger (the 'sex fiend' of sensationalist newspapers). It was also often seen as 'provoked', and therefore largely excusable, if a woman had in any way encouraged a man to think his attentions were welcome (perhaps by wearing a short skirt, or by smiling at him, or by getting drunk, or by saying 'please don't' rather than screaming 'get off!').

Such assumptions around the nature and prevalence of rape have long been challenged by many feminists, who have shown that rape is much more common than most people think, that it often involves someone known to the victim and that it can occur within marriage. Most feminists also argue that rape should never be blamed on the woman, and that all women have an absolute right to decide whether or not they have sex: as the feminist slogan says, 'Whatever we wear, wherever we go, yes means yes and no means no!'

The idea that a woman has the right to refuse to have sex with a man, even if she is married to him, was a central issue for some nineteenth-century feminists (Bryson, 2016:36–8, 42–3, 80–1). By the 1970s, some radical feminists were going much further, arguing that rape is not only a violation of women's right to say 'no', it is also about men's collective power over them – something that many were now describing as 'patriarchy'. From this perspective, a man does not rape, sexually assault or harass a woman because he is overcome by uncontrollable lust. Rather, for some men in positions of economic, social or political authority over women, coercive sex is simply an expression or extension of their power: they do it because they can. For some other men, it will be a way of asserting or reasserting their authority when this is threatened or absent: it is a way of punishing women, 'bringing the bitches into line'. For others, the exercise of power will itself be a source of sexual satisfaction. Others will only target particular groups of women, such as black women, white women, trans women or sex workers, whom they see as undeserving of the respect due to the 'proper' women in their own social group. And at a more general level, the actions of individual men serve both to reflect and to maintain a whole system of male domination.

This kind of view was expressed most unequivocally by Susan Brownmiller, who claimed that rape 'is nothing more or less than a conscious process of intimidation by which *all men* keep *all women* in a state of fear' (1977:15, emphasis in original). Brownmiller's formulation of her ideas in this widely quoted phrase is neat but misleading, almost suggesting that there is some kind of deliberate plot amongst men, and that a rapist might be thinking 'it's hard work, but someone's got to do it if patriarchy is to survive'. There are clearly also many women who would deny living in a 'state of fear', and Brownmiller seems to be generalising from the experience of white western women, forgetting the ways in which sexual violence has been bound up with slavery and colonialism, and the complex effects of this on black men as well as women (Bhandar and da Silva, 2013). However, Brownmiller's overall argument was not that all men rape or approve of those who do, but that they indirectly benefit from the subordinating position that women's fear puts them in, as this fear curtails their lives and leads them to seek the protection of one man against all the rest. This claim should not be pushed too far, and it should be combined with the kind of intersectional analysis discussed in Chapter 3. Nevertheless, I believe that Brownmiller's argument can provide insight into the role of sexual violence in the maintenance of patriarchy; I will return to this point in Chapter 2.

Many other feminists reject radical claims about the nature and significance of rape (see in particular Greer, 2018; Roiphe, 2018); the claims are of course also opposed by many non-feminist women as well as by many men. Nevertheless, old assumptions have at least been challenged, and in many countries the law increasingly reflects the understanding that rape can be committed by an acquaintance, friend, partner or husband, not just a stranger in a dark alleyway; that 'no' should indeed mean 'no'; and that consent to sexual activity can never be assumed but must be actively given. There is also a growing understanding that acts of rape should be treated not as isolated incidents but as part of a wider culture in which women are routinely depicted as sex objects and in which less violent forms of unwanted sexual attention have only gradually come to be named and recognised as 'sexual harassment'.

Sexual harassment

While 'rape' has to some extent been redefined, the newer term 'sexual harassment' has further challenged dominant assumptions around what constitutes acceptable behaviour, and its use has increasingly helped women call men to account. The term, which some feminists were already using, erupted into the political mainstream in 1991 during the Senate confirmation hearings into the appointment of Clarence Thomas to the Supreme Court of the United States, during which Thomas was accused of having sexually harassed a woman law professor, Anita Hill, some years earlier. Thomas's appointment was approved by an all-male committee in a Senate of ninety-eight men and just two women. Many women were outraged by the decision, by the attacks on Hill's character and by a widespread sense that, when it came to women's experiences of unwanted sexual attention, most men simply 'didn't get it'. One result was a surge in feminist activism in the US, and 1992 was hailed as 'the year of the woman' as the number of women elected to both the Senate and the House of Representatives reached an all-time high (although in retrospect the then record 6 per cent female Senators and 10.3 per cent female House Representatives seems somewhat unimpressive).

Although Hill's complaint of sexual harassment had not been taken seriously by male Senators, the case brought discussion of men's thoughtless, damaging or exploitative behaviour into the public domain; and, although few women were willing to speak out publicly, there was an increased sense of the extent to which apparently isolated individual experiences were both widely shared and linked to more general issues of power. Grassroots campaigns, support groups and networks helped keep awareness of sexual violence alive in the following years, and, as a steadily increasing number of women were moving into positions of social, cultural or political influence, they were able to give feminists' concerns a wider hearing. By the second decade of the twenty-first century, 'sexual harassment' was not only a familiar term in many countries but also one that identified certain forms of behaviour as unlawful discrimination in the workplace; the prevalence of sexual harassment was also increasingly treated as a serious issue on university campuses and in other public spaces.

At the same time, however, there was no consensus about how sexual harassment should be defined, with subjective perceptions and assumptions sometimes making the same behaviour seem perfectly acceptable to some, and deeply upsetting and exploitative to others. Even legal definitions are open to a range of conflicting interpretations. Thus the law in England and Wales defines sexual harassment in the workplace as a form of unlawful sexual discrimination through 'unwanted conduct of a sexual nature that has the purpose or effect of violating someone's dignity or creating an intimidating, hostile, degrading, humiliating or offensive environment for them'. In its 'advice to employers', the Equality and Human Rights Commission gives examples of such behaviour that range from 'unwelcome touching, hugging, massaging or kissing' and 'making promises in return for sexual favours', to 'sexual comments or jokes' and 'suggestive looks, staring or leering'; it also notes that 'The recipient of the behaviour decides whether or not it is unwanted', and that behaviour can have a discriminatory effect even if this was not expected or intended (EHRC, 2017). In this context, many claim that 'normal' workplace relationships have become impossible and that they have no idea what they can or cannot say or do in the workplace; here worried men might bear in mind the brisk advice offered by Jude Kelly, founder of the London-based Women of the World festival:

> One of the things I say to people at work is: 'Anything you wouldn't do with your boss, don't do.' So would you suddenly fling your arm around your boss's shoulder and tickle her on the ear? You probably wouldn't do that, would you? Would you wolf-whistle your boss? Probably not. So don't do it to anyone else either. (2018)

#MeToo

While the groundwork had been laid gradually, the issue of sexual violence and harassment seemed to explode in 2017 as the #MeToo movement went viral, women's accusations ended or damaged the careers of some powerful men, and women all over the world and from all kinds of backgrounds testified to their bad treatment. This does not mean that there is a new consensus around what constitutes bad or inappropriate behaviour or that women are now somehow controlling the world. Indeed, there has been a strong backlash against the movement, particularly by those men who now feel that women will interpret their gestures of affection as sexual assault and take offence at their mildest joke, or that some youthful indiscretion or thoughtless tweet will be used in evidence against them.

Many women too, including some feminists, are critical of both the #MeToo movement and what they see as a more general fear of male sexuality amongst feminists. Some such critics, of whom Germaine Greer is probably the best-known example in the UK, blame women for being over-sensitive or for not standing up for themselves, and they have little sympathy for what they see as the self-centred, individualistic preoccupations of successful and privileged women who seem to equate any minor assault on their self-esteem with violent humiliation, and an unwanted pat on the bottom with violent rape. They also dislike the demonisation of men, and insist that, far from being inherently exploitative, heterosexual intercourse can be a freely chosen source of pleasure for many women (for an overview of the debate, see Donegan, 2018).

Some of the movement's feminist critics also condemn the fact that although #MeToo had been started in 2006 by a black, grassroots activist, Tarana Burke, her contribution was at first ignored when the movement took off in 2017, with glamorous white Hollywood stars seeming to represent the acceptable face of aggrieved womanhood while the much greater vulnerability of black women attracted little attention. The voices of black women had already been marginalised during the 1991 Clarence Thomas hearings discussed above: both Thomas and Anita Hill were black, and while many white women empathised with Hill and many black men could agree with Thomas that he was experiencing 'a high-tech-lynching', black women's more complicated perspective went largely unheard. However, the women who have used #MeToo to share their stories come from a very wide range of backgrounds. By 2017 there was, at least in some feminist circles, a much greater awareness of the ways in which gender, race and other dimensions of inequality intersect, and of the distinctive experiences of black women (see Chapter 3 below), and Hill herself has endorsed #MeToo, saying at the end of 2017 that it had contributed to a change in attitudes, so that 'In today's atmosphere, there would be more people who would understand my story, who would believe my story' (quoted in Onwuachi-Willig, 2018).

By the end of 2018, the sense that attitudes were changing was supported by research in the UK for the Fawcett Society, which found that a majority of people, particularly in younger age groups, thought that what is acceptable has changed because of #MeToo (Fawcett, 2018a). By linking apparently minor incidents to more serious assaults, #MeToo has also had the effect of putting the kind of analysis that some radical feminists were making in the 1970s more firmly into the public domain: it provides a sense of shared experiences amongst women across their many differences, it tells women that they are not alone and that they are not to blame for some men's bad behaviour, and it reveals that such behaviour is far more common and often much more damaging than most people realise. It therefore provides a basis for female solidarity and a challenge to men's sense of entitlement that logically extends to challenging wider structures of power.

Of course, this apparent change in attitudes has been far from universal, and it did not prevent Brett Kavanaugh, Donald Trump's nominee for the Supreme Court, being confirmed by Senate in 2018 despite allegations that he had committed a serious sexual assault against Christine Blasey Ford, when he was a young man of 17 and she was just 15 years old. Moreover, while employers and politicians are increasingly likely to condemn abusive behaviour in principle, they are less willing to act or to commit resources to address it. This may be partly because many cases are highly complex, involving tricky issues around evidence, perception and memory, or because the range of behaviour and attitudes that are described as abusive seems exaggerated to some, or because the problem seems so complicated that it is impossible to know where to start. It also reflects the priorities that are set by powerful political, economic and cultural groups, which are still highly male-dominated and which inevitably contain many who use their power to abuse.

Violence against women in politics

The above discussion indicates that men's violence against women is bound up with power. This link is at times direct, aimed at restricting women's political participation. Mona Krook has shown how feminist understanding of this link has developed since the end of the twentieth century, initially arising from the experiences of women in Bolivia, across Asia and in Kenya, then gathering knowledge, feeding into regional and global initiatives and drawing strength from the separate rise of #MeToo.

The resulting analysis sees 'violence against women in politics' as a specific form of violence, which includes sexual violence and harassment and is directed at women *because they are women*; this violence is not simply a subset of political violence in general. Naming this violence has been a vital first step in opposing it as a violation of women's human rights, and Krook identifies a series of measures that are being taken at international and global level to identity, condemn and end it. While it is unclear to what extent laws and statements of intent will end the problem, the very fact that global documents now recognise this form of violence is a step forward, and Krook argues that this represents 'a collective achievement, giving a name to women's experiences, and in so doing, contributing to the ongoing advancement of democracy, human rights and gender equality' (2019:90–1).

Understanding the wider power context within which different forms of violence, harassment and abuse occur is a key part of challenging it, and this wider power too needs to be named. Here a number of feminists use the terms 'sexism' and/or 'patriarchy'. These terms are the focus of the next chapter.

2

Sexism and patriarchy

I N THIS CHAPTER, I use the terms 'sexism' and 'patriarchy' to develop issues raised in Chapter 1. In line with my earlier discussion, I will sometimes use the term 'gender' to discuss the experiences of 'women' and 'men' at the same time as recognising both that these are socially created categories rather than the inevitable outcome of biology, and that the categories can have very different meanings for different groups within the same society. In this context, readers should again note that the ideas discussed in this chapter were initially developed largely by white feminists; as such, they represent only a starting-point for inclusive feminist analysis.

Sexism

The term 'sexism' first came into use in the late 1960s in the context of the movement for black civil rights in the US. There, and in the anti-war, new left and student movements in North America, Europe and Australia, many young women found that supposedly 'progressive' anti-racist and left-wing groups were not immune from the 'feminine mystique' that had been identified by Betty Friedan (see previous chapter), and that they were expected to act as sexually available secretaries and housewives rather than equal partners or decision-makers. Labelling men's behaviour as 'sexist' was a way of asserting the political seriousness of women's claims and complaints by saying that prejudice, discrimination or ill treatment based on gender was every bit as important and every bit as unjustifiable as that based on race.

In subsequent decades, the terms 'sexism' and 'sexist' have proved a highly useful shorthand for identifying a wide range of beliefs, attitudes and behaviour that reflect, maintain or create an environment or outcomes that disadvantage one sex (usually women). Examples include conscious acts of discrimination, intimidation or exclusion (such as refusing to employ or promote women, or sexually harassing them in the street), and also the unthinking acceptance of gender stereotypes (for example, boys don't cry, women are naturally suited to housework), the use of non-inclusive language (such as referring to all potential students at a school open day as 'he'), treating women as objects to be looked at (in art, advertising or pornography) and the classification of children's toys into those for girls (pink, decorative, domestic and nurturing) and those for boys (blue, mechanical, adventurous and warlike).

Like racism, sexism is not just about individual acts of discrimination, and it can take institutional forms: an organisation may be full of well-intentioned people intent on treating everyone equally, but it may also be riddled with assumptions that systematically favour men over women. For example, when political activists are selecting a candidate to stand in a parliamentary election they may look for someone, male or female, with trade union or business experience while failing to see that setting up a play scheme for local children also involves politically relevant skills. Today, institutional sexism can occur even without deliberate human involvement, as computer algorithms learn from people's previous patterns of behaviour; for example, on Facebook and Google advertisements for particularly well paid or traditionally male jobs have been targeted at men (Gibbs, 2015; Hicks, 2018).

Although the term sexism is most often used to 'call out' individual acts of bad or inappropriate behaviour, it can also help us see their wider social context: to describe our society as sexist is not just to say that some people do or think discriminatory things, but to see the connections between different instances of this discrimination. This connection was clearly made by Laura Bates, who founded the online 'Everyday Sexism' project in 2012 in response to her own low-level, bad experiences, such as being shouted at on the street and groped on a bus. Bates argued that 'reams and reams of tiny pinpricks' had a cumulative effect, and that they were linked to more serious forms of abuse:

> the steady drip-drip-drip of sexism and sexualisation and objecti-fication is connected to the assumption of ownership and control over women's bodies, and the background noise of harassment and disrespect connects to the assertion of power that is violence and rape. (Bates, 2014:12, 19)

Identifying a range of diverse experiences as 'sexism' enabled Bates to articulate her findings and, by naming the problem, to take the first steps towards challenging it. She argues that grassroots activism is important in shifting the culture of sexism, and she campaigned with others to encourage companies whose Facebook advertisements had been appearing on pages that seemed to condone or encourage sexual violence to withdraw from the site (after fifteen advertisers, including Nissan, withdrew, Facebook promised a number of measures, including improved moderator training and updated user guidelines: Bates, 2014; Mantilla, 2015).

The word 'sexism' continues to be widely used today, and it has a clear role to play in creating a view of the world that reflects and communicates many women's experiences and that can inform practical feminist politics. It can, however, often be difficult for a woman to employ the term without being portrayed as an old-fashioned, negative, humourless complainer who finds problems where none exist and sees the world through a distort-ing, feminist lens. This means that, while silence or participation in sexist culture often goes unremarked, criticism of sexism is often punished, so that 'When we name what we come up against, we come up against what we name' (Ahmed, 2015:10). In this context, Sara Ahmed finds that female academics have often ceased to engage in the exhausting and apparently pointless work of identifying sexism wherever they find it, and that as a result 'sexism seems to have "dropped out" of feminist theoretical vocabu-laries' (2015:6).

In some respects, academic neglect of the term might seem no bad thing, for feminist academic theory can sometimes seem almost deliberately obscure, a way of signalling membership of an elite group whose language is impenetrable to 'outsiders' (a category that includes most black and/or working-class women). At its best, however, feminist theory can both bring apparently unrelated insights together and inject more rigour into public debates. My sense is that the term 'sexism' is now almost too easy to use and that it is bandied around to an extent that threatens to rob it of its power; here it may be that a lack of academic interest contributes to its apparent lack of analytical or critical edge.

Some problems with the term 'sexism'

While 'sexism' is sometimes applied to institutional behaviour, it is most often understood in relation to *individual* acts and intentions, losing sight of the deep-seated processes and outcomes that underpin them. The term also often isolates gender-specific forms of ill-treatment and bad behaviour from the other structural inequalities with which they intersect, focusing on the put-downs and discriminatory incidents experienced by relatively privileged women, rather than the constant abuse and exploitation experienced by those who are more vulnerable.

Another problem with 'sexism' is that it is a gender-neutral term. As Bates says, men too are sometimes treated unfairly because of their sex, that is, they too experience sexism. However, as she also says, such sexism is very different in terms of 'frequency, severity and context' from that experienced by women (2014:315). It is also different because of the overall gendered power context, discussed in the next paragraph, within which sexist incidents or actions take place. In this wider context there is, for example, a world of difference between jokes that mock privileged men and jokes that are at the expense of disadvantaged women. As has often been said, this is the difference between 'punching up', aimed at subverting existing inequalities by puncturing the unreflective and self-satisfied worldview of privileged people, and 'punching down', which humiliates those who are already downtrodden. This context is often forgotten, so that feminists can find themselves accused of lacking a sense of humour if they fail to find misogynistic jokes funny, while also being accused of sexism if they make a joke at men's expense; this accusation might itself tempt them to invoke a much-quoted observation by the novelist Margaret Atwood, generally paraphrased as 'Men are afraid that women will laugh at them. Women are afraid that men will kill them.'

When discussion of sexism treats sexist acts in isolation from wider patterns of male power, this can underestimate the difficulty of achieving substantive change. Thus, although Bates, reflecting on her project in 2014, said that she soon discovered that positions of power and authority in the judiciary, politics, culture and the media are dominated by men, she did not really explore the relationship of this institutionalised public power to sexism or its connection to other forms of male privilege, such as men's generally higher financial resources. Moreover, rather than seeing that male vested interests might make ending sexism both very complicated and very difficult, Bates was pleased to find that many men supported her project, and she insisted that ending sexism is a relatively simple question of cultural change: 'This is not a men versus women issue. It's about people versus prejudice', and 'The thing about sexism is that it is an eminently solvable problem' (2014:313 and 380). In contrast, a more analytical approach would see that the general privileging of men over women is not simply a matter of culture or attitudes but a complex, multidimensional system that contains a number of linked and mutually reinforcing economic, political, legal and physical as well as cultural elements. In this context, support from well-intentioned men is welcome, but it needs to take the form of action as well as words.

These criticisms do not mean that the term 'sexism' should be abandoned. Indeed, in identifying discriminatory practices and behaviours and labelling them as unacceptable, it continues to provide an accessible and politically very useful starting-point for feminist awareness and political action. However, it remains descriptive rather than analytical, and it needs to be used as part of a wider investigation of 'patriarchy', discussed in the following section.

Patriarchy

The concept of 'patriarchy' emerged in the late 1960s from the same ferment of left-wing ideas and experiences as 'sexism', as young women in a number of western countries, often white and relatively privileged, found that many apparently egalitarian and progressive men did not extend their political principles to their treatment of women. Sharing their bad experiences in 'consciousness-raising groups', these women began to discover that apparently individual and personal problems were widely shared; they also realised that they built up into a general pattern of male use and abuse of power. In this context, they began to argue that it was not only black people who were oppressed but women too, and that women should take immediate action to liberate themselves from what they soon learned to describe as 'patriarchy'.

The concept of 'patriarchy' went further than 'sexism' in clearly labelling men's collective power over women, 'joining the dots' between different aspects of women's experiences in both their political and their private lives, and linking these individual experiences to wider social structures and institutions. Today, if we see the world as not just 'gendered' but also as 'patriarchal', we can see that the gender disadvantages and inequalities outlined in the Introduction are both cumulative and interconnected and that they also take less tangible or measurable forms. It is not just that women generally earn less and are more likely to live in poverty than men in the same class or race-based group; nor is it just that they are under-represented in economic and political decision-making positions; nor is it just that their experiences, needs and perceptions have often been marginalised or ignored; and nor is it just that they are all too often subject to sexual harassment and violence and denied the right to make their own reproductive choices. Rather, individual and/or apparently separate examples of discrimination, exploitation or injustice build up into a more general picture of a world characterised by a gender hierarchy that is so ubiquitous and pervasive that, paradoxically, it can often seem as unremarkable and invisible as the air we breathe.

Some much earlier feminists had also been aware of the multifaceted nature of the injustices and disadvantages facing women, the need to campaign on a wide range of issues and some of the more subtle ways in which men maintained their power. For example, when the nineteenth-century philosopher John Stuart Mill argued that women had a right to education, employment and the vote, he also argued that they had a right to protection from abusive husbands. He further wrote that 'Men do not want solely the obedience of women, they want their sentiments ... They have therefore put everything in practice to enslave their minds' (1869/1983:26–7). At the same period in the United States, Elizabeth Cady Stanton was campaigning on the same public issues as Mill; she further argued that all forms of organised religion were used by men to oppress and manipulate women, she refused to listen to male 'experts' on how to bring up her children, she asserted her right to dress for comfort and convenience rather than male approval, and she insisted on keeping part of her own name when she got married (refusing to be known as 'Mrs Henry Stanton'). She also said that women themselves would have to fight for change against the contrary interests of men and that 'When I think of all the wrongs that have been heaped upon womankind, I am ashamed that I am not forever in a condition of chronic wrath, stark mad, skin and bones, my eyes a fountain of tears, my lips overflowing with curses' (quoted in Griffith, 1984:164). However, like Mill and other feminists of her day, Stanton had no word that could capture her ideas or that could analyse as well as describe the diverse wrongs that she identified. It was not until 1970, with the publication of Kate Millett's *Sexual Politics*, that feminists had an accessible and systematic way of conceptualising the interconnections between very different and apparently unrelated issues.

Describing her ideas as 'Notes towards a theory of patriarchy', Millett argued that all known societies have been structured around the power of men over women, that this patriarchal power extends into every area of human life and that, precisely because it is so universal and all-pervasive, it seems natural rather than political. She argued that 'patriarchy's chief institution is the family', and that it is primarily maintained by a process of socialisation, whereby women are taught about their own inferiority and unimportance from childhood; this early 'interior colonisation' is then confirmed by the whole of education, literature and religion. Patriarchy therefore rests on the consent of women as well as men. However, it is also underpinned by state power, the legal system and the economic exploitation of women and, like all systems of domination, it ultimately relies on the use or threat of physical force; this threat extends into intimate life, where it often takes the form of sexual violence and rape. In the context of such domination, Millett said, love can only be a confidence trick that disguises the power inevitably involved in all relationships between women and men.

At the time, many women found that labelling their society as 'patriarchal' provided a powerful new way of seeing the world and making sense of their lives, and many described a 'click experience' as separate pieces of knowledge and experience fell into place (Tobias, 1997:5, 192). Since 1970, the concept has been developed by a number of feminist writers, and heavily criticised by others; at the beginning of the twenty-first century it was somewhat out of favour, but today it is quite widely used in popular discussion of #MeToo or the gender pay gap. While it can be used carelessly, or to make over-inflated claims, I believe that the concept of patriarchy continues to provide critical insights that can and should inform effective feminist politics. Here I identify three key areas where it seems particularly helpful, before looking at its limitations.

Rejecting the 'normality' of a male-centred worldview

Perhaps the most fundamental contribution that the concept of patriarchy has made to feminist or human knowledge has been to take women and their experiences as its starting-point. This has the immediate effect of decentring men; it thereby challenges both the 'normality' of their perspectives and the underlying assumption that they are the measure of what it is to be human and that society should be organised in accordance with their needs. It also exposes the particularity of men's supposedly objective way of knowing the world, in which women become an optional extra or special interest – as for example in the distinction between 'history' and 'women's history', or 'novels' and 'women's novels'. This means that, despite its universalistic pretentions, the 'mainstream' of political, social, economic and cultural life is effectively a 'male-stream' that marginalises or excludes half the population.

The dominant assumption that men are 'normal' can have dangerous and/or discriminatory effects. As Caroline Criado-Perez (2019) has shown, practical effects include women's greater risk of injury or death in a car crash (because safety tests have been based on the average male body); failing to recognise the symptoms of heart attacks (which typically differ between women and men); and producing tools that are too large for the average woman to use. More generally, women have to conform to male standards if they want equality. This means that any 'difference' (such as giving birth or raising children) is treated as a sign of women's inferiority and inability to compete with men, while their domestic and caring responsibilities are invisible to economists and political analysts. From this partial and inadequate perspective, political and economic equality between the sexes means little more than 'business as usual plus a few more women'.

In contrast, women-centred perspectives remind us that the world of paid employment would collapse without women's unpaid work, and that genuine equality cannot be on the terms that have already been written by men; rather, it requires a radical reordering of priorities and assumptions in all areas of life. Such reordering should not, however, constitute a simple reversal of earlier values and arrangements. As discussed below and in Chapter 3, there is no one 'women's perspective', but a kaleidoscope of shifting, overlapping, fragmentary and sometimes clashing viewpoints, reflecting both the diversity of women's experiences and the ways that these can change over time. Displacing men is, therefore, only the first step towards moving beyond the limitations of a worldview based on either 'side' of a binary division. Here the difficult trick is to balance awareness of differences amongst women and the instability of the terms 'women' and 'men' with recognition of the often grim realities of a world that is, in general, not only gendered but also patriarchal.

Expanding the notion of the political

Until recently, conventional political thinking in the west has generally accepted the liberal assumption that there is a clear and necessary distinction between public and private life, with politics firmly restricted to the public sphere. From this dominant perspective, what happens in personal or family life has nothing to do with political principles like justice or equality; rather, it is a matter of personal choices and preferences that concern only the individuals involved. For example, when John Rawls wrote his influential *Theory of Justice*, first published in 1971, he initially assumed that the 'individuals' whose interests the creators of a just society should consider were male heads of households, and that justice already existed in the family (for feminist responses, see Okin, 1990; Abbey, ed., 2013). Economic theories have similarly focused on the public world of paid employment and monetary exchanges, seeing raising children, caring for others or cleaning the house as unproductive activities that economists can safely ignore.

In contrast, the concept of patriarchy shows us that how we define politics is *itself* a political issue, and that the conventional belief that private life should be kept separate from political analysis is based on an artificial and self-serving distinction that helps sustain patriarchy by concealing its private bases. Once we see that 'the personal is political', we can see the ways in which men generally benefit from conventional family arrangements, and that these can have knock-on effects on other areas of life, helping to explain both the gender pay gap and the relative paucity of women in political life: quite simply, it is harder for people with domestic and caring responsibilities to pursue either well-paid employment or a political career.

As discussed in the previous chapter, an expanded notion of politics and power also enables us to see that acts of domestic and/or sexual violence should be seen not as rare and isolated incidents carried out by a tiny minority of evil men but as part of a continuum of aggressive behaviour and a wider system of power and control that starts with sexualised 'banter' and wolf-whistling, and that can turn public spaces or workplaces into hostile environments for women. The concept of patriarchy also helps explain why states have historically ignored, tolerated or even encouraged such sexist behaviour. In general, it seems that it is only when women gain a degree of political power that such behaviour is seriously challenged and recognised as part of a wider pattern of power; even today, when governments are increasingly aware of the extent of misogynistic violence, they are unwilling to allocate adequate resources to challenging it.

Joining the dots: from a vicious to a virtuous circle

The expanded notion of politics outlined above exposes the interconnected nature and cumulative effect of apparently random and unrelated manifestations of male power and privilege; it also shows how the foundations of this are laid down from the earliest years. This means that inequalities or injustices in one area reinforce those in another, and that issues that at first seem trivial, or even benign, can reinforce more obvious abuses of power.

In my Introduction I outlined some of the inequalities and problems faced by women around the world. The litany of injustices could go on and on, and it can seem both overwhelming and deeply dispiriting, particularly when we understand that, as I argue in later chapters, patriarchy is entangled with both racism and the international capitalist economy. Listing problems can also encourage what some feminist critics see as a negative obsession with victimhood that ignores all signs of progress (Wolf, 1993; Walter, 1998; Williams, 2017). However, the flip side of arguing that patriarchy is a *system* and that problems are interconnected is to see that the same thing applies to potential solutions; this means that even minor positive changes in one area can have knock-on effects on others, and that any kind of action can gain significance and strength when accompanied by other forms of political engagement. In other words, the vicious circle of mutually reinforcing spheres of domination can be broken into at a number of points and gradually converted into a virtuous circle of progressive change.

Today, feminists in the UK are acting as individuals and campaigning collectively on an extraordinarily wide range of issues that includes equal pay, political representation, support for women's refuges, abortion rights, affordable childcare, objecting to sexist jokes in the workplace, choosing gender-neutral toys for their children, researching women's history, exposing the misogynistic behaviour of powerful men and campaigning to get more statues of women in public spaces. If we see these issues as interconnected, part of a wider system of opposition to male power and privilege, we can see that the effects of apparently unrelated actions and campaigns can be complementary and cumulative; from this perspective it is not always necessary to argue about their relative importance or to complain about the misdirection of feminist energies on to apparently trivial issues. Interconnected activities are also building up to produce global feminist networks, and Cynthia Enloe (a major writer on feminist international relations) argues that 'both UN and member state officials now have to spend more energy and political currency trying to explain away their complicity with efforts to sustain patriarchy' (2017:57).

These interconnections also help explain the anger that is often provoked by apparently minor feminist claims. For example, in 2013, Caroline Criado-Perez successfully campaigned to have Jane Austen's face on a UK banknote (without Austen, no woman other than the Queen would have been depicted on any note). This might not look like a serious blow to patriarchy. However, if we see Criado-Perez's campaign as part of a wider challenge to the authority of men and the silencing of women, we can better understand why some men seemed to find it deeply threatening, and why some reasserted their power by threatening to rape or kill her.

Patriarchy: a complex concept, to be handled with care

While I believe that the concept of 'patriarchy' is an important feminist tool, I also believe that it is often misused. This subsection contains interconnected warnings against simplistic interpretations that distort our understanding and can be politically counterproductive.

First, 'patriarchy' should not be treated as a stand-alone concept. It is not the only form of oppression, and it needs to be treated as part of a wider analysis that explores how the structures of male domination intersect with other dimensions of inequality and exploitation and the ways in which they are bound up with the logic of the global capitalist economy. The implications of such a multidimensional approach are developed in later chapters, in which I argue for broadly socialist solutions.

Second, this means that I disagree with some early proponents of the concept, including Mary Daly (1973), Adrienne Rich (1977) and Robin Morgan (1984) as well as Millett. These writers have sometimes seemed to say that, because all known societies are patriarchal, they are all essentially 'the same', that all women are united as victims of global patriarchy, that patriarchal power necessarily overrides divisions of class and race, and that, therefore, 'sisterhood is global' (Morgan, 1984, book title). As I have shown, there are indeed patterns to be found, and women in radically different societies often have experiences in common involving sexual exploitation, lack of reproductive choice, economic exploitation and/or exclusion or marginalisation from mainstream social, cultural and political life. At the same time, however, some women oppress other women, and over-generalised claims risk trivialising the depths of suffering and humiliation inflicted on some by equating them with the slights and inconveniences experienced by others.

The problem with over-generalising is not simply that women's experiences are vastly different, but that relatively privileged women assume the centrality of their own concerns in much the same ways as men have assumed the centrality of theirs, so that 'There are disturbing parallels between what feminists find disquieting in Western political thought and what many black women have found troubling in much of Western feminism' (Spelman, 1988:6). However, I believe that the concept can be rescued from exaggerated simplifications and generalisation if, as I argue throughout this book, it is combined with analysis of race and class and used to explore the interconnections between different forms of discrimination, inequality and oppression.

A third, related, warning stems from the untenable notion that patriarchy is somehow timeless and unchanging. A moment's reflection shows this to be nonsense. Millett herself said that, although the overall system of patriarchy remained in place, by 1970 it had become 'much altered and attenuated' in the US and Europe (1970/1985:26). She attributed this to the campaigns of women in the past, and her own work was motivated by the belief that her writing could help achieve further change. In the half century since Millett outlined the concept, it looks at first sight as if the foundations of western patriarchy have been decidedly shaken, if not yet overturned. Most obviously, the western world that Millett described, in which women were virtually absent from political life or high-status employment, most were economically dependent on a husband and 'nice girls' did not have sex before or outside marriage, is not a world familiar to most young women today (although the sexual double-standard remains strong). As outlined in the Introduction there has also been a widespread shift in official attitudes, so that gender equality and/or an end to violence against women are now the stated goal of many national and international organisations. By 2017, the feminist writer Naomi Wolf was arguing that the ability of the #MeToo movement to call some powerful men to account had 'torn the fabric of patriarchy' while a headline in the *Guardian* newspaper asked 'Is the patriarchy over?' (Saner, 2017).

However, as other feminists have argued, recent changes represent not the end of patriarchy but only a shift in its nature. For example, Enloe says that:

> Patriarchy is a system – a dynamic web – of particular ideas and relationships. That system ... is not brittle; it is not static. Patriarchy can be updated and modernised. It is stunningly adaptable. (2017:16)

In much of the world, such adaptation has historically involved a general movement away from private patriarchy, based on individual control within the home, to public patriarchy based on structures in the world outside. From this perspective, most western women are no longer entirely economically dependent on their husband, but many are dependent on the male-run state for employment or benefits; similarly, most are no longer sexually controlled by family members, but the rising use of pornography represents 'a more collective, impersonal, male control of women's bodies' (Ferguson, 1989:115). Such arguments have been neatly summarised by Sylvia Walby: 'Women are no longer restricted to the domestic hearth, but have the whole society in which to roam and be exploited' (1990:201) – although as she also said, there is no neat division between private and public forms of patriarchy, and she subsequently (1997) sought to analyse the complex gains and losses experienced by different groups of women in different areas of their lives.

One reason for the changing nature of patriarchy is the changing nature of the capitalist economic system with which it is inexorably entangled. As Beatrix Campbell has argued, our era of global capitalism is seeing a new form of patriarchy; she describes this as 'neopatriarchal neoliberalism, an ugly name for an ugly deal' (2013:5). This new system at first sight appears to have responded to feminist pressures, so that in principle it allows girls to become astronauts, bankers or anything else they want, but in practice it resists any genuine change to the division of labour between women and men, it exploits women on a global scale and, in line with neoliberal economic theory, it dismantles the welfare provisions and state benefits that have provided a safety net for the poorest women (for related arguments, see Chapter 6). While this can sound like a counsel of despair, it can serve as a reminder of the complexity rather than the impossibility of the task facing feminists; here Enloe, who shares many of Campbell's concerns, also insists that 'Updated patriarchy is not invincible', that feminist campaigns are having a measure of success across the world, and that what we need now is 'organized, cross-race, inter-generational, transnational resistance' (2017:159, 166).

Seeing patriarchy as a dynamic and complex system also means that we should resist referring to 'the patriarchy'. This formulation, which has recently crept into feminist vocabulary, seems to suggest some kind of stable, monolithic control by a uniform group. I believe it is unhelpfully simplistic, and that it makes no more sense to talk about 'the patriarchy' than it does to talk about 'the capitalism' or 'the democracy'.

Finally, to say that the concept of patriarchy can help us understand the world is not to label all women as helpless victims and all men as active oppressors. This is self-evidently not the case: there have always been many brave women who fight their own corner and the oppression of others, and many feminist women have received personal and/ or political support and encouragement from men. If we see societies as patriarchal, we are identifying men's collective power as the underlying problem, and we need to focus on this rather than on the bad behaviour of individual men. As Jessa Crispin says, we cannot eliminate misogyny 'individual by individual', while the 'casual demonization of white straight men follows the same pattern of bias and hatred that fuels misogyny, racism, and homophobia ... the same lazy thinking, easy scapegoating, and pleasurable anger that all other forms of hatred have' (2017: 100, 101–2).

At a fundamental level, the privileging of men's interests and concerns is systematic, in the sense that it is not random. However, patriarchy does not have the same necessary dynamic as the capitalist economic system, which is based on the remorseless pursuit of growth and profit as ends in themselves. This dynamic means that in the long term it is impossible to be a good, non-exploitative capitalist without going out of business. In contrast, in principle it is possible to be a good man, even a feminist or pro-feminist man, in a patriarchal society – although this is not easy, and many men are more privileged than they realise (not least by the comfortable, unreflective sense of their own 'normality'). It is also clear that men do not all benefit from living in a patriarchal society. In particular, as discussed in the previous chapter, many men cannot hope to achieve western society's expectations of masculinity; for those men whose lives are blighted by poverty, racism and/or homophobia, any idea that their interests are systematically privileged must seem like a bad joke.

Reflections and conclusions: challenging patriarchy, renaming the world

A first step towards challenging patriarchy is to name it. This is not an academic exercise, but part of a shift in understanding that helps rob male power of its 'naturalness'. Such naming can contribute to 'real world' change. It is therefore important to retain the concept even if it makes people feel uncomfortable; as Enloe says, 'The fact that patriarchy is a term so many people shy away from using is one of the things that enables it to survive' (2017:15).

The other terms discussed in these opening chapters can similarly contribute to change by helping women see things they previously knew but had no way of expressing. In doing this, they can also reframe public perceptions and debates. I have therefore argued that, despite its problems, the sex/gender distinction remains a useful reminder that socially ascribed gender roles, attributes and behaviour are not the inevitable outcome of biology, while the terms 'sexual harassment' and 'sexism' enable us to identify and contest oppressive and/or discriminatory forms of behaviour that were previously experienced as isolated events. In this context, 'patriarchy' constitutes an umbrella concept that pulls such insights together and reveals the cumulative and interconnected nature of apparently unrelated aspects of life from the bedroom to the boardroom, the classroom to the government, and the rape crisis centre to the internet.

A few newer terms such as 'mansplaining' and 'manspreading' have also gained widespread currency. Some feminists dislike these terms as trivial and/or unfair to many men. For example, Rebecca Solnit, who has often been erroneously credited with coining the term 'mansplaining' (after she described how a man insisted on telling her all about a book *which she herself had written*), fears that the term blames all men for the bad behaviour of a few (2014). However, 'mansplaining' has clearly struck a chord with many women, suggesting that it describes a widely shared experience that had not previously been articulated. The subversiveness of this and other new terms does not lie in accusing all men of something, but in looking *at* men through women's eyes, in the context of a wider social environment that endows many of them with a privileged sense of superiority and entitlement. Here I would like to make a pitch for greater feminist use of the term 'phallic drift', identified by Diane Bell and Renate Klein as 'the powerful tendency for public discussion of gender issues to drift, inexorably, back to the male point of view' (1996:561).

Some feminists have also sought to reclaim terms that have traditionally been used to insult women. For example, the 'slutwalk' movement began in 2011, after a Canadian police officer said women should stop dressing like 'sluts' if they wanted to avoid getting attacked; the feminists who then marched and demonstrated under the 'slutwalk' banner in many nations were not only protesting against the view that women were to blame if they were assaulted, they were also redefining a negative term for feminist ends (Mendes, 2015; Teekah et al., 2015). Similarly, the homepage of the feminist magazine *Bitch* explains its use of the term:

> When it's being used as an insult, 'bitch' is an epithet hurled at women who speak their minds, who have opinions and don't shy away from expressing them, and who don't sit by and smile uncomfortably if they're bothered or offended. If being an outspoken woman means being a bitch, we'll take that as a compliment. (www.bitchmedia.org/about-us)

Reclaiming terms like 'slut' and 'bitch' can clearly make some women feel powerful. However, this may be easier for some groups than others, and some women of colour have opposed the use of 'slut' by feminists, arguing that this fails to understand the power, depth and virulence of the contempt it expresses when it is applied to black women (Black Women's Blueprint, 2011/2016). Similarly, it can seem subversive if feminists reject conventionally 'ladylike' language in favour of swearing, but if such taboo-breaking involves a viciously negative portrayal of women's genitals this is hardly empowering: thus at the end of what she had found a very funny (and feminist) show by a young woman comedian, my friend Penny was moved to queue up at the end to congratulate her but also to say that her frequent use of 'cunt' as a term of abuse (which she mainly directed at men) made her feel uncomfortable 'because, you know, I've got one'.

More generally, the development of a feminist language that both articulates women's particular experiences and places them in a wider context is an important part of collective political engagement. It is a way of contesting the silencing of women, and also guards us against getting dragged into debates on terms we would never use. As Solnit says: 'If the right to speak, if having credibility, if being heard is a kind of wealth, that wealth is now being redistributed' (2017:23). So far, such redistribution has only just begun, and it remains critically important for feminists to develop the terms they have. Any redistribution is also heavily skewed in favour of the most privileged women. As I argue throughout this book, issues of gender inequality and oppression cannot be understood or challenged in isolation from their economic, political and cultural context, and they are entangled with other forms of inequality and oppression. These entanglements are the focus of the next chapter.

3

Intersectionality: a dry word that can make a lot of sense

IN THE PREVIOUS chapter, I 'named' patriarchy as a multifaceted, inter-connected and self-reinforcing system that generally privileges men's perceptions and interests but which is also entangled with other forms of structural power and inequality. In this chapter, I agree with those who use the term 'intersectionality', first developed by black feminists in the US, to address such entanglements and place the most oppressed and disadvantaged women at the heart of feminist analysis. In line with the socialist feminist approach that I develop in this book, I also argue that such analysis must recognise the central importance of class, as well as gender and race.

I cannot remember when I first encountered the term, but I do remember thinking at first that it was just a bit of passing feminist jargon, before quickly seeing it as a necessary restatement of what should be blindingly obvious but is all too often ignored. In this respect, I find myself in partial agreement with the UK politician Dawn Butler who, when she was appointed Shadow Minister for Women and Equalities in 2017, described intersectionality as 'my new favourite word', adding that 'it takes a while to get used to' (Photiou, 2017). Today, in line with the arguments of Kimberlé Crenshaw, the black American academic generally credited with introducing the concept, I see intersectionality as a very useful analytical tool that has important and radical practical applications. I also agree with Crenshaw when she says that it is not a 'grand theory', and that it does not offer causal explanations as to why the world is as it is.

I open the chapter with Crenshaw's classic exposition of the term, before exploring both its antecedents in earlier black feminist thought and its reception in the context of late twentieth-century intellectual and ideological developments. In the next section I tackle developments and debates that have emerged as intersectionality has 'travelled', focusing on arguments about which differences and identities can, should or must be included in intersectional analysis. The final section explores some practical examples of intersectional analysis and politics.

As a black feminist concept, intersectionality has troubled the assumptions of many white western feminists by revealing the unthinking racism that has permitted them to think they can speak for 'women'. However, now that the term is on the brink of assimilation into 'mainstream' feminist vocabulary, it sometimes seems little more than a sloppy buzzword, thrown around by feminist groups to indicate a wish to be inclusive, but without any serious self-examination or real content. Such usage also tends to focus on individual experiences rather than on structural forms of oppression. Throughout the chapter and in its conclusion, I seek to defend intersectionality's subversive potential against these deradicalising tendencies.

Crenshaw's metaphor: who injures the pedestrian when two roads intersect?

Intersectional thinking did not originate with Crenshaw. She was, however, probably the first to use the term, in an article first published in 1989. Writing in the context of radical ideas and approaches around feminism, social justice, postmodernism, civil rights, critical race studies and critical legal studies that were circulating in US law schools at the time, her aim was to expose and contest the way that black women's specific needs, experiences and very existence were rendered invisible by US anti-discrimination legislation. In particular, she wanted to convey the inability of this legislation, ostensibly in place to defend the interests of women and black people, to see, let alone meet, the needs of those who were in both categories – that is, *black women.*

Crenshaw based her initial arguments on the case of a group of black women who had lost their jobs but who were unable to claim that they had been unfairly discriminated against on grounds of either sex or race: white women remained employed (so there was no sex-based discrimination) and so too did black men (so there was no race-based discrimination either). She likened this to the situation of an individual knocked down at the intersection of two roads, who may have been injured by a vehicle coming from either direction, or both at once, but who can call for an ambulance only once the driver who caused the accident is identified: if this is unclear, 'the tendency seems to be that no driver is held responsible, no treatment is administered, and the involved parties simply get back in their cars and zoom away' (1989/1998:322).

Crenshaw further argued that the single-axis mindset of anti-discrimination legislation extends into wider political claims for racial or gender equality, which are generally based on the experiences of the most privileged members of subordinated groups: that is, black men in the case of racial inequality, and white women in the case of gender inequality. Within these dominant frameworks, black women simply disappear, and white feminists have felt able to make generalised claims, such as the assertion that society teaches us that 'men' are powerful and 'women' are weak and passive, without noticing that these teachings do not apply to black people.

In a slightly later (1991) article, Crenshaw applied her metaphor to highlight black women's particular experiences of domestic and sexual violence, arguing that these have been largely ignored in both anti-racist and anti-sexist movements, in which the interests of 'people of colour' and 'women' are often treated as if they are in opposition. More recently (2016; 2018), she has drawn attention to other dimensions of black female experience that have received little public or political attention in the US, particularly the high number of black women who have been killed by the police and of black girls suspended from schools (the killing of black men and the suspension of black boys have received far more publicity). Here she has again used intersectionality as a metaphor to highlight both what is actually happening in many women's lives and the inability of dominant approaches, which focus on either gender *or* race, to see this; she argues that we must not lose sight of what occurs at an intersection, and we must see that this is qualitatively different from events on the main highway.

Historical background

Like the term patriarchy, intersectionality provides a neat and memorable way of capturing insights that women had reached in earlier generations, but that had tended to disappear from public consciousness. In her original article, Crenshaw invoked the call for inclusion made by Sojourner Truth, a black campaigner and former slave who, at a women's rights convention in 1851, was reported to have rebutted the claim that women were too weak and frail to deserve the vote with a reminder of the strength and suffering of women like herself, who had toiled under the lash and seen their children sold into slavery – 'and ain't I a woman?' Ironically, this refrain was probably never actually spoken by Truth herself, but written into an account by a white feminist over ten years later (Painter, 1997). Nevertheless, it summarises important insights, for Truth was challenging not only men's view of women but also the invisibility of black women and the falsity of white women's assumption that they represented the whole of their sex.

White feminists' erasure of black women's perspectives was particularly clear in the years after the American civil war, when many of them rejected the argument that they should set aside their own claim to voting rights because 'this is the negro's hour'. Faced with an apparent choice between the claims of sex and race, these women chose their sex, and many were quite overtly racist. Meanwhile, the 'negro's hour' was of course understood as the hour of black *men*. This understanding was, however, contested by some black women, including Sojourner Truth, who warned that 'if the coloured men get their rights and not the coloured women theirs, you see the coloured men will be the masters over the women, and it will be just as bad as it was before' (quoted in Giddings,

1984:65) A generation later, Julia Cooper famously asserted that black men could not speak for all black people, and that

> Only the BLACK WOMAN can say 'when and where I enter, in the quiet, undisputed dignity of my womanhood, without violence and without suing or special patronage, then and there the whole *Negro race enters with me.*' (1892/1988: 31, emphasis in original)

By the 1930s and 1940s, a number of black women who were in or connected to the US Communist Party were further analysing the specific situation of black women in relation to *class* politics. Activists such as Marvel Cooke, Ella Baker, Louise Thompson Patterson and Claudia Jones argued that black women were particularly exploited as domestic workers, and that they experienced 'triple exploitation' or 'superexploitation' 'as workers, as women, and as Negroes' (quoted in McDuffie, 2011:112). They even persuaded the party to recognise officially that these black women were the most exploited group of all workers, although in practice its male leaders continued to see their situation as something to be addressed 'after the revolution'.

Few of the white women in the civil rights, anti-war and feminist movements of the 1960s and 1970s knew about these earlier analyses. They were not deliberately racist but, like the white feminists of Sojourner Truth's day, they tended simply to forget that some people are both female and black – a tendency epitomised in the titles of Gayle Rubin's 1970 essay 'Woman as nigger' and John Lennon and Yoko Ono's 1972 song 'Woman is the nigger of the world'. In this kind of context, many black women agreed with bell hooks when she complained in 1981 that

> black women have felt forced to choose between a black movement that primarily serves the interests of black male patriarchs, and a white women's movement which primarily serves the interests of racist white women. (1981:9)

hooks herself argued (1984) that the white feminist idea of 'sisterhood', which concealed differences amongst women, should be replaced by that of 'solidarity', which enables different groups of women to support each other without insisting that their situation is all the same; it also enables them to form alliances with oppressed groups of men. Other more class-based black feminist ideas re-emerged in the work of Angela Davis, probably the best known woman in the 1960s black liberation movement, and a member of the US Communist Party until 1991. In *Women, Race and Class*, first published in 1982, Davis argued that a feminist movement which begins with middle-class white women will only change their position at the top of the social pyramid, leaving the lives of other women untouched. We should therefore aim at improving the situation of those at the bottom – that is, working-class black women – because this would transform the entire oppressive structure of society.

At around the same time, one of the first anthologies written by black feminists was published. Its title, *All the Women Are White, All the Blacks Are Men, But Some of Us Are Brave* (Hull et al., eds, 1982), memorably captured the combination of erasure with the contrary determination to insist on black women's presence, and Crenshaw used it as 'a point of departure' in her original article (1989/1998:314). Other influential books published in the early 1980s also insisted that black women's voices should be heard and treated as central to feminist analysis: these included Audre Lorde's *Sister Outsider* (1984), bell hooks's *Feminist Theory: From Margin to Center* (1984) and the edited collection *This Bridge Called My Back: Writings by Radical Women of Color* (Moraga and Anzaldua, eds, 1983/2015). This last collection included the important 'Combahee River Statement' by the Combahee River Collective, written in 1977. The Collective identified 'racial, sexual, heterosexual, and class oppression' as 'interlocking' systems, and argued that none of these could be addressed in isolation, but that '[i]f Black women were free, it would mean that everyone else would have to be free since our freedom would necessitate the destruction of all the systems of oppression' (1977/2015:210, 215). From this perspective, including black women in feminist politics is not an optional extra or a friendly gesture; it is an essential starting-point for meaningful change.

Intersectionality by the end of the twentieth century

Related or similar ideas had been developing independently in Europe. For example, Lola Olufemi (2020) argues that black feminist groups in the UK were practising intersectionality well before Crenshaw had coined the term, while Nira Yuval-Davis (2006) has pointed out that from the 1980s she and others were exploring the relationships between gender, class and ethnic divisions in the UK, and Amrit Wilson (1978/2018) showed how race, class and patriarchy impacted on the lives of Asian women. Many British Asian feminists were particularly aware of the competing interests involved when they sought to confront issues such as domestic violence and forced marriage in communities which experienced the authorities, particularly the police, as sources of racist oppression or immigration control rather than protection (Siddiqui, 2000; https://southallblacksisters.org.uk). However, these home-grown ideas lacked a ready label, and the imported term 'intersectionality' has become firmly established amongst European feminists, not only in academic discourse but also at the level of policy-making and political activism.

Intersectional thinking was also in evidence at the 1995 United Nations World Conference on Women in Beijing, which identified the multiple barriers faced by many women, and it has provided the basis for global initiatives. These include the 2001 United Nations World Conference Against Racism, Racial Discrimination, Xenophobia and Related Intolerances, held in Durban, South Africa, and Crenshaw herself was involved in the preparatory work for this (Collins and Bilge, 2016).

Meanwhile, the surge of black feminist theory-making in the US continued into the 1990s. Much of this built on Crenshaw's insights in highlighting the interactive, interlocking and interdependent nature of different forms of oppression. In her influential *Black Feminist Thought*, first published in 1990, Patricia Hill Collins described this as a paradigm shift in feminist knowledge that opened up the way to a more general awareness of how different systems of disadvantage and oppression interact as part of a larger, interconnected whole.

Collins herself said that all individuals are positioned in a *matrix* of disadvantage and privilege, and that few will be purely victims or purely oppressors. She also drew on feminist standpoint theory to argue that the perspective of those who are disadvantaged by a system of oppression is not only different from that of those who are advantaged by it, it is also more accurate, so that if black women's perspectives are excluded from feminist thought, then its attempt to understand even the situation of white women will be seriously flawed. By the end of the twentieth century, some white feminists agreed with this analysis, and attempted to move beyond earlier 'confessions' of shortcomings to a critical awareness of their own racial identity.

The understanding that previously marginalised people can best define their own reality, and that they should be at the centre of analysis, is also found in the postcolonial feminist ideas that developed from the 1980s and that are particularly associated with Chandra Mohanty and Gayatri Spivak (although the latter has been critical of intersectionality, her analysis shares many of its assumptions). Other scholars have explicitly developed intersectional analysis to argue that, if we are to understand the impact of globalisation on women in the south, we must go beyond a narrow focus on gender to explore the ways in which this is mediated by intersecting identities, such as caste, class, ethnicity, race and religion (Patil, 2013).

Intersectionality and postmodernism

Intersectional and postcolonial approaches both also have some affinities with the post-structuralist and postmodernist ideas around language, knowledge and power that had come to dominate much of western intellectual life by the late twentieth century. Rather than accepting that terms such as 'woman' have any stable or inherent meaning, these new approaches stressed the fluid, multiple and artificial nature of any identity category and, in her 1991 article, Crenshaw explicitly agreed with the postmodern finding that categories such as 'black' and 'women' are socially constructed, and that we should question their 'naturalness'. Postmodernism also supports the idea that, although dominant groups will attempt to impose their ways of seeing on to the world, this can be challenged by those on the margins of society.

The strong position of postmodern theory in many universities meant that by the late 1990s, when black feminist theory was beginning to become established as an academic discipline in the US, its key idea of intersectionality fell on fertile academic ground. This has in some ways served to legitimise it and give a veneer of respectability to its more subversive and unsettling claims. Conversely, intersectionality's black feminist origins were useful to postmodern feminist theorists, as its apparently similar conclusions could provide political credibility to their more abstract analyses.

However, as Crenshaw also saw, postmodernism can be a dangerous tool for any kind of progressive politics. Categories such as 'women' or 'black women' may be artificial, but they can have very real consequences, and in practice it may be necessary to organise politically around them. Here Crenshaw believes that intersectionality can provide a way forward beyond the indefinite open-endedness of postmodern analysis, because it allows us to act on the basis of group identity at the same time as seeing that particular groups are not fixed or uniform; rather, they are actual or potential coalitions. This means, for example, that we can continue to organise politically around 'race' but we should also reconceptualise this as 'a coalition between men and women of color' that can also be 'a coalition of straight and gay people of color' (1991:1299).

I find the idea that social groups are coalitions extremely useful, but I am not clear that we need to employ postmodernism to see this. I therefore agree with Collins's more critical position. She finds that, at best, postmodernism might provide a 'corrective moment' that supports black feminism's claim to speak from the margins and its challenge to false universalism. However, Collins also finds that postmodernism is unable to see major structural inequalities and that, far from genuinely giving voice to the marginalised, it merely 'provides some relief to intellectuals who wish to resist oppression in the abstract without decentering their own material privileges' (1998:150). As many other critics have said, postmodernism's stress on fragmentation and its denial of the 'reality' of categories such as 'women' or 'class' are also in tune with the individualistic assumptions of the neoliberal ideology that is used to justify economic policies that have disproportionately damaged those who are already disadvantaged (see Chapters 5 and 6).

Differences and identities: which ones 'count'?

Both Crenshaw and Collins initially focused on the intersection between race and gender. However, they also opened the door to the analysis of other intersecting forms of oppression, including class, sexual orientation and age (see for example Crenshaw, 1991:1299, 1245 footnote 10; Collins, 2000:129; Guobadia, 2018). This raises the question of whether an intersectional approach must be endlessly open-ended, requiring us to list all forms of oppression or difference, starting from the 'big three' of gender, race and class, through sexual orientation, gender identity, age, physical ability and citizenship status to what Judith Butler has termed 'the embarrassed "etc"' (1990:143). Such an approach can easily drift into an individualistic and narcissistic form of identity politics that gets stuck at the level of personal self-expression, conceals the reality of collective experiences and structural oppression, and encourages individuals who are highly privileged in many ways to identify as members of an oppressed group. It can also have a paralysing effect on political analysis and activism, suggesting that we cannot address any one form of discrimination or oppression without simultaneously addressing them all (Russell, 2018).

These problems are not, however, inherent in intersectional analysis. To see the importance of such analysis and avoid the problems associated with it, we need to understand five interconnected points, which I develop in the rest of this section. First, individual experiences should not be equated with structural forms of privilege, oppression and power, but they may be connected to them. For example, when the newly elected MP Dawn Butler was in a lift in the UK House of Commons, she was told by a Conservative member that she should not be there as the lift was not for cleaners (Wren, 2018). This was not a random personal experience, but clearly reflected her identity as a black woman, and the social role that such a person is expected to play in a society structured by inequalities of race and gender.

Second, privileges and oppressions are not self-contained and separate but interlocking and mutually constitutive. This means that they cannot be understood in isolation from one another. This point is absolutely critical to intersectional analysis. To repeat Crenshaw's primary example: men and women are not only men and women, they are white men, black men, white women and black women – for the experience and meaning of gender is always racialised and the experience and meaning of race is always gendered. This means that it is not simply meaningless to compare 'women' with 'black people', it is also both racist and sexist, because the comparison leaves no way of seeing *black women*. When a white feminist held up a sign on a 'slut walk' (see Chapter 2) in 2011 that referenced the Lennon/Ono song title to proclaim that 'Woman is the Nigger of the world', she was therefore widely condemned for her lack of intersectional awareness; this reaction was summed up by Flavia Dzodan (2011), whose much-quoted response to the sign was: 'My feminism will be intersectional or it will be bullshit!' More generally, Collins and Sirma Bilge have condemned a 'resurrection of the tendency to draw parallels between the experiences of oppressed groups for the purpose of advocating on behalf of one's own group … [This] breaches the most basic premise of intersectionality: analogies such as these erase multiply disadvantaged groups' (2016:106).

The 'basic premise' identified by Collins and Bilge leads into my third point: that any identity or social group is inevitably a *coalition* of people who are all also members of other groups, and that there is no one foundational or explanatory category from which everything else flows. No one is ever simply a woman, or a black person – or a young person, a politician, a fat person, a poor person, an immigrant, a man, a teacher, a tax payer, a sex worker, a parent, a socialist or a lesbian. As Anna Carastathis has said, this understanding can be deeply challenging, as it asks us not only to think about different aspects of our own and others' identity but also to 'think about how we think' and to 'grapple with and overcome our entrenched perceptual-cognitive habits of essentialism, categorical purity and segregation' (2016:4). It also rules out any kind of identity-based politics that suppresses differences within groups, reifies particular aspects of group culture and/or promotes separatism rather than alliances with other disadvantaged groups.

The coalitional nature of identity, and the ways in which this can be used to claim a political voice, is illustrated clearly in relation to marginalised sexualities and gender identities. These have gained a degree of political and cultural recognition through the LGBTQ+ 'community', as a self-consciously open-ended coalition of those who define themselves as lesbian, gay, bisexual, trans, queer/questioning, or in other ways outside the dominant two-gender, cis-gender, heterosexual norm. As I show in the next chapter, this 'community' is far from united, while its coalition members are also inevitably members of other groups, including black and white, old and young, and rich and poor. An intersectional analysis shows that LGBTQ+ people who are disadvantaged in these other social dimensions are likely to face particularly difficult economic and social situations (including destitution and greater vulnerability to physical aggression). However, they are also likely to find that their particular experiences are further marginalised or forgotten, as the more privileged members of this coalition of coalitions are most able to express and gain a hearing for their own priorities, and they may unthinkingly claim to speak for the wider group.

This is linked to my fourth point: that, because intersectionality is about power and inequality, it is about those who are advantaged as well as those who are oppressed, although it may not be in privileged people's immediate interest to recognise this. An intersectional approach does not simply say that people who are female, black, poor, gay, trans or disabled are 'different' from dominant groups, it also challenges the idea that dominant groups are 'normal' and that they should be the starting-point for social analysis. As I said above, this also means that those who are oppressed in one way cannot automatically speak for all members of 'their' group.

In this context, the mantra 'check your privileges' can provide a useful reminder to some white western women that they should not be the automatic starting-point for feminist analysis, and that they should not simply listen to those who are more disadvantaged and marginalised, but allow them to take centre stage. Taken seriously, this message can and should be deeply troubling to those whose privileges are normally unremarked. In Crenshaw's original formulation, it meant focusing on black women, rather than white women or black men. However, although she has worked on behalf of working-class black women, Crenshaw herself sometimes seems to neglect the class-based inequalities that put her and some other high-profile black feminists in a much more privileged material position than many white as well as black women in her own society. And of course even poor black women in the US are often legally and materially privileged in comparison with many women elsewhere in the world.

Finally, the question of which identities and forms of privilege and oppression are the most important is not an abstract one, and the answers will partly depend on the situation in which they arise or are found. Crenshaw herself has said that, although intersectionality can be used 'to illuminate and address discriminatory situations that would otherwise escape articulation', it 'does not anticipate or call forth a listing of all differences' (2011: 233, 232), because these will not all be relevant in any particular situation. This point did not seem to be taken on board by Dawn Butler who, when she described intersectionality as her 'new favourite word', also said that she saw it as 'all about women in all their different forms – black, white, disabled, rich, poor, working-class, middle-class, overweight and underweight. It is about everything you can think of' (Photiou, 2017).

The categories on Butler's list may indeed all intersect with each other and with other dimensions of social experience and identity to produce different meanings for different groups of women: for example, an expensively dressed woman who weighs more than average may not be judged as negatively as a bedraggled, overweight benefits claimant (on the intersections of fat with other social divisions, see Friedman et al., eds, 2020). However, intersectionality is not a kind of dumping ground for 'everything you can think of'. All differences and identities do not have equal social significance, and, as discussed above, it is important to distinguish between bad personal experiences and more structural forms of oppression. I therefore agree with Crenshaw that only some differences or identities will be immediately relevant in any given situation, and that their relative importance is inevitably context-dependent.

This leaves us with a number of socially significant differences and identities that systematically privilege some groups and disadvantage others. These clearly include sexuality, cis/trans/other gender identity, citizenship status, ability/disability and age (although the last two are particularly fluid categories, as a moment's inattention when crossing a road can turn an able-bodied individual into a wheelchair user, while of course any older person was once young, and both youth and age can sometimes confer advantages and sometimes be a source of negative treatment). In some societies religious identity too is not simply a matter of status or power but a matter of life and death. Nevertheless, I am largely in agreement with those who argue that, although other categories can be highly relevant and important, at a general level we should focus on the 'big three' of gender, race and class, if we are to understand the most basic society-wide and international structures of privilege and oppression. I will attempt to justify this position in the rest of this section.

The 'big three': gender, race and class

Gender

Earlier chapters have, I hope, shown that gender is a basic organising principle of all human societies and that this almost always works to the general and collective disadvantage of women (or rather, what we should now see as the coalitional group of people categorised as women). As discussed in later chapters, the subordination of women is also central to the capitalist economic system, which depends upon the unacknowledged exploitation of women's unpaid labour, with different groups of women affected in different ways. This means that gender-based forms of discrimination and ill-treatment cannot be reduced to the prejudices and bad behaviour of individual men; rather, they reflect deep-seated processes, assumptions and power relationships that are so much a part of society that they are often invisible. It also means that, if we are to challenge patriarchy successfully, we must also challenge the economic processes and ideological assumptions of the capitalist system that benefits from it; in other words, feminists should look to more socialist solutions.

Race

Race and racism also have deep historical roots, and the legacies of slavery, colonialism and imperialism are built into the social, cultural and economic assumptions and practices of western societies and the global capitalist economy (Lugones, 2010; Nash, 2019). However, it can be uncomfortable for white feminists to accept that they are racially privileged – or indeed to accept that they should be labelled as 'white', let alone racist. As the young British writer Reni Eddo-Lodge argues in *Why I'm No Longer Talking to White People About Race* (2017), to feel that one has no racial identity is itself a form of privilege; as she also says, racism 'does not go both ways' because it is about power as well as prejudice and, while black people can be individually prejudiced, they do not have structural, collective power over white people. Robin Diangelo, a white American woman, makes similar points, and highlights the defensiveness of white people who are unaware of their own histori-cal role and unused to being 'raced' (2018). Such defensiveness was clear when Munroe Bergdorf (who is queer and trans as well as black) was sacked by L'Oréal as the face of its 'True Match' make-up range for alleged 'racism': in the aftermath of the killing by a white extremist of a black anti-racist protestor, Bergdorf had told her Facebook followers that 'Most of ya'll don't even realise or refuse to acknowledge that your existence, privilege and success as a race is built on the backs, blood and death of people of colour' (Iqbal, 2017). Meanwhile, Emma Watson, the white British actor named as UN Goodwill ambassador for women in 2014, was at first puzzled when she heard herself described as a 'white feminist', but she says that she experienced a moment of realisation when she read Eddo-Lodge's book (Okolosie, 2018; Watson, 2018).

Although it is deep-seated, racism in Europe is often unconscious and unintended. However, more overt racism has risen in recent years, partly because changing patterns of migration have been exploited by unashamedly racist right-wing political organisations. Migration itself often reflects responses to economic instability, climate change and political upheavals that are the direct or indirect consequences of economic, political and military interventions by western governments and organisations from colonial times to today. In recent years, racist hostility towards visible minorities has become entangled with fear of Islamic extremism, and Islam as a whole has been equated with the oppressive practices of a small minority. This in turn has fed into a general scapegoating of non-white people, who have been blamed for all manner of economic, social and cultural ills. In the UK, hostility towards migrants has been explicitly entrenched in official policy since Theresa May, then Home Secretary, stated in 2012 that the aim was to create 'a really hostile environment' for (allegedly) illegal immigrants; subsequent legislation effectively requires schools, healthcare professionals, landlords and others to act as immigration enforcement officers and to refuse services to those who cannot prove their right to remain (Grierson, 2018; Liberty, ed., 2018).

Despite the structural and increasingly virulent nature of racism in western countries, academic feminists in Europe working on intersectionality have, as Gail Lewis says, tended to see this as a problem in the United States and possibly the UK, disavowing 'the relevance and toxicity of the social relations of race as a pan-European phenomenon' and displacing its significance to a 'series of "elsewheres"' (2013:870). Such thinking supports a trend, also occurring in the US, to 'move intersectionality on' from its focus on black women and to use the concept to seek ever-greater inclusiveness. As Jennifer Nash says, this appears to draw on black feminist insights, but '[w]hen intersectionality is imagined as feminism's future, intersectionality sheds black women' (2014:19).

Black feminists are also having to defend the term itself against criticisms by some female journalists, who claim that it is used to unfairly attack feminist writers who deviate in any way from 'politically correct' inclusiveness (Adewunmi, 2012). For some such critics of intersectionality, the term itself is 'too academic', comprehensible only to 'those armed with an MA in Gender Studies, and a large vocabulary to match' (Cosslett and Baxter, 2012). In this vein, Julie Burchill (2014) wrote, in an article entitled 'Don't you dare tell me to check my privilege', that she was 'hoping that the in-fighting in-crowd of intersectionality disappear up their own intersection really soon, so the rest of us can resume creating a tolerant and united socialism' (See also the response by Lewis, 2014). As Collins and Bilge have argued, this kind of argument reverses the reality of racial privilege, turning 'women of color' into 'the oppressors of uneducated white women via their alienating word – intersectionality', while Eddo-Lodge says that 'The backlash against intersectionality was white feminism in action' (Collins and Bilge, 2016:106; Eddo-Lodge, 2017:167).

Class

Despite her intemperate language, Burchill's claim that intersectional theory is elitist has a degree of truth in relation to some usages of the concept. It also ties in with socialist and Marxist feminist critiques, which argue that intersectionality loses sight of class and capitalism, and that its apparently open-ended list of oppressions fails to see there is an economic *necessity* to capitalist exploitation and inequality. As discussed in the following chapters, capitalist exploitation goes far beyond personal greed or prejudice, for capitalism 'is not a code word for a cabal of evildoers … it is an impersonal system of material social relations' (Lewis, 2016:6). Race and gender as well as class are built into these social relations in very complicated ways, so that any serious challenge to gender-based or race-based oppressions also involves challenging the economic system that requires them.

In this context, some Marxist feminist critics echo the complaint that has often been made by socialist men against feminism in general: that intersectionality is both divisive and elitist and that it serves the interest of economically dominant groups, 'pitting workers against each other, exacerbating sexism, racism, xenophobia, and nationalism' (Giminez, 2018:263, 266; see also Eisenstein, 2018; Foley, 2018; Vogel, 2018). I agree with these critics that intersectionality has sometimes moved feminists away from radical politics and into apparently endless reflections on individual identity that seem to become an end in themselves and make collective actions extremely difficult. However, this problem is not inherent in the concept. Rather, as Sara Salem argues, Marxist feminists can work *with* intersectionality, so that we can see that capitalism requires gender inequality and then 'push further through an intersectional lens to ask which women are affected in which ways?' (2018:410). Without this intersectional lens, socialist working-class movements are always at risk of being movements of and for white working-class men. At the same time, intersectionality needs to focus more clearly on class and economic exploitation if it is not to lose sight of the material foundations of gender and race oppressions.

Beyond the 'big three'

The above arguments do not deny that other aspects of identity can also be sources of real, material oppression. The sometimes state-sanctioned discrimination and violence experienced by sexual minorities and trans people can be genuinely life-threatening, as can hostility to particular religious groups, while negative treatment experienced by many older people or people with disabilities can result in social isolation and economic exclusion. Discrimination and prejudice against minority groups can also be very useful to political and economic elites, by providing scapegoats, splitting opposition and diverting attention from genuine problems.

These experiences and the society-wide forces behind them are often sidelined by those mainstream feminists who are not directly affected by them. For example, lesbian and queer feminists have been angered by the apparent denial by some socialist feminists that issues of sexuality are as important or 'real' as those of class. In particular, Judith Butler (1998) has asserted that, because these feminists have shown that capitalist production depends on the heterosexual family, they should also see that the family itself depends on the ill-treatment of those who do not conform to sexual norms; this means that, contrary to the view that queer politics is 'merely cultural', homophobia is central to the functioning of the capitalist economy, which has also been able to treat gay people as a separate 'class' that was ripe for exploitation by profit-driven organisations during the AIDS epidemic. Today, the severity of oppression based on sexual orientation is widely variable, but homophobia remains prevalent, even in apparently tolerant countries such as the UK.

Nevertheless, it is not impossible to imagine a capitalist society in which sexuality is freely expressed. In many countries, same-sex couples can now marry, free choice in the 'private' matter of sexuality is highly compatible with the individualistic principles of neoliberalism, discussed in Chapters 5 and 6, and the 'pink pound' has been widely welcomed as a new source of profit. In this context, I agree with Nancy Fraser (1998, 2000) that injustices based on sexuality, unlike those based on class, race and gender, are not really *necessary* for the continued existence of capitalist societies, even though they may often be *useful*; it is therefore 'highly implausible that gay and lesbian struggles threaten capitalism in its actually existing historical form' (2000:146). Fraser further argues that the injustices experienced by gay men and lesbians are analytically distinct from economic injustices (which she refers to as 'maldistribution') and that they represent a form of 'misrecognition', whereby the negative messages received by a group that is devalued and denigrated by the dominant culture make it difficult for its members to develop a positive, self-affirming culture of their own or to participate as equals in the wider society. Such injustices, she says, can involve serious, material harms; although they are as important as the harms of maldistribution, they are not the same, and they cannot be addressed by the same methods. However, as Butler and other writers have argued, political and economic realities are messier and more complicated than such binary categorisation suggests, and different forms of injustice are often deeply entangled (see for example Alcoff, 2007). Here I would add that poverty too can be an issue of misrecognition for poor people who not only lack the resources to participate in society but are also treated as if they have no right to participate, while an intersectional approach always alerts us to different experiences within as well as between groups and tells us that people are never *only* gay or *only* poor.

Related arguments apply to issues around religious identity, including Islamic identity. With a rise in both Islamic extremism and Islamophobia, these have become particularly important in recent years, as public perceptions of Islam have tended to equate the whole religion with its most extreme forms, focusing on its association, both real and imagined, with terrorism and with ill-treatment of women, while right-wing anti-immigration groups use anti-Islamic feeling as a proxy for race (Olufemi, 2020). In this context, Muslim women are widely portrayed as victims of a particularly misogynistic and oppressive culture that at best expects them to be passive and submissive, and at worst mutilates their genitals, forces them into arranged marriage, kills them if they 'dishonour' their family, confines them to the home and/or forces them to cover their bodies and faces.

In contrast to their race (which of course varies), Muslim women's religion can look like a freely chosen identity, and for some individuals, particularly converts, this can be the case. However, for people born into a religious community, and perhaps particularly for those in a minority ethnic community that faces discrimination and hostility from the wider society, their religion may be experienced as the core aspect of both their personal and their racial, ethnic or social identity, central to who they are and the group to which they belong. For many European Muslims, such identity is not readily shed. As Mariam Khan shows in *It's Not About the Burqa* (2019), an edited collection of writings by British Muslim women, their Muslim identity is also often very much at odds with non-Muslim perceptions of it – as Khan says, none of the contributors to her book could be described as passive or submissive, Muslim women are certainly not a uniform group, and their religion is about much more than the clothes they wear.

To the extent that Islam in the west is closely linked to issues around immigration and race, Islamaphobia is bound up with structural forms of economic exploitation that go beyond prejudice and discrimination, however virulently or even violently expressed. Nevertheless, it is not built into society in the same way as oppressions based on class, gender and race. This means that the 'big three' will generally have primacy in intersectional analysis. At the same time, however, I do not want to overstate this primacy, for the relative importance of different identities or dimensions of oppression will, as I have argued throughout this chapter, also depend on their context.

Intersectionality in practice: some examples from the UK and Europe

This section briefly explores some of the ways in which intersectionality has been applied to 'real world' politics. Its main focus is on developments in the UK and the EU, looking first at the legal situation and then at two well-established and widely respected feminist groups before turning to more grassroots research and political activism.

The law and political developments

In mainland Britain, the 2010 Equality Act, initially introduced by a Labour government, legally protects people from discrimination in the workplace and in wider society in relation to nine 'protected characteristics'; these are (in alphabetical order) age, disability, gender reassignment, marriage and civil partnership, pregnancy and maternity, race, religion or belief, sex, and sexual orientation. It also requires public bodies to consider how their decisions and policies affect people in relation to these characteristics. The Act replaced and consolidated many earlier pieces of legislation, and it operates under the oversight of the Equality and Human Rights Commission (EHRC).

At first sight, treating all forms of discrimination under the same law might seem to open up the possibility of an intersectional approach. This was indeed the hope of some of those involved drawing up the legislation, which initially allowed individuals to bring cases on two (but no more) grounds of discrimination; it also required public authorities to have 'due regard' to socio-economic disadvantage when taking strategic decisions. However, both these sections of the Act were vigorously opposed by powerful business organisations, and they were not taken forward when a Conservative-led coalition government came to power after the 2010 election (Hepple, 2010). Although British equality law now protects people against discrimination on more grounds than in the recent past, it therefore still officially supports the kind of single-axis thinking that is unable to see the situation of those situated at the intersection of two or more forms of discrimination, and it ignores class-based disadvantages.

A single-axis approach is also the basis for most anti-discrimination law in the rest of the EU, so that inequalities are generally juxtaposed rather than analysed together; as in the UK, class-based discrimination is excluded from the list of legally protected characteristics (Lombardo and Verloo, 2009:490). While some feminists are calling for the 'mainstreaming' of more intersectional approaches, many commentators are pessimistic about this succeeding, particularly in the context of other problematic developments in the EU, including the widespread imposition of austerity measures and the entry of some countries with more 'traditional' ideas around gender and sexuality. The editors of a recent volume therefore fear that gender equality in the EU will be addressed only 'through a reactive, individually based, anti-discrimination approach, rather than through a proactive, group-based, preventative approach' (Kantola and Lombardo, 2017:12).

A 2016 report for the European Commission that draws on evidence from all the member states and candidate countries is more optimistic. Its author, Sandra Fredman, finds not only that it would be possible to incorporate an intersectional approach within the provisions of current EU law but that equality bodies in member states are increasingly recognising multiple and cumulative forms of discrimination, and that this is informing their research and the information they provide. Such signs of progress are themselves partly a response to ideas emanating from advocacy and research groups such as the Berlin-based Center for Intersectional Justice, an independent and non-profit-making organisation, which aims to bridge the gap between academic research and policymaking (www.intersectionaljustice.org). Fredman reports that the most vulnerable groups, whose members experience intersecting forms of disadvantage, are already being helped by practical proactive measures. She says that such measures can be more effective than litigation, and she therefore argues that equality bodies should use what powers they have to mainstream them: here she gives the example of making language teaching accessible to migrant women with childcare responsibilities as a proactive measure that addresses the intersecting difficulties they face.

Fredman's report is clear in its focus on structural forms of disadvantage that go beyond legal definitions of discrimination, and it goes far beyond attempts to appear inclusive by simply sprinkling the term 'intersectionality' into political discussion or using it as a tick-box exercise. A similarly progressive step was taken in 2018 when the European Network Against Racism and the Center for Intersectional Justice brought activists, EU civil servants and government officials together for the first European symposium on intersectionality. As the report on the symposium made clear, the aim was not to provide any instant solutions but to share ideas and good practice, to resist the tendency to depoliticise intersectionality and to recentre race as a political category at the heart of intersectional analysis (Chandler, 2019).

Meanwhile, some feminist politicians in the UK too have started to explicitly use the language of intersectionality to argue against a single-axis approach. For example, in 2018 Dawn Butler, as Shadow Minister for Women and Equalities, promised that a Labour government would 'acknowledge intersectionality' to recognise that 'different layers of discrimination interact with each other'. She said that a Labour government would therefore enact the section of the Equality Act that would have allowed individuals to bring a case on two grounds, but that had been rejected by the Conservative-led coalition in 2010 (Wren, 2018). Such change would end the legal invisibility experienced by doubly disadvantaged groups, such as black women, that had provoked Crenshaw's original analysis of intersectionality in 1989. Also in 2018, the All Party Parliamentary Group on Sex Equality reached similar conclusions in its report *Invisible Women*. This additionally argued that women's diverse economic, social and legal needs could best be met by including users in the design of services. As with some of the recent developments in the EU, such an approach would involve a radical change of mindset to one in which disadvantaged groups have an active role rather than being seen simply as passive victims to be 'helped' by others.

Intersectional research and feminist politics

In the UK, increased awareness of the intersectional nature of inequalities informs the research of some leading feminist campaigning and research groups. This is clear in the work of the Women's Budget Group (WBG), which describes itself as 'an independent network of leading academic researchers, policy experts and campaigners', and which has been scrutinising the gender implications of UK budgets and government spending plans since the early 1990s (https://wbg.org.uk/about-us/). For example, its 2017 report on *Intersecting Inequalities*, produced jointly with the Runnymede Trust (a race equality think tank), assessed the cumulative impact of the government-imposed austerity measures by gender, race and income, to show that negative effects were disproportionately concentrated amongst the poorest black, Asian and minority ethnic (BAME) women. Subsequent WGB reports have continued to unpack the particular consequences of policies for different groups of women (see https://wbg.org.uk/category/analysis/reports), and in 2020 it was immediately able to see that the coronavirus crisis 'impacts on different groups, including women, BAME communities and disabled people differently' so that 'a response that takes into account different groups' positioning in society and in the economy is necessary' (Women's Budget Group, 2020a).

The Fawcett Society, which has roots going back to the late nineteenth century and which was involved in the *Invisible Women* report discussed in the previous section, now says that 'We live in an increasingly and consciously intersectional world, and the language of intersectionality must become second nature to all of us' (Fawcett, undated). It has accordingly recommended that equality law should recognise multiple discrimination, perhaps initially with a limit of three combined grounds (Fawcett, 2018b). It is also looking at ways of involving grassroots women's organisations and ensuring that diverse women's voices are heard and fed into policy-making. This principle was reflected in the society's response to the COVID-19 crisis in March 2020, when it co-ordinated a wide range of national and local groups in a joint call to the government 'for women and girls in all their diversity to be visible, heard and have their needs met' (Fawcett, 2020).

The need for subordinated people to speak for themselves is central to research by Leah Bassel and Akwugo Emejulu, who have developed an intersectional approach to explore the impact of austerity policies on minority women in England, Scotland and France. This approach enables them to see that, although terms such as 'minority women' or 'women of colour' can be important identifiers, these are only a starting point, for we should also name 'the particular interests, inequalities and demands' that any identity contains. They interviewed activists, people working in third-sector (voluntary, community and charitable) organisations, and civil servants and local government officials with an equalities brief, and found not only that minority ethnic women are particularly badly affected by austerity policies but also that their experiences are erased and their voices silenced as 'experts' claim to speak for 'victims'. This silencing is reinforced, they argue, by the attitudes of many on the left of European politics, who deny or forget that 'Europe is constituted by a racial logic of exclusion, violence and exploitation', and who reject claims around gender or race as a threat to a united working-class movement (2017:28, 21).

Bassel and Emejulu link their findings to a critique of the increasing focus on enterprise and individualism that is compelling many third-sector organisations to model their behaviour on the private sector. However, they also found evidence that some activists were still managing to use social enterprises 'as a tool for advocacy and activism', they identified a 'ray of hope' around some new anti-austerity and self-consciously intersectional groups led by minority ethnic women, and they argued that the less visible work of others in informal, self-help and grassroots organisations represented a 'politics of survival and self-care ... survival as a radical action in and of itself' (2017:68, 110, 85). In research for a new project, Women of Colour Resist, they find that such action and survival strategies by women of colour have a capacity to disrupt mainstream ways of thinking and to build solidarity through lived experiences. They argue that these women can be 'radical agents for social change' and that, as some of them work to build anti-austerity coalitions, they are 'already enact[ing] intersectional justice' – that is, a form of justice that 'treats race, class, gender and legal status as integral, not superfluous, to re-imagining and re-building social citizenship and the social welfare state' (2019:23).

Bassel and Emejulu identified the UK group Sisters Uncut as an example of an intersectional organisation led by women of colour. The group is also the subject of research by Armine Ishkanian, an academic, and Anita Saavedra, an activist and member of the group, into how its members deal with inequalities within their organisation as well as in the wider society (2019). Sisters Uncut was originally set up in London in 2014 in response to the failure of the wider anti-austerity movement to explore the gendered and intersectional impacts of austerity, particularly the cuts in support for survivors of domestic and sexual violence. It is now a national movement, and it is a self-consciously diverse group (Spratt, 2016).

The group's intersectional approach was clearly established in its 2018 'Feministo', which argued both that different struggles for economic and social justice are connected and that an equal society can be brought about only by a movement that strives to eliminate hierarchy and privilege within its own ranks. However, Ishkanian and Saavedra found that such ideas can be difficult to put into practice, and that differences in class and education created greater barriers to participation in the group than race, gender identity or sexuality, with some members complaining that 'a lot of Gender Studies speak and terminology' made it difficult for less well educated working-class women to get involved (quoted in Ishkanian and Saavedra, 2019:11). As many critics of intersectionality have observed, there is also a danger that open-ended attempts to be inclusive can be paralysing, and that they can represent a naïve statement of intent rather than a coherent political strategy (see for example, Evans, 2015:54–5; Russell, 2018:288). Nevertheless, Ishkanian and Saavedra's findings were generally positive, stressing the importance of people moving out of their comfort zones, and seeing the acknowledgement of hierarchy and privilege as an essential first step towards more progressive and genuinely inclusive forms of politics.

Intersectionality and feminist politics: some conclusions

This chapter has not attempted to argue that intersectionality is an explanatory theory. It is, however, an important analytical tool that should be at the heart of feminist politics. Its key messages can sometimes seem obvious, even trite, but are still too often ignored. Here I pull out just four interconnected points, before adding some cautionary notes.

First, the inequalities and injustices that are built into our societies do not run in parallel, and they are not free-standing. Rather, they intersect, and they produce qualitatively different experiences for different groups of women. For multiply disadvantaged women, these experiences can include being invisible to dominant groups or being subject to policies that, even if they are well-intentioned, ignore their specific needs.

Second, a single-axis thinking that isolates patriarchy or gender-based discrimination from other dimensions of social inequality and injustice cannot be an adequate basis for feminist politics and understanding. This need not mean that we can never talk about or organise around 'women' or other structural group identities. Instead, it means that we should recognise that 'women' constitute a coalition of people whose experiences are sometimes shared but sometimes very varied, and whose membership of other social groups means that they are often hierarchically placed in relation to each other.

Third, we should treat the needs of the most disadvantaged women as central, rather than an optional extra: when a few well-educated white women succeed in breaking some glass ceilings, society does not need to change very much, but if the claims of poor black women were taken seriously, the world would look very different. In this sense, as Collins and Bilge argue, '[i]ntersectionality is not simply a method for doing research but is also a tool for empowering people' (2016:46).

Finally, intersectional analysis is not just for or about women who are disadvantaged but also for and about those of us who are privileged in relation to structural inequalities other than our gender. Here the call to 'check our privileges' need mean not some breast-beating, guilt-tripping exercise but a requirement to consider whom we might be speaking about and for, and who might be excluded, marginalised or damaged by a particular idea or policy that seems beneficial to us.

These arguments do not mean that self-described intersectional approaches are always useful. The term has sometimes been swallowed up by academic discourses that treat theory as an end in itself. Its radical potential is undermined if it is carelessly extended to include an individualistic form of identity politics that talks about 'overlapping identities' rather than structural injustices (Chandler, 2019) and promotes 'a "micro-political" understanding in this globalizing world' (Mojab, 2015:16), or if it takes the form of an 'ornamental intersectionality', used by businesses and establishment-oriented organisations to make statements about inclusivity without addressing underlying exclusionary structures (Bilge, 2013:408). As Carbin and Edenheim have said, such developments risk turning intersectionality into a 'liberal, consensus-based project' (2013:245).

None of this should stop us from using and developing intersectional analysis. If, however, we are to retain it as part of a radical approach, we also need to develop it more clearly in relation to economic class, rather than treating this simply as one of many dimensions of identity, and we need to focus on the relationship between different aspects of oppression and the global capitalist economic system. Such analysis indicates that feminists need to challenge the economic status quo, and points the way to some kind of socialist solution. Meanwhile, the idea that the interests and experiences of different groups of women are cross-cutting, so that we can be united and divided in many different ways, is very much in tune with both the rejection of either/or thinking and the recognition of complexity that we need to draw on to address the claims of trans women, discussed in the next chapter.

4

Trans women and feminism: thinking beyond binaries

Although people who call themselves feminists differ widely in the issues they prioritise and the solutions they propose, they share an underlying focus on the experiences and needs of women, or particular groups of women. Recently, however, the rapid rise of movements for transgender rights has thrown open the basic question of which people should 'count' as women. This has produced a series of intense and sometimes ugly disputes between some feminists and some trans women and their supporters, underpinned by the basic question of whether people who were identified as male at birth can ever become 'real' women.

In this chapter, I attempt to disentangle some of the arguments involved and suggest some ways forward. Throughout, readers should be aware that trans women and feminists are not two mutually exclusive and necessarily oppositional groups, and that many trans women see themselves as feminists, while many cis feminists are fully supportive of trans rights.

I start by stepping back from immediate disputes to link the intersectional approaches discussed in the previous chapter to wider feminist critiques of binary thinking. I then look at the diversity of perspectives, experiences and arguments covered by the 'trans' umbrella before focusing on disputes between some trans people and some feminists, and suggesting how these might be reframed in less confrontational ways. My arguments throughout are linked to my earlier discussion in Chapter 1, where I gave a qualified defence of the distinction that many feminists make between biological sex and socially produced gender. I conclude with a 'modest proposal' to abolish legal classification by sex.

Theoretical context: feminist critiques of binary thought

The intersectional approaches discussed in the previous chapter indicate that we are never simply 'women' or 'men', for these categories are inevitably coalitions of people who are also members of other groups, producing complex, cross-cutting interests and power relationships. This understanding is in tune with some other developments in feminist theory that have challenged the basic either/or framework of 'modern' western thought.

Feminist critics have argued that this dominant framework oversimplifies a complex world, and that its binary and oppositional assumptions involve a series of false dichotomies that are both gendered and hierarchical; these work to exclude women and devalue the qualities traditionally associated with them (from a large literature, see for example Coole, 1993; Squires, 1999). Thus the mind is set against the body, reason against emotion, the public against the private, the universal against the particular and civilisation against nature; all this is underpinned by the contrast between men and their supposedly superior qualities, associated with the first category, and women and their supposedly inferior qualities, associated with the second. This simplistic logic falsely assumes that the world can be neatly classified in terms of distinct and mutually exclusive categories. In practice, it also means that women can be fully part of the male worlds of paid employment and politics only to the extent that they can reject female qualities; meanwhile, their traditional, life-sustaining contributions to society are invisible.

In contrast, many feminists argue that women's gendered experiences, particularly their socially ascribed caring role, can help develop ways of thinking that are less oppositional and individualistic than those associated with men, but which men can and should learn too. This position sees women-centred perspectives as complementary to those based in male experiences, rather than entirely replacing them. It also shows that categories that appear to be mutually exclusive, such as the public and the private, are in fact interconnected and mutually constitutive: most obviously, the ways in which private family responsibilities are distributed between women and men affects how they can participate in the workplace. As with intersectional approaches, this points towards recognising complexity and cross-cutting interests rather than taking polarised positions. This in turn means that we should strive to take a 'both/and' rather than an 'either/or' approach as the starting point for political analysis and debate.

Such a both/and approach has the potential to reduce the adversarial nature of political debates, not only between feminists and non-feminists, but also amongst feminists themselves. For example, it has helped feminists move on from disagreements over whether we should try to work through conventional political structures (and risk getting co-opted or compromised) or retain feminist integrity by working outside dominant systems (and risk total ineffectiveness) to a widespread agreement that both forms of involvement are needed, that they can support each other, and that feminists should therefore work both 'in and against' the state.

While criticising binary thinking in general, many feminists have continued to assume both the 'real world' existence of 'women' and 'men' as separate, sometimes even 'opposite', categories of people, and the distinction between biological sex and socially produced and ascribed gender. They therefore continue to depend on some binary distinctions. At the same time, some of their arguments merge with or draw on the post-structural and postmodern approaches that had become highly influential by the late twentieth century. These not only overturned any idea that there are fixed dichotomies such as truth/falsehood, or public/private but insisted that *all* categories, including sex, gender and the distinction between them, are unstable and fluid, conjured up and maintained through discourse and social interactions rather than reflecting any underlying 'reality'.

To some extent, postmodernism has provided a useful counter-narrative to the generalisations to which some feminists, particularly the most privileged, have been prone, and which have served to exclude or marginalise the experiences of 'other' women. However, as I said in Chapter 3 in relation to black women, if we question the existence of collective identities, and if we see everything as constantly shifting, then we lose sight of the existence of power structures. Even if the categories of 'women' and 'race' are artificial, sexism and racism have a real existence; a postmodern perspective can therefore make it difficult to see, let alone challenge, the ways in which 'women' are disadvantaged in the patriarchal societies in which we all live.

In terms of 'real world' politics and activism, it is important to develop a careful balance that avoids simplistic notions of 'sisterhood' that mask the inequalities and competing interests that divide women, but is able to see and contest shared exclusions, disadvantages or exploitation. Here some feminists have taken up the notion of 'strategic essentialism', derived from the postcolonial theory of Gayatri Spivak; this suggests that women can temporarily unite around particular goals or against particular injustices, while recognising that they are also divided in other respects and that 'woman' itself is a contested category. Others have similarly talked about 'strategic sisterhood' as a way of building alliances between differently placed groups of women without forgetting the historical and cultural specificities of their different experiences. It is, however, probably the idea of 'solidarity' that is most widely used by feminists who wish to unite with or support women and men who are experiencing or campaigning against particular forms of injustice or oppression, without assuming that they all share the same situation. Here the idea of 'solidarity in difference' seems particularly useful: this does not reduce us to one aspect of our identity, but instead seeks to 'build in difference into the very fabric of the political project' (Lister, 2003:82) at the same time as recognising that women face particular difficulties *because they are women*. The idea of solidarity also leads beyond single-issue politics, to show that because different forms of oppressions are often interconnected, so too are movements against them. This does not, however, mean that solidarity between differently oppressed people is automatic: indeed, while we can sometimes come together as 'women', other aspects of our identity and material situation may often seem more significant, and may at times divide us.

Most obviously, in countries divided by civil war or by serious ethnic or religious conflicts, differences between women can appear much more significant than anything they have in common. However, some feminists have used the idea of *transversal politics* to argue that dialogue is possible across divisions even in the most difficult circumstances. The term was first used by Italian feminist activists who were trying to support women in war-torn countries during the 1990s; it was subsequently developed by Nira Yuval-Davis, and Cynthia Cockburn (2015) has described how women have put it into practice in very divided societies (Israel, Northern Ireland and Bosnia-Herzegovina), albeit without themselves labelling their activities in this way. The idea does not assume that all conflict can be overcome, but it refuses to see differences as exclusive or essentialist. It advocates a process of dialogue involving 'rooting', whereby political actors reflect on and try to understand their own position and identity, and 'shifting', whereby they try to put themselves in the situation of those who are different, thereby discovering differences within as well as between groups and 'keep[ing] one's own perspective on things while empathising with and respecting others' (Yuval-Davis, 1998:185). As Cockburn says, it requires imagination both to try to think what the world might look like to those in a very different situation and to allow for the belief that the world and our identities in it could look very different in the future.

Such imagination is needed today, not only in or between countries where divisions have erupted into extreme and widespread violence but also in relation to the increasingly abusive nature of social and political differences within western countries, including the UK. In this context, the need for feminists to work together and with a wide range of people is particularly urgent. I will return to these ideas later in this chapter, when I discuss how we might move on from the current heated debates around whether the rights of trans women are a threat to the majority of women: that is, those who have been identified and brought up as female since birth.

Trans politics

This section sets the scene for the current high-profile disputes between some trans activists and some feminists. It provides a brief overview of the terminology currently used by many of the former, and outlines the diversity of identities, interests and theoretical perspectives that trans politics involves.

Terminology and labels

The terms that people who are outside conventional gender and sexual norms use to describe themselves are often self-consciously political. From the use of 'gay' in the 1960s, they have variously been used as badges of identity and pride, to make marginalised groups visible, to enable individuals to make sense of their own experiences, and to provide a basis for claiming rights. In recent years a host of new identities have been given names, and 'LGBTQ+' (see Chapter 3) is now widely used as a shorthand for people who see themselves as outside of normative sexualities and/or sex/gender identities in a wide range of ways. This expanding vocabulary is particularly important for the growing number of people who do not feel that they are either female or male and who previously had no way of expressing this, even to themselves.

Trans activists have also introduced the term 'cisgender', to refer to people whose gender identity is in line with their legal sex, based on the appearance of their genitals at birth. Giving this label to the majority of people highlights the fact that their experience of gender is common rather than universal or 'normal', for 'just as we cannot describe being gay without having a word for straight, we need a word to describe experiences which are *not* trans, as well as experiences which are' (Lester, 2017:8).

Since the 1980s, 'queer' has been reclaimed by some activists from its earlier use as an insult. Although sometimes used as a synonym for 'gay', it is generally seen as more transgressive and open-ended; it is also sometimes seen as an overarching term for all LGBTQ+ identities. From the perspective of queer theory, all sexual or gender identities, whether gay or straight, male or female, are artificial and provisional; to describe oneself as queer is therefore to claim an identity that knows itself to be always on the point of dissolution. The related queer politics aims not at achieving respectability and a conventional lifestyle within existing society but at disrupting ideas of normality and acceptability. By asserting the instability of the male/female dichotomy that underpins binary thinking, it seems to take the critique of this to its logical conclusion.

The language used around trans identities is laden with political significance. It is also slippery, often used carelessly and sometimes highly confusing; this reflects the shifting diversity of trans experiences and perspectives discussed in the next sections. In this chapter, I tentatively use 'trans' as an umbrella term for a wide range of non-normative sex/gender identities. Although 'transgender' is also used as an inclusive term, it risks conflating sex and gender, pre-empting discussion of a distinction that some trans people want to retain. The term 'transsexual' is used by some trans people who seek to change their bodies by surgery and/or hormonal treatment; others, however, strongly reject it.

As trans issues have attracted greater attention and some campaigning groups have gained political voice, trans people have increasingly been able to define their own experiences; this is reflected in changes in both everyday speech and the language used by the medical profession and official bodies. Thus doctors and consultants now often talk about 'gender reassignment' or 'gender confirmation' rather than 'sex change' surgery: this newer terminology means accepting that an individual knows what their gender is, and that their body is being brought into line with this. For example, Thomas McBee reports that he was enabled to have surgery 'because of the therapist who wrote that I was, in his professional opinion, a man, and in acute distress because I did not look like one' (McBee, 2018:64).

Although medical language still generally assumes that people who reject their legally assigned identity want to change to the 'opposite' sex, many official forms, including those used by the UK civil service, now allow people to choose from a range of identities beyond the male/female binaries. Increasing numbers of educational establishments, employers, public opinion surveys and service providers are also using inclusive options; and by the mid-2010s Facebook was offering its members a choice of over fifty terms to describe their 'gender'. As well as allowing trans people to change their legal identity, increasingly on the basis of self-declaration, a growing number of countries now recognise the existence of a third sex or gender (Hines, 2018; Reed, 2019). Accepting that sex and gender identities need not be closed and binary also involves making the use of pronouns more inclusive. Here some writers (for example Monro, 2005) advocate the introduction of new, neutral pronouns such as 'ze' or 'hir', while the use of 'they' to refer to an individual without reference to their gender is in increasingly common use; for some, 'they' has the added advantage of indicating the plurality of their identity.

Diversity, disagreements and divisions

Trans people are often divided by a wide range of identities, experiences and political positions. As in the cis population, these divisions may be underpinned by competing or conflicting theoretical perspectives. This section links different examples of trans identity to these wider theoretical and political issues, and explores their relationship to feminist approaches.

Many trans people reject the popular perception that they feel 'trapped in the wrong body' (Fiani and Han, 2019). However, others such as Jack Halberstam (a trans man and academic writer) say that the phrase offers a kind of explanation that helps make sense of their experience. The sociologist Raewyn Connell provides a vivid description of what such experience can feel like, when she talks of the terror of 'the moment of knowing that one is a woman despite having a male body ... And there is no walking away from this terror: gender is intransigent, both as a structure of society and as a structure of personal life' (2012:867–8). Connell's perspective does not deny the feminist claim that sex is about biology and gender is socially constructed. However, she argues that the contradiction between her knowledge of who she was and how she was supposed to be arose in a process of embodiment; it therefore had to be handled at the level of the body.

Juno Dawson, who currently identifies as a straight trans woman, agrees that gender is produced by society. She says that she was born a *baby*, that she is not and never was a man, and that 'a person identifying as "man" or "woman" is, in fact, aligning themselves with a fiction'. She also says that 'I am changing some elements of my sex [through surgery] because I feel much more attuned to the female *gender* ... [which] feels to fit me much more than the binary alternative' (2017:14, 16). Stephen Whittle, a trans man, makes the related point that, while gender is 'an idea, an invention, a means of oppression and a means of expression', many who see themselves as oppressed by it nevertheless use 'its icons and signifiers to say who they are', so that many trans people 'are seeking a form of sanctuary in the gender roles they adopt' (quoted in Davidman, 2010:191). However, while Connell and Whittle seem to see their gender identities as stable, Dawson says that hers could change, because 'What it *means* to be a man or a woman, our perception of masculinity and femininity, is constantly in flux' (2017:15, emphasis in original).

C.N. Lester, who was raised as a girl, but now describes themself as 'transgender' or 'genderqueer', says they needed surgery to free them from their sense of a constant clash between 'what my body knows *should* be there ... and the sexed characteristics that, bizarrely, impossibly, seem actually to exist ... [producing] the continual pain of discord, as wrong as a broken bone' (2017:68). While Lester rejects any gender identity, some trans activists see gender as at least partially innate: for example, Julia Serano argues that 'certain aspects of femininity ... are natural and can both precede socialization and supersede biological sex' (2007:6).

In different ways, the experiences of Dawson and Lester both feed into an emerging 'politics of non-recognition' amongst those who describe themselves as neither male nor female (Hines, 2013:64). In the UK, the Government Equalities Office (2019) has found that this movement has gone furthest amongst young trans people. These ideas have also influenced the general population: a survey of eight thousand people for the Fawcett Society in 2016 found that 44 per cent believed that there can be more than two genders, rising to half of 18–34-year-olds (Olchawski, 2016), while a YouGov poll the same year found that only 2 per cent of young men felt completely masculine, compared to 56 per cent of those over 65 (Dahlgreen, 2016). This growing sense of gender complexity is part of a global trend and owes much to social media, where people can find information and supportive communities, and to the publicity attracted by high-profile individuals, such as Miley Cyrus, who has described herself as 'queer', 'gender neutral' and 'gender fluid'. It is also supported by the growing use of a range of new gender descriptions on official forms, outlined in the previous subsection, and by increased knowledge and awareness of the diversity of gender arrangements at other times and in non-western societies (for an overview of these, see Menon, 2012; Hines, 2018).

The increased sense of the 'normality' of gender diversity and fluidity is welcome to many who would otherwise be isolated, while queer theory positively endorses bold displays of gender nonconformity. These developments support feminist ideas around the artificiality of gender, and they seem to take feminist critiques of binary thinking to their logical conclusion. However, they generally lose sight of the feminist analysis of the structural relationships of power that the expression of gender in a patriarchal society inevitably involves.

Meanwhile, some self-identified transsexual people reject any idea of challenging the gender binary; instead, they want to establish their 'correct' position in it. These people do not say that they are 'choosing' their gender, or that they 'believe' they are a man or a woman; instead, they say that they *know* it. From this perspective, successful medical treatment means that their body reflects who they really are, rather than merely enabling them to 'pass' as a woman or man. Some therefore find it offensive to be described as a 'trans man' or a 'trans woman' rather than simply a 'man' or 'woman', and many resent those trans people who seem to trivialise their often painful and deeply felt experiences by taking a 'pick and mix' approach to gender identity. Those whose aim is to assimilate into 'respectable' society also fear that the 'queering of transsexuality' (Eliot, 2010:33) will discredit the whole idea of 'transsexual rights', including the right to change legal gender identity and access appropriate medical care.

In this context, writers such as Viviane Namaste, Jay Prosser and Henry Rubin argue that queer theorists and activists are elitist, self-indulgent and out of touch with reality, and that they fail to understand the needs of those who, once they have crossed the gender binary, have to conform to established gender norms in order to access employment, housing and healthcare. Against this, their queer opponents claim that it is 'respectable', self-identified transsexual people who can afford expensive bodily and cosmetic surgery who are elitist, and they point out that many poor people and people of colour identify as genderqueer (for an excellent overview of these debates, see Eliot, 2010).

Many trans activists further accuse those who successfully 'pass' of denying their own existence. Such denial offers no validation or support to other trans people, and makes it harder to act politically against discrimination. As Sandy Stone argued over thirty years ago, 'it is difficult to generate a counterdiscourse if one is programmed to disappear' (1987/1992:230), while Roz Kaveney has said 'We cannot claim freedom from discrimination as transsexuals by denying that we are transsexuals' (quoted in Monro, 2005:186). However, while some such people will deliberately choose to leave their past behind, many others may see 'passing' simply as a survival strategy in a world in which transphobia is rife, while some can feel compelled to play along with gender stereotypes in order to access surgery and hormone treatment.

Disagreements amongst trans people at times mirror political disagreements amongst feminists, as both can involve differences between those who seek individual rights within existing societies and those who look to more collective, egalitarian and socialist solutions. The latter position, which I argue for in this book, is implicit in Halberstam's rejection of the middle-class agenda of 'assimilationist projects promoting marriage, securitization, conventional family, and tax benefits' (2018:82), because this agenda seeks acceptance by an unjust and unequal society and does nothing to improve the impoverished conditions in which so many people, including a disproportionate number of trans people, live. From this perspective, a focus on rights seems like a sell-out that leaves structural inequalities intact and fails to understand the socio-economic context of trans-specific issues such as gender-reassignment surgery: as Connell (2012) points out, this is now a highly profitable, market-driven industry that is increasingly rationed by people's ability to pay rather than by genuine need.

The pursuit of rights is part of a more general mainstreaming of trans politics, epitomised in the front cover of *Time* magazine (2 June 2014), headlined 'The Transgender Tipping Point'. Campaigns for trans people's right to have their 'correct' identity entered on their passport and birth certificate, to equal marriage conditions (particularly important where same-sex marriage is not allowed), to access the medical treatment they need, and for legal protection from transphobic discrimination and hate crimes have met with success in many countries. The successful mainstreaming of LGBTQ+ issues can also be traced through the shift away from the kind of radical politics that helped produce both the 1969 Stonewall uprising in New York against police treatment of gay and trans people and the gay liberation movement of the 1970s, which drew on ideas around black power and Marxism. Instead, we now have family-friendly, corporately sponsored and officially endorsed Pride events (as prime minister, Theresa May sent messages of support to London Pride, and Barack Obama held Pride receptions at the White House during his time in office). Many trans people are also entering conventional politics; these include Sarah McBride, a young, white trans activist in the US Democratic Party, whose 2018 book includes a 'Foreword' by Joe Biden.

Disagreements amongst trans people are criss-crossed with intersecting social, economic, cultural, political and ideological differences. This means that trans people will inevitably sometimes have less in common with those who share their trans status than with those who share other aspects of their background and identity. The first decades of the twenty-first century have also seen a growing generational gulf of expectations, assumptions and experiences amongst trans people. On the one hand there are older people, who often struggled in isolation and waited many years, in many cases marrying and having children, before coming out, even to themselves. On the other hand there are the rapidly rising numbers of young trans people, including pre-school children, who have learned about trans issues from an early age. While many will experience difficulties, including mental health problems, many will also have support, both from online communities and in the 'real world', where the doctors, teachers and other adults around them will often be much more informed and supportive than in the recent past. These adults are increasingly likely to believe a child who insists that they are a boy or a girl, despite the appearance of their bodies, rather than to tell them they are talking nonsense – indeed, Halberstam even suggests that in some white middle-class families a trans child 'might now be displayed as a trophy, a mark of the family's flexibility, a sign of the liberal family's capacious borders' (2018:60). Halberstam also recognises that many young trans people experience hostility, ridicule or a complete lack of understanding from everyone around them, and he points out that trans children who grow up in poverty, particularly children of colour, are more likely to end up in the criminal justice system or as sex workers than as respectable members of mainstream society. Nevertheless, a generation of young trans people are growing up in a world in which some people 'like them' are not only tolerated but hold positions of influence, and are able to act as positive role models.

Trans women versus feminists: a binary too far

The complicated and contested nature of trans identities, experiences and politics means that the relationship between trans and feminist politics is far from straightforward. In this section, I discuss disagreements between some feminists and some trans women over what it means to be a woman, before turning to the practical implications of their competing claims. I hope to show that, while there are some incompatible theoretical perspectives involved, these represent differences amongst feminists and amongst trans women as well as between the two 'sides'. There are also some competing interests, which need to be handled with empathy and sensitivity, but which have developed into well-publicised, head-on clashes, sometimes involving 'no platforming' (refusing to allow someone to speak because of their allegedly damaging views), physical assaults and death threats. These disputes are currently taking up the political energies of people who otherwise have much in common. In seeking to find a way forward, I draw on the ideas of solidarity and transversal politics that I discussed in the first section of this chapter;

again, these are in tune with the socialist feminist approaches I develop throughout this book.

Before going any further, I should perhaps put my own cards on the table. As a cis woman and a feminist I reject the idea that our lives should be restricted by artificial gender stereotypes. I can also appreciate the strength and seeming naturalness of these stereotypes, and I sometimes feel irrationally concerned that I fall short of what a 'proper' woman should be like. I see the development of ideas around gender fluidity and non-binary identity as potentially liberating at personal and political levels, although I am also concerned that broader political concerns can get lost in an open-ended exploration of individual identity and fulfilment.

While my own body tells me that I am female, and I have no real problem in agreeing with it, I can just about grasp the idea that someone can experience their sexed body as frighteningly alien and at odds with who they really are. I can also understand how someone might look at their society and think 'If that's what it means to be a man, then I want no part of it; I feel much more like a woman, and I want people to see and treat me as such'. And I can see that such a person might or might not find it necessary to change their body in pursuit of this goal.

I reject the idea that biological sex is an inevitable or clear basis for binary classification, and I agree with the Butlerian idea that the significance of genital differences is in many ways socially produced by pre-existing notions of gender (see Chapter 1). Nevertheless, I also see biological sex as having a physical reality that gender does not. Gender is entirely artificial; it has no necessary natural or material basis. *It is also about the collective power of men over women.* Although it is a fiction, gender is powerful, and our subjective sense of gender identity is an important part of being a woman or a man. Gender is, however, far more variable and far more open to change than biological sex could ever be. In this context, cis and trans feminists should work together to contest gender stereotypes and the broader injustices of our patriarchal world; if we are to improve the lives of the majority of women, we also need to address socio-economic injustices and the logic of the economic system in which they are produced.

What does it mean to be a woman?

The phrase 'real women' is, I think, unhelpful in many ways. It can erase the existence of people who are identified as female at birth but who are later discovered to have intersex characteristics. It often equates women with their reproductive role, forgetting that many women are infertile and implying that the menopause must involve a loss of womanhood. It can work to exclude lesbians and any women who seems 'unfeminine', and to conceal the huge diversity of women's experiences. And, of course, it can be used to say that trans women are not really women. At the same time, it can divert attention from the feminist argument that women are collectively disadvantaged or oppressed.

When someone with a male anatomy says that they are a woman and want to be treated as a woman they probably do not mean that they want to be paid less than men or to be sexually assaulted. However, their declared identity makes them a member of a subordinate group and means that they are disproportionately likely to be on the receiving end of sexist discrimination and misogynistic violence. Politically, this makes them women; unlike cis women's, trans women's experiences will be compounded by transphobic discrimination and violence.

In practice of course, trans women's claim to womanhood is usually much more about their gender identity than about their place in gendered power structures. Here some feminists have a number of concerns.

Some feminists' concerns

The vast majority of those feminists who argue against the 'naturalness' and 'reality' of gender are in no way denying the right of anyone to live, dress and identify as they want, or to adopt whatever gender feels right for them. However, they fear that trans people are endorsing damaging gender stereotypes around acceptable behaviour and insisting on the reality of something that is socially created. They also argue that, although transitioning may represent a solution for some individuals, it is far better to challenge these stereotypes and the way that women and men are treated in society, so that people can live as they want without having to worry if this is how a man or a woman is supposed to behave.

Some go further, and argue not only that trans women are different from cis women but that they are not 'real women'. Arguments here include the belief that a woman must have certain objectively observable biological characteristics; that trans women cannot share the female experiences of menstruation, pregnancy and childbirth; that trans women have not had the experience of being raised as girls in a patriarchal society; and that both their upbringing and their bodies mean that trans women are in important respects still men, with the predisposition to violence that this seems to involve. Some also say that, because they have been raised as members of a dominant group, trans women expect to carry their patriarchal privileges into their lives as women. As discussed in later subsections, these arguments have led some to argue that trans women should be excluded from some 'women-only' spaces.

While these arguments are often expressed in temperate terms that invite debate, some writers are decidedly aggressive. The tone of the most critical discussions of trans women was set in 1979, with the publication of Janice Raymond's *The Transsexual Empire*. In this, Raymond describes trans women (whom she refers to as 'She-Males' or 'deviant males') as a direct threat to women in general and lesbians in particular. Although she says that '[i]t is my deepest hope that this book will not be viewed as an unsympathetic treatment of the anguish and existential plight of the transsexual', her language is frequently hostile and inflammatory, as in her hyperbolic claim that 'All transsexuals rape women's bodies by reducing the real form to an artefact, appropriating this body for themselves', her insistence on referring to trans women as 'he', and her assertion that those she describes as male-born transsexuals are claiming to be lesbian feminists in order to 'possess the creative power that is associated with female biology' (1979/1994:175, 134, xxi). More recently, Sheila Jeffreys argues in a similar vein that 'transgenderism on the part of men can be seen as a ruthless appropriation of women's experiences and existence' (2014a:7). Although her other concerns, for example around the prescription of puberty-delaying drugs to children, can be the subject of debate, her arguments are not helped by this aggressive language.

Such language has become the trademark of Germaine Greer: once an outspoken feminist pioneer, she now sometimes seems simply outspoken. She insists that she is only expressing an opinion when she says that a person who has, or has had, a penis is not a woman, and she says she is happy to use the personal pronouns (he/she etc.) that an individual prefers. However, to say on television 'Just because you lop off your dick and then wear a dress doesn't make you a fucking woman', or to describe trans women as 'ghastly parodies … with too much eye shadow' (quoted in Dawson, 2017:195) seems a good way of turning a potentially rational discussion into a confrontation. Similarly, the journalist Julie Bindel is concerned that young women, particularly lesbians, who feel constrained by gender stereotypes are now being encouraged to risk their health by having a 'sex change' instead of challenging these constraints. Again, this point could be the basis of reasonable discussion, but it has been overshadowed by her personal distaste for the appearance of those who transition: 'fuck-me shoes and birds-nest hair for the boys; beards, muscles and tattoos for the girls – Think about a world inhabited just by transsexuals. It would look like the set of Grease' (2004).

Meanwhile, as discussed in later subsections, some feminist organisations (such as Women's Place UK and Fair Play for Women in the UK) are trying to exclude trans women from 'safe' women-only spaces, and to highlight the potential danger that their presence allegedly poses to cis women's safety. Although these organisations take care not to appear transphobic, Lorna Finlayson, Katherine Jenkins and Rosie Worsdale note that they sometimes seem to show 'an almost obsessive spot-lighting of the statistically tiny incidence of violence by trans women against cis women' (2018:9); they argue that this parallels the way that right-wing racists draw attention to crimes by Muslim men against white women and girls, while ignoring the fact that the vast majority of rapists are white. A minority of lesbians have gone further: for example, some shouted down a trans speaker who had been invited to a lesbian event, and handed out leaflets describing her as 'a misogynistic, anti-feminist, lesbian-hating man' (Hines, 2019:150), and protesters disrupted a hustings for the 2020 Labour leadership election, hosted by *Pink News* and *Diva* magazine (Butterworth, 2020).

Some trans women's concerns

Trans women often feel under attack in a world in which many experience or fear transphobic violence and, along with their supporters, they have reacted with anger to the more inflammatory feminist statements. They have succeeded in getting some prominent UK feminists, including Greer and Bindel, no-platformed at a number of UK universities; when they have been invited, their appearance has been greeted by angry protests. Woman's Place UK has had its meetings disrupted and its members intimidated, and other individual activists have been abused and threatened for criticising some trans activists' beliefs (see for example Steel, 2017).

For some trans women, any debate begins and ends with the statement 'trans women are women', and anyone who questions this statement is automatically seen as transphobic. For example, although Jenni Murray, presenter of BBC Radio 4's *Woman's Hour*, told trans women to 'be trans and proud', she added 'but don't call yourself a "real woman"'; she has since been no-platformed (Kennedy, 2017). The writer Chimamanda Ngozi Adichie was accused of 'killing trans women with her words' after arguing that the experiences of trans women are distinct from those born female. She later said she meant that 'The vileness that trans women face is *because* they are trans women – there are things trans women go through that women who are born female will *never* have to go through ... If we are going to pretend that everything is the same, how do we address that?' (Adichie, 2018).

Can there be a middle way?

I think that Adichie's position makes it possible to use 'women' inclusively, while also recognising that this term covers many different kinds of 'women', with a wide range of cross-cutting identities and character-istics. These different kinds of women include cis women (the majority) and trans women. Here it is important to recognise that both cis and trans women are divided politically amongst themselves, and that their political differences include both their relationship with feminism and their understanding of trans issues. They are of course further divided by socio-economic factors including education, class and ethnicity. There also appears to be something of a generation gap amongst both femi-nists and trans women: younger cis feminists seem generally much more relaxed about the status of trans women than older ones, while younger trans women may find it easier than those of previous generations to gain mainstream acceptance (if they want it). It also seems possible that, as more people define themselves as outside of the sex/gender boundary, the whole question of 'who is a woman and who is a man?' will become increasingly less significant.

Meanwhile, the deep theoretical disagreements amongst and between cis feminists, trans women in general and trans feminists about the meaning and nature of sex, gender, and what it 'really means' (if anything) to be a woman or a man cannot easily be resolved. We can however, continue to debate these issues without agreeing *either* that anyone who says that cis and trans women are in any way different is a TERF (trans-exclusionary radical feminist) whose views must be shouted down, *or* that the views of trans women can be dismissed as misguided and/or harmful to the major-ity of women. The next sections address some more practical concerns in this spirit.

Gender self-identification and the law

In the UK, disputes around the status of trans women gained in urgency in 2018, when the government announced a consultation into proposed amendments to the 2004 Gender Recognition Act. This Act allows trans people to change the sex recorded on their birth certificate in line with their gender identity if they can satisfy a panel of experts (whom they do not meet) that they fulfil a number of conditions. These include a medical diagnosis of gender dysphoria (defined by the NHS as 'a condition where a person experiences discomfort or distress because there's a mismatch between their biological sex and gender identity'), a report of any relevant medical treatment and proof (for example payslips and passport) of having lived for at least two years in their desired identity. Surgery or hormone treatment is not an official requirement, and the fee of £140 can be reduced or removed for those who can prove their income is low.

This all sounds relatively simple, but in practice the process of documentation can be difficult, lengthy, costly and highly bureaucratic. Many people find it intrusive and demeaning, many particularly dislike the idea that to be transgender is to have a medical disorder or mental illness, some have been asked to provide detailed evidence of medical treatment and some appear to have had their application rejected because they have not had surgery (Reed, 2019). By 2018, only five thousand trans people had been issued with a Gender Recognition Certificate (GRC), out of the approximately two to five hundred thousand trans people that the Government Equalities Office (2018) 'tentatively estimate[s]' are in the UK.

The government consultation, which promised that all views would be heard, was a response to concerns about the difficulty in obtaining a GRC, and it raised the possibility of self-identification through a simple legal declaration. Contrary to what some believe, this process would still be legally regulated: it would not mean that someone could change their gender according to their mood that day. Such a process is already in place in a growing number of countries, including Argentina, Ireland, Denmark and Norway (for details and a fuller list, see Reed, 2019).

Meanwhile, the rights of trans people are already protected by the 2010 Equality Act, *regardless of whether or not they have a GRC*. This means that they can be excluded from a single-sex service or facility only if this is 'a proportionate means of achieving a legitimate aim' – for example, a female-only domestic violence refuge could provide a separate service to a trans woman if including her in the regular service would be 'detrimental to its other users' (Government Equalities Office, 2018). The 2010 Act also gave trans people with or without a GRC the right to use public facilities, including toilets, that match their gender identity, and to change the sex or gender recorded on many documents, including their passport. The equalisation of the pension age and the right to marry another person regardless of their sex are also making an individual's sex or gender identity increasingly irrelevant in law.

A move to full self-identification would have little immediate practical impact on the general population, and the government has been clear that 'there will be no change to the provision of women-only spaces and services' (Government Equalities Office, 2018). Change would, however, represent progress for those trans people who do not want to disclose their past and/or fear that they would face discrimination if someone discovered their birth certificate.

Some of those who oppose a change in the law are clearly and obviously transphobic; many are also anti-feminist and opposed to gay as well as trans rights. In contrast, most feminists who express fears about the consequences of change do not see themselves as against the right of people to live and identify as they please, and groups such as Woman's Place UK call for 'respectful and evidence-based discussion' about the impact of change. As discussed in the previous section, some trans activists refuse to engage in debate. Others, however, argue that feminist fears should be responded to and rationally assessed. The next subsections attempt such a rational assessment of competing views in relation to both the law and more general issues.

Some feminists' fears: is there a threat to women's safety in refuges, prisons and toilets?

Given that male violence against women is endemic in every country of the world, some feminists believe that allowing trans women into women-only spaces constitutes a threat to the safety of other women. Their concern is particularly acute in relation to those trans women (the majority) who have not had genital surgery. They are not arguing that all trans women are dangerous, but that because trans women are biologically male and have been raised as males, 'they will inevitably carry patterns of behaviour and entitlement associated with that group' (Gender Critical Greens, 2016).

Domestic violence refuges and rape crisis centres

In the case of refuges and rape crisis centres, concerned feminists are particularly worried that the presence of trans women who look like men would be deeply disturbing for already traumatised women.

The findings of research conducted in 2018 for the LGBT campaigning group Stonewall amongst the professionals delivering domestic and sexual violence services did not support these fears (Stonewall and nfp-Synergy, 2018). Rather, it found that trans women have been accessing these services for some time without causing problems for other women, and that robust safeguarding procedures are in place that would prevent a violent man pretending to be a woman from gaining access to the service. Rather than seeing trans women as a threat, some of the professionals interviewed felt they might not be providing them with adequate levels of support.

In contrast, another study, conducted later in the same year for Fair Play for Women (2018), found both that some professionals and survivors had very different views and that they feared the consequences for their service and/or jobs if they expressed them. Some professionals cited this fear as a reason for not taking part in the Stonewall study, which they did not think was fully representative of the sector, and many rejected the claim that security measures were 'robust'. Some said that Muslim women would find it particularly difficult to access their service once word got out that trans women with male anatomy might be there, and some of the survivors said that their own horrendous experiences had resulted in a deep-seated fear of biological males, whose presence could trigger panic and post-traumatic stress.

A number of issues arise from these contrasting findings, which need to be disentangled and addressed in turn. First we might establish one key, double-pronged point that feminists can agree on, regardless of whether they are cis or trans, and whether or not they have doubts about enabling trans people to self-identity: that the real problem is not other feminists but male violence against women (cis and trans) and the lack of funding for services to support abused women (again both cis and trans). As feminists, we can agree that it is profoundly wrong that 64 per cent of women who were referred to refuges in England in 2019 were turned away, mainly because of lack of funding (Women's Aid, 2020); we should focus on this, rather than fighting each other.

Given that some trans women are already accessing these services, and that they do not require a GRC to do so, it seems unlikely that the proposed legal change would have much immediate impact on provision. It is of course possible to construct a scenario in which a deep-voiced, heavily bearded person is demanding admission to a refuge while brandishing a certificate that says they are a woman, and threatening legal action if they are turned away. The person may be an abusive man, claiming to be female only in order to gain access. However, even if risk-assessment procedures are less robust than they should be, the idea that the proposed shift to self-identification will enable this person to be admitted seems somewhat fanciful.

The claim that trans women's male biology and/or socialisation make them more prone to use violence than cis women is hotly disputed by many trans women, who reject the idea that their bodies represent a threat. For example, Julia Serano says that 'What I have between my legs is not a phallic symbol, nor a tool of rape and oppression; it is my genitals. My penis is a woman's penis and she is made of flesh and blood, nothing more' (2013:31). Finlayson, Jenkins and Worsdale (2018) argue that the effects of socialisation into manhood will be different for boys who feel that they are boys and those who feel that they are girls; indeed, the very fact that trans women see themselves as women makes them unlike cis men. These differences may include a reduced propensity to violence; *we simply do not know*. They agree with those who say it is 'better to be safe' than sorry, but argue that we need to give as much consideration to the safety of trans women as to cis women. This means balancing the theoretical risk that trans women, or men pretending to be trans women, may pose to cis women against the real, known dangers facing trans women. They conclude that trans women should not be turned away.

Even if this argument is convincing, two problems remain. First, whether or not trans women pose a significant statistical risk to the physical safety of other women, the very presence of those who 'look male' is likely to be difficult for some abused women to deal with. Second, the difficulties faced by some ethnic-minority women in accessing services will be compounded if it is known that people who are biologically male may be present. Unlike the concerns that seem to obsess some feminists, these problems have nothing to do with whether trans women still have a penis, which presumably will not be apparent. There is, however, no easy way of resolving the apparently conflicting interests involved. There is also a danger that attempts to avoid distress or difficulty for some cis women could involve dividing trans women into an 'acceptable' minority (those who look sufficiently like a biological female to 'pass') and those who are too 'different'.

Here the methods involved in 'transversal' politics, discussed in the first section of this chapter, might at least help us understand what lies below the surface, as these methods require us both to reflect on our own position and to try to see why others disagree. In this case, this would involve trying to see the world from the point of view of both a terrified trans woman seeking sanctuary and a cis woman who might be traumatised by her presence, or who would be unable to return to her community after sharing living space with a biological male. It would also require us to think hard about why we hold the views we do, and what their wider implications might be in terms of how trans people are generally treated. Hopefully, such reflection would also lead campaigners to direct their attention to the need to fund refuges properly, so that these could ensure both more thorough risk assessment procedures and more private space for women using the service. However, as I have indicated, refuges are often already grossly underfunded, partly as a result of government-imposed austerity measures; if we are to ensure that no woman, cis or trans, is turned away from a refuge when she needs one, we need to accept the urgent need for adequate financial support.

Prisons

At first sight, the situation in prisons appears simpler, and some feminists believe that their fears about the danger of changing the law to enable trans women to self-identify have been amply confirmed by the case of Karen White. White, who had previously been imprisoned as a man for offences including sexual assaults on children, re-entered the prison system in 2017, by which time some earlier allegations of rape were being investigated. She now identified as a woman, and was transferred to a women's prison, where she sexually assaulted two women prisoners. She has subsequently been given a life sentence for crimes that include rape.

White's appalling case could be dismissed as a one-off example that should not be used to make generalisations about other trans prisoners; however, figures from the Ministry of Justice show that, in 2018, sixty of the 125 transgender prisoners known to be held in prison have been convicted of one or more sexual offences (Parveen, 2018; BBC Reality Check Team, 2018). A year later, a survey by the official jail watchdog found that one in fifty male prisoners was identifying as trans, making a much higher total of around fifteen hundred (a ratio of trans to cis that is at least four times the number in the general population: Hyman, 2019). If the law were changed to enable all these men to self-identify as female, and they were all transferred to women's jails, the danger to other women's safety might appear to be clear. However, there may be other reasons for this rise in trans prisoners, indicated later in this subsection, making it unlikely that the ratio of sex offenders will approach the Ministry of Justice figures. It is also important not to equate trans sex offenders with trans women prisoners more generally.

Meanwhile, men's jails can be dangerous places for anyone held in them, especially if they are a trans woman. In 2014 the Howard League for Penal Reform (a long-established and well-respected organisation) found that in the previous year there had been 165 'sexual assault incidents' in male prisons and detention centres in England and Wales; it also found that trans women held in these prisons were particularly at risk.

Clearly, no prisoner should be placed in close quarters with someone who is likely to assault them, and the prison authorities have been attempting to respond to the apparently competing concerns of those concerned about the safety of trans women and those who focus on cis women's safety. White's transfer to a women's prison reflected changes introduced after two trans women committed suicide while on remand in a men's prison (Parveen, 2018). However, revised guidelines introduced in 2019 state that prisoners should stay in a prison reflecting the gender they were assigned at birth, unless a new gender identity has been legally recognised (Walawalkar, 2019). White had not sought such recognition and, even if it becomes easier for people to change their legal identity, widespread forward thinking by cis male criminals wanting to be held in a female prison if they are convicted seems unlikely. More importantly, safeguarding and risk-assessment procedures, which were grossly inadequate in White's case, are now much more robust.

Meanwhile, more positive moves are being taken in a number of prisons, where transgender prisoners are entitled to shower alone and to sleep in single cells; in 2019, one men's prison has also introduced a separate wing for trans women prisoners (Hyman, 2019). These 'perks' may help explain why so many male prisoners have started to describe themselves as trans. If such measures were widely adopted, they might go a long way to help resolve the danger of sexual assault against either trans or cis women. They are of course costly, and they are unlikely to be widely adopted in a prison system that is under great strain from the combined effects of reduced spending and an increased prison population. Adequate solutions involve asking why so many people are in prison for minor crimes, spending enough on the prison service to enable all prisoners to be adequately supervised, and transforming prisons from institutions that focus on punishment and containment to places aimed at rehabilitation. Anyone genuinely concerned about the welfare of prisoners should prioritise these issues, rather than the often notional dangers that trans women might pose.

Toilets and changing rooms

While most women will never be in either a domestic violence refuge or a prison, the vast majority will use public toilets or changing rooms.

Arguments over whether trans women should be allowed to use these has come to dominate much public discussion around trans rights.

Women's safety is again a key issue, but those feminists who oppose trans women's right to access female toilets often seem only to take cis women's safety into account. As discussed above, Finlayson, Jenkins and Worsdale (2018) argue that trans women are different from cis men *because they identify as women*, and that we do not have the evidence to show whether or not they share cis men's propensity to act violently towards women. In practice, trans women have been using women's toilets for years without anyone noticing, and it is widely accepted that they would be at risk of attack by men if they were forced to use male toilets, both because they are women and because they are trans. Meanwhile, there are no proposals to prevent male sex offenders who have assaulted other men from entering male toilets: as Sarah McBride says, we are therefore 'holding transgender people's rights to safely access a restroom to a higher standard than ... actual, certified sex offenders' (2018:108).

As I said earlier, the 2010 Equalities Act already allows trans people in the UK to use the facilities that match their gender identity, whether or not they have a certificate to prove it. There is therefore no reason to suppose that much would change if the law were to allow for gender self-identification. In particular, a predatory cis man pretending to be a trans woman has no need to provide a certificate to prove his right to use a female toilet – and of course he would be open to criminal charges if he were to abuse someone there.

Many feminist opponents of trans women's right to use women's toilets and changing rooms are particularly concerned about the danger posed by those who remain anatomically male. This anxiety was epitomised by the 2014 Twitter hashtag #NoUnexpectedPenises, and debates around this often seemed to equate men's sexual violence with the presence of male genitalia (Hines, 2019). In practice, all female toilets have cubicles, so there would be no way of knowing whether someone using female facilities had a penis or not. Some feminists have trawled the world and found multiple examples of women being assaulted by men in toilets

(Jeffreys, 2014b); trans women, however, seem guilty only by association. The situation in changing rooms and showers is somewhat different, as these often provide little privacy and, while the actual risk of a cis woman being attacked is probably low, many would find it disturbing to see someone who looks like a naked man next to her in the shower. Some of the many women who have been sexually harassed or assaulted by men are likely to find such proximity deeply upsetting.

The issues around access to women's toilets can seem to attract an undue level of attention, distracting from more important issues facing both cis women and trans people, such as workplace rights and economic injustices. As McBride says, this attention is partly because people feel particularly vulnerable in the toilet. As she also says, however, those who support excluding trans women from women's toilets are also feeding into a much more virulently anti-trans movement in the US which feels to her like 'an attempt to legislate transgender people out of public life' (2018:202). This movement is also opposed to 'progressive' politics in general, including feminism.

In this situation, it is perhaps time for feminists to try some more transversal thinking, rather than squaring up for yet more confrontation. We can presumably agree that people have a right to be able to use a toilet in safety when they need to. To deny anyone this is effectively to deny them the right to free movement that other citizens should be entitled to (hence the campaigns for more toilets that can be accessed by disabled people). We can perhaps further agree that it must be unpleasant and embarrassing for someone to be treated as a potentially violent predator when they use the toilet or take a shower, while also understanding that some cis women may well be scared by a trans woman's presence in an intimate space, and that they will be very uncomfortable knowing that someone who looks like a man may be in the next cubicle while they are urinating, defecating or changing their sanitary protection (Greed, 2019).

In these situations, neither the trans woman who needs to use the toilet nor the cis woman who finds her presence unsettling is being unreasonable. However, it would not be reasonable for a trans woman with a male anatomy to deliberately display her body in a changing room or shower.

Nor would it be reasonable for a group of cis woman to aggressively challenge the right of a trans women to be there, when she is simply using the toilet and washing her hands.

In working towards solutions that meet the needs of both cis and trans women, we should also remember that some cis women whose appearance does not conform to conventional expectations of what a woman looks like may face difficulties; in particular, the attention that is being given to trans women seems to have produced an increase in hostile 'policing' that extends to questioning their right to use women's spaces. Non-binary people face particular problems, and some report being turned away from both male and female toilets (Lester, 2017). Although toilets for disabled people are sometimes unisex, they are sometimes placed within male and female toilet areas, creating problems if they need assistance from a carer or relative of the 'opposite' sex; the same difficulties arise for those looking after children who are too young to go to a toilet or changing room on their own. Putting the needs of these groups into the mix hopefully helps to extend our thinking beyond a simple cis versus trans impasse.

There are a number of apparent solutions, but the best are very costly. Jeffreys suggests that concerns for the safety of both trans women (whom she calls 'male-bodied transgenders') and cis girls and women could be met by 'the creation of individual toilets which contain washbasins, and are entered through individual, full-length doors from a corridor, or public space' (2014b:19). Similarly, private showers and changing cubicles could be provided in sporting facilities for those uncomfortable with shared facilities. Others suggest that there should be an additional, gender-neutral space; as well as being potentially helpful for some trans and gender nonconforming people, this might be useful for those caring for someone of a different sex.

Meanwhile, some public authorities, schools and service providers in the UK are starting to 'degender' existing toilets. Such unisex provision should avoid the embarrassment and risk of challenge that some trans women currently experience when they use women's toilets. It would also resolve the dilemma faced by non-binary people, and it could help transgender schoolchildren. At the same time, however, unisex toilets can cause severe embarrassment to other adults and children. They also do nothing to reduce the danger that trans women currently fear if they have to use men's toilets, and in many cases they would create a risky or frightening environment for cis women: here it seems highly unlikely that the hordes of drunk and boorish young men who dominate the streets of many UK towns and cities in the evenings, often routinely making suggestive comments to any women they see, would suddenly change their behaviour when queuing for a toilet. A blanket provision of unisex toilets would also reduce the already inadequate facilities available to women, because men who like the privacy of a stall would be able to access those in the formerly female toilet, while women would be able to access the (usually fewer) stalls in the formerly male toilet only if they were prepared to walk past the urinals.

I therefore agree with Clara Greed, a well-respected authority on town planning who has researched toilet provision for women for years, that toilet provision should reflect broad demographic trends, including the rise of transgender identities, but that any new kinds of facilities should be *in addition to*, not at the expense of, those already established for women. This solution represents a compromise that will not entirely satisfy everyone. However, that is the nature of compromise. As Greed says, we need to recognise and address 'the particular biological, social and personal needs of cis and trans men, women and non-binary people', and we should explore these needs in a spirit of 'open, frank discussion' that does not simply place these needs in opposition to one another, and that does not overlook the problem of male violence towards all women, cis and trans (2019:920, 921).

Ideally, any introduction of unisex toilets should be done very carefully and the facilities should be designed with safety in mind. Such toilets should also be restricted to places that are adequately lit and where there are likely to be other people about, such as many workplaces, restaurants, sports venues or theatres. In many cases, it would require greater provision, as queues for the female toilets are often already uncomfortably long. School toilets, which have long been a site of bullying, should always be properly supervised. All this costs money; as Greed says, this makes it particularly important that 'toilet users are not pitched against each other for ever diminishing resources' (2019:921).

I have argued throughout this section that if we are to move beyond current disputes we need to recognise the needs, perceptions, strengths and vulnerabilities of those in a range of different situations. This will involve recognising and respecting marginalised, denigrated and subordinated identities. I have also argued that practical solutions to contested issues around refuges, prisons and toilets will require greater public spending and investment, as private, profit-making organisations will be unable or unwilling to provide the quality of services that is required or to adequately address their underlying causes. This means that, in terms of the distinction between the injustices of 'misrecognition' and 'maldistribution', discussed in Chapter 3, we are necessarily talking about both.

Women's right to their own social and political space

Feminists have long seen it as important to spend time talking, organising and socialising without men being present. As discussed in Chapter 2, the women-only 'consciousness-raising groups' that developed from the late 1960s helped many women to see that their apparently personal experiences were widely shared and should be understood as part of a wider system of patriarchy. They argued that it was important to exclude men from their meetings so that they could talk more freely, and because if men were present they were liable to take over and undermine them; they also argued that men's presence was incompatible with the aim of understanding how patriarchy played out in all areas of life. In other words, 'women need to be able to meet and organise without members of the ruling group present' (Jeffreys, 2014a:145). Women-only spaces were also often important for reasons of personal safety and, in an era when the idea of a 'girls' night out' was much less common, deliberately meeting as women was often both liberating and fun.

The question of whether trans women could be included in feminist spaces was not on the agenda of most feminists before the late twentieth century, when the numbers of openly trans people began to increase. Many trans women now seem to be working in feminist groups and organisations without it becoming an issue. However, their presence is sometimes disputed.

For example, some feminists have questioned whether trans women should be part of women-only 'Reclaim the Night' marches. These can provide an empowering expression of female solidarity, and aim at shocking onlookers into awareness of the extent of male violence against women. Finn Mackay, a self-defined radical feminist who revived the London march in 2004, is clear that trans women *are* welcome, and this is stated on the march's website (www.reclaimthenight.co.uk); in contrast, men are welcome only as helpers, not as marchers. Some trans women have, however, reported feeling excluded. Mackay herself is clear that individual trans women are not a threat of any kind, and that it is male domination and violence that are the problems. However she also says that, in the context of 'the fact of sex inequality and the epidemic levels of male violence against women', she can understand why some women will fear or mistrust 'people who have previously inhabited the male sex class'. She therefore says that it will sometimes be necessary for both trans and cis women to work separately: 'Both are members of oppressed groups under patriarchy, and taking space separately is as important as working together to defeat that shared enemy' (2015:250).

Mackay's conclusion certainly does not preclude also working together. Indeed, because trans women are a doubly disadvantaged group, they may see some structural inequalities more clearly. As Mackay says, the learning process may be uncomfortable, but '[h]aving different angles on patriarchy, including different positions of personal privilege, is what will help us find cracks in the system, those places where it needs to be fixed first, as well as where it might be vulnerable' (Mackay, 2015:258–9).

However, some differences and fears have gone beyond easy solutions. Building on the arguments of Janice Raymond's 1979 *Transsexual Empire*, discussed earlier, some lesbians are extremely hostile to what they see as the excessive influence of trans activism and ideology; as discussed in earlier subsections their responses have included physical disruption. They have three key immediate concerns: that trans women are 'invading' lesbian spaces; that they are sexually aggressive to cis lesbians; and that young girls who are attracted to other girls are being pressurised into seeing themselves as boys, rather than accepting that they are lesbians. I know of no evidence either way in relation to the first issue. In relation to the second, one online article (Wild, 2019) claimed to provide research-based evidence that some trans women who have not had genital surgery are presenting themselves as lesbians, pressurising or forcing cis lesbians into having sex, and accusing those who reject them of transphobia; unsurprisingly, the article has been disputed, and by April 2020 it seemed to have disappeared from the internet. I will address the third issue later in the chapter, when I discuss the rising numbers of transgender children.

Abusive trans and cis lesbians are a tiny minority of their respective groups. However, hostile views rapidly escalate as they circulate through social media. Here it would be helpful if less confrontational feminists on both 'sides' could actively seek to de-escalate disputes and remember both that bad behaviour is not confined to one group and that trans women and cis lesbians are both part of often stigmatised minority groups that could do with a sense of solidarity in difference.

Unfair competition?

This section looks at some of the issues around who 'counts' as a woman when people are competing against each other in politics and in sport.

All-women shortlists

Women have had more or less the same political rights as men for around a hundred years in most countries. For a range of cultural, socio-economic and political reasons, including sexist discrimination, this has not been reflected in the numbers of women elected into political office, and some countries have introduced positive measures to address this. In the UK, the Labour Party has greatly increased its number of women MPs through a policy of all-women shortlists for candidate selection in fifty per cent of safe and winnable seats. Party policy since 2018 has been that all self-identifying women have been eligible for these shortlists. At least one trans woman has since been on an all-women shortlist, and at least one has been elected to the women-only post of Women's Officer in her constituency.

Predictably, these developments have been strongly opposed by those who say that this once again represents trans women taking over women's spaces, keeping out 'real' women, and reclaiming the patriarchal privileges they had when they lived as men. Many say that those who have been brought up as boys and men cannot possibly represent the majority of women; some fear that cis men will pretend to be trans; and others say that, because trans women embrace traditional stereotypes of femininity, their selection would be positively harmful.

An obvious problem with these arguments is that, because our experiences are so diverse, *no* woman can represent the whole of her sex – and in practice it has generally been the more privileged women who have claimed to do so, even though they appear to have little in common with those who are not educated, not white, not economically comfortable, not straight and/or not able-bodied. Women in the UK today have not all been brought up in the same way, and there is a world of difference between the experience of a young woman who has always been encouraged by her family and school to see herself as the independent equal of men and one who has been taught that her duty is to marry a man chosen by her parents and to submit to his authority. Yes, both are likely to encounter sexist discrimination and male sexual violence, but so too are trans women. Moreover, if trans women were to be excluded from women-only shortlists or positions, it would also seem logical to say that trans *men* could be included.

When feminists try to exclude trans women from political opportunities open to other women, they are effectively 'pitting women against each other in a competition for scarce seats at the table' (Fawcett, 2019:6). Rather than expend their political energies in this divisive way, it would surely be much better to focus on the underlying problems facing all women, including the continuing male dominance of positions of political power.

Sport

In contrast to men's socially produced political advantages over women, their competitive advantages in sport are generally the 'natural' consequences of biological differences; hence the widely accepted need for the sexes to compete separately. However, this gives rise to two sets of problems: how to treat women identified as female at birth, but who are later found to have some typically male biological characteristics (that is, they are intersex); and whether trans women should be allowed to compete against cis women.

The UK 2010 Equalities Act recognises that male bodies are, on average, able to outperform female bodies in most sports. Although it otherwise outlaws discrimination against trans people, it therefore allows them to be excluded from competing in sports as women, if their physiological and/or anatomical sex can be objectively shown to give them a competitive advantage: in such cases, UK law clearly states that trans women do *not* count as women.

The rules regulating international sport are rather different. In the past, the main concern of international regulatory bodies has been to exclude men pretending to be women. From the 1960s this was checked by a basic genital inspection, later changed to a swab to verify that all female competitors have XX chromosomes. This is currently supplemented by tests to check that their testosterone levels are in the normal female range. In practice, this testing has affected cis women with intersex traits, rather than fraudulent men or trans women, effectively saying that not all cis women should count as women when it comes to elite sporting competitions. The most famous case is probably that of Caster Semenya, a cis woman and former world champion in the women's 800 metres: Semenya's testosterone levels are naturally much higher than average for a woman, and she has been banned from competing unless she takes hormone treatment to reduce it. Meanwhile, trans women can compete internationally as women if they have taken hormone therapy to reduce their testosterone level to the same level as that required for cis women for at least a year (Rowbottom, 2019); critics say that this does not eliminate the natural advantages that their bodies have developed since puberty, and many cite the example of the women's world record-holding cyclist Rachel McKinnon, a trans woman (Freedman, 2019; Guest Author, 2019).

There seems to be a basic conflict here between two conflicting principles: the principle of inclusion, which would allow both trans women and cis women with naturally high testosterone to compete with other women, and the principle of fairness, that says that trans women and some cis women have natural physiological advantages over 'normal' cis women, and that this makes nonsense of any idea of fair competition. Here I find it difficult to see why average differences between women and men should be seen as so much more important than those between different ethnic groups, and why some kinds of natural advantage are seen as unfair, while others (such as height) are not. I am therefore in agreement with those such as Taryn Knox, Lynley Anderson, and Alison Heather (2019) who argue that the conflict between inclusion and fairness will never be resolved without challenging the attempt to 'squeeze everyone into a gender binary' around which sport is organised. Instead of attempting to divide all competitors into men and women, they advocate a complex algorithm that would basically enable people to compete with those whose characteristics, including weight and testosterone levels, they share (for a similar argument, see Davis, 2017).

Such radical suggestions would be complicated to introduce, and they would not satisfy everyone. However, as the numbers of trans people increase around the world, only a radical solution can cut through the apparently conflicting principles at stake.

Trans children

The second decade of the twenty-first century has seen a dramatic increase in the number of children who are questioning their sex or gender. In the

UK, figures for the Gender Identity Development Service (GIDS), the only NHS clinic providing specialist support for young people on these issues, show referrals rising from fewer than seven hundred in 2014–15 to over two and a half thousand in 2018–19. This increase has been disproportionately high amongst those identified as female at birth, who by 2018–19 were nearly two-thirds of total referrals (http://gids.nhs.uk/number-referrals).

Many feminists, cis and trans, see the rise in referrals as a welcome reflection of a more open, aware and tolerant society, in which children and their parents can more readily access the information and support they need, and teachers and medical professionals will show understanding of their needs. Other feminists, again both cis and trans, are more cautious, fearing that at least some of the children who present with gender-identity problems are reacting to the pressures of a society which expects them to behave in restrictive 'gender-appropriate' ways. If so, from a feminist perspective, it is much better to challenge gender stereotypes than to help boys and girls to transition (Fawcett, 2019).

Some feminists also share a wider social unease that the rise reflects an element of 'social contagion', even a sense that a transgender identity is becoming fashionable, and that social media's focus on celebrity trans people can make transitioning look much easier than it really is. They also fear that some parents or teachers will too readily affirm a child who announces that they are 'really' a girl despite their boy's body, and that the fine line between giving inappropriate significance to a momentary whim and supporting a child with genuine issues around their gender identity is sometimes too readily crossed. Similarly, while changing their gender can feel like a solution to children who, for all kinds of reasons, are unhappy, they might often be better supported in other ways. In this context, some feminists are concerned about the over-medicalisation of childhood, in which quick fixes are sometimes sought for socially created problems, and pharmaceutical companies are often the only real winners. Against all this, Julia Serano (2017) reminds us that many trans people who transitioned as adults report having been unhappy with their gender since childhood, and she asserts that

You don't need to concoct half-arsed theories to explain the mysterious appearance of transgender children. All you need to do is recognise that we have always existed. It's just that we were long rendered invisible via stigma, punishment, and ostracism.

This sounds convincing, up to a point. However, it does not rule out the possibility that at least some children today are being encouraged along a path that will not solve their problems, and Serano's argument does not address the question of why the apparent rise in transgender children should be concentrated amongst those who were labelled female at birth.

Another set of concerns arises from the possible health consequences for children of medical interventions. In practice, the GIDS clinic provides a range of counselling and support services, and many of its users do not take any medication; cross-sex hormones are not prescribed to anyone under sixteen, and gender affirmation surgery is not available to anyone under eighteen. However, GIDS now prescribes puberty blockers to a minority of the children referred to it from the age of 11. These can provide breathing space for young people dreading the arrival of changes to a sexed body they no longer identify with, and many trans children and their families experience such acute distress that they are the only solution. Their long-term health effects are, however, not yet known.

Legitimate concerns about health are also being cranked up, and feelings are running particularly high, amidst allegations that some children are being encouraged to see themselves as transgender, when they may actually be gay or lesbian (a view which has gained support in the wake of the resignation of five clinicians at GIDS: McCall, 2019). This is a long-standing issue. Thus Julie Bindel wrote in 2007 that

As someone who spurned dolls and make-up as a child, I find it deeply troubling that, had I gone to one of the specialist psychiatrists while growing up and explained how I did not feel like a 'real girl' (which I did not, because I wanted to be a lesbian), I could be writing this as a trans man.

Today, the rise in the number of girls being referred to GIDS (which is part of an international trend) gives these concerns a new urgency, and seems to some to validate Raymond's 1979 claim, discussed earlier, that a transgender takeover is denying the validity of lesbian identity. In this context, some former members of the LBGT organisation Stonewall have labelled its policies on trans children homophobic, and they have set up a new organisation, the LGB Alliance; this has in turn been labelled transphobic (Gibbons, 2019). An alternative feminist explanation for the rise in the number of trans girls is, of course, that some are simply taking the opportunity to reject the subordinate status of being a woman in a patriarchal society.

Stepping back from the dispute, it seems at least possible that GIDS, an overstretched service, may have fast-tracked some children without taking their sexual orientation fully into account, and that Stonewall's support for trans children's right to their identity may sometimes lose sight of other issues. This does not, however, mean that there has been a deliberate attack on the right of women to be lesbians. Meanwhile, hostile clashes are compounded by the fear of both groups that the other is denying their existence or right to exist: some lesbian feminists believe that because 'gender' has no real existence trans women cannot be really women; while, if trans people focus on enabling children to change their gender identity, they seem to be telling girls that they can be trans men, or non-binary, but not that they can be lesbians. It is therefore understandable that each side is highly sensitive about how it is portrayed, and that, because they are so often insulted, they may see insults when none are intended.

Where do we go from here?

Today, a small minority of trans women are locked into an angry battle against a small minority of feminists, who see them as a threat and deny that they are really women. Unlocking this impasse requires using our imagination to try to see the world from the other 'side' and to work towards a politics of 'solidarity in difference' that can recognise that trans and cis women share the experience of living in a patriarchal world, even as we are affected by this in different ways. We have a common interest in opposing all forms of violence and discrimination against women, and the misogynistic culture that underpins them; this is more important than the issues that appear to divide us.

This common interest is accepted by many feminist organisations, who therefore welcome all 'self-identifying women'. It is also in line with one of the pledges that the Labour Campaign for Trans Rights (LCTR) asked the candidates in the 2020 Labour Party leadership contest to make: this committed them to agree that 'there is no material conflict of interests between trans rights and women's rights, and that all trans women are subject to misogyny and patriarchal oppression' (https://twitter.com/labour_trans?lang=en). However, the idea that there 'is no material conflict' between the interests of trans and cis women is hard to sustain if vulnerable women are forced to compete against each other for scarce resources. I therefore believe that Labour politicians should focus their energy on campaigning for these resources, rather than escalating disputes by also pledging to agree that Women's Place UK is a 'trans-exclusionist hate group' and that those who hold its views should be expelled from the party. Similarly, members of Women's Place UK who are concerned that some women will be unable to access refuges if trans women are present should remember that far more women are denied access because there are not enough places, and campaign accordingly.

All three of the final leadership candidates agreed that 'trans women are women' and all supported a legal change to self-identification; however, while Rebecca Long-Bailey, Lisa Nandy and all deputy leadership candidates signed the LCTR pledges, the winner, Kier Starmer, signed another, less confrontational, list of pledges issued by LGBT+ Labour (www.lgbtlabour.org.uk/leadership_pledges). From an intersectional perspective, the fact that two pro-trans groups disagreed is unsurprising, as any social group is a coalition of differently situated people with a range of experiences and interests that may at times come into conflict. An intersectional approach also argues that real, progressive change must start with the most disadvantaged; because trans women are disproportionately likely to be poor, they would disproportionately gain if a Labour Party with a strong commitment to reducing economic inequality were to gain office.

Meanwhile, many trans women around the world recognise that women have common interests in combating patriarchy, and many explicitly identify as feminists. For example, Rawyen Connell says: 'Given the depth and interwoven character of gender inequalities, the best guarantor of justice for transsexual women is a gender-equal society' (Connell, 2012:872); Julia Serano says 'most of the anti-trans sentiment that I have had to deal with as a transsexual woman is probably better described as misogyny' (2007:3); and Sarah McBride says 'I was so focused on the transphobia I might face after transitioning that I didn't realize just how pervasive the sexism and misogyny could be' (2018:45).

Many other trans people agree. For example, as a transgender/genderqueer person C.N. Lester says that they need feminism, not because they are a woman but because they are 'subject to gender-based abuses, founded on the idea that there is one, hierarchical, coercive gender system … Feminism is my method of resistance, my road map to change' (2017:172); and Meg-John Barker and Alex Iantaffi write as non-binary feminists that we need to reframe the current debate to focus on the essential fight, which is not against other feminists, but 'to dismantle patriarchy' (2019:190). Some trans men also support feminism because they are aware that the new respect and rewards they gain after they transition reflect undeserved privilege: for example, Thomas McBee reflects on 'how race and masculinity were inventions that benefited me, and what I could do to challenge that' (2018:153: see also Davis, 2017; for research showing how trans men gain in the workplace, see Schilt, 2006, 2011).

Seeing through a feminist lens can help us all – cis and trans – to see that gender is not simply about individual identity or personal fulfilment. Nor is it simply symbolic, for it is also about economic, political and social power, while feminist solutions to apparent conflicts of interests between trans and cis women would often require public spending and a re-allocation of scarce resources. In other words, the resolution of disputes around trans issues must be about redistribution as well as recognition, and part of a wider feminist struggle that, as I discuss in the following chapters, also involves a movement away from a capitalist economy driven primarily by the pursuit of profit rather than the satisfaction of people's needs.

Meanwhile, I suggest in the next subsection that there may be a way of side-stepping one current problem: how the law should classify people who are trans.

A modest proposal

At a conference in 1996, I argued that there was no criterion that would allow the human race to be divided into two exclusive sexes, and that to make binary classification by sex the basis of our legal identity was therefore to create a legal fiction (published as Bryson, 2000). I found that the law has played a powerful role in defining what it means to be a 'woman', and that any progress towards full equality was being limited by its confirmation of 'the parameters of binary division and essential difference'; I therefore concluded that such classification should be abolished (2000:46).

I hold to this position today. Indeed, I believe that increased awareness of the needs of trans and intersex people makes abolition increasingly relevant, as it provides a practical way forward that cuts through deep-seated and complex disputes over the difference between sex and gender and our right to affirm our own identity. I now therefore propose that when a child is born, their birth certificate should simply record their date and place of birth and who their parents are (without labelling them as 'mother' and 'father'). Meanwhile, their medical records would show whether they appear to be male or female, or whether they may be intersex. As now, these records would be private and confidential, and they would be updated throughout a person's life to show whether they have had children, a heart attack or anything else that might affect their medical treatment. They would also show if the individual had had medical interventions to help them transition towards a sex they were not born into.

In addition, I now suggest that, when they reach the age of 18, anyone who wanted to could obtain a certificate that would recognise their gender identity. They would be given an open-ended list of options, and if their gender identity later changed, they could amend the certificate. Because it makes no sense to give legal recognition to something as personal and potentially fluid as an identity, this would have no legal status; however, many would see it as an empowering source of social legitimacy. Unveiling the gender identity certificate might even become a central feature of eighteenth-birthday celebrations, and it could be particularly important for those who have transitioned away from the sex they appeared to be at birth.

For most people, these changes would have little practical impact. They would still be able to tell the world whether their baby was a boy or girl, and many would continue to choose clothes and toys according to conventional gender stereotypes. Most boys and girls would probably never question their sex or gender. However, if they started to feel that their gender identity was out of line with their sexed body they should, as now, be able to access support; this could include puberty blockers and, when they were older, cross-sex hormones and/or genital surgery. All this would be on their medical records, so that calls for them to attend screening sessions for cervical or prostate cancer would be in line with their bodies, rather than anything recorded on an original or amended birth certificate.

My proposal would not work in countries where women are legally subordinate to men and/or where restrictive gender roles are enforced by law. However, in many western countries, including the UK, the sex recorded on our birth certificates already has few legal consequences: women and men receive the state pension at the same age, virtually all occupations are open to both sexes, and both same-sex and mixed-sex marriage and civil partnerships are available. At first sight, more complicated issues arise in relation to maternity and paternity leave; however, these already arise for adoptive and/or same-sex couples, and can be resolved without ignoring the specific needs of the birthing parent. In the rare cases where sex might be relevant in relation to employment or service provision, for example in a rape crisis centre, people might be asked to indicate their gender identity, and their referees could be asked to validate this.

Sex-based data are of course still needed for policy-making purposes, particularly to monitor inequalities in pay, education and political representation, and to document patterns of criminal behaviour, especially sex-based violence. Without such data, it would be harder to analyse shared oppression or to campaign collectively as women. However, this does not require legal classification by sex. After all, we also need data to identify inequalities and discrimination based on race and ethnicity, and we are able to collate information on this without recording it on birth certificates (although this was standard in most of the US before the 1960s: Davis, 2017:37). Moreover, the monitoring of sex/gender inequalities could usefully follow the example of race/ethnicity monitoring in identifying an expanding number of categories; this would recognise the diversity of sex/gender identities rather than forcing us all into binary female/male boxes.

My proposal will be disliked by many, and it would not magic patriarchy away. However, it would represent a powerful symbolic move that disempowers the law as a way of constructing our identity as male or female. As such, it could play a role as part of much wider movements against sex-based inequalities and oppressions. It also seems in tune with observable social trends towards increasingly fluid and open ideas around gender identity. And it is of course one way of putting feminist critiques of binary thought into practice.

Conclusions

If we are to move debates around trans issues forward, we need to move beyond adversarial thinking and competitive notions of individual or group rights. Instead, we should focus on ideas around solidarity in difference, and when rights appear to come into conflict we should adopt a transversal approach, making a leap of imagination to see the situation from the perspective of someone with very different experiences, expectations, needs and priorities, rather than simply treating them as opponents. We need to retain the insights of the intersectional approaches discussed in the previous chapter, to see that neither cis nor trans women constitute a singular interest or identity; rather, both are coalitions of women whose interests and allegiances cut across any idea of a binary division. We also need to look at wider socio-economic issues, to hold capitalism and the ideology that sustains it to account and to investigate whether alternative ideologies and socialist policies can offer better feminist solutions.

5

We need to talk about capitalism

I HAVE ALREADY made some quite sweeping claims about the exploitative nature of capitalism and the extent to which it is bound up with
patriarchy and other forms of structural inequality. I have also been critical
of the neoliberal ideology that has dominated much economic and political
thinking over the last forty years, claiming that this has been used to justify
harsh policies that are particularly damaging for the poorest and most vulnerable women, who often exist at the intersection of multiple inequalities
and must compete against each other for scarce resources. My aim in this
chapter is to lay the foundations for the rest of the book by making the
economic theories and arguments involved in these claims accessible to
readers unfamiliar with them.

I begin by outlining the changing nature of capitalism and its effects on
living standards and inequality, before providing a critical overview of
liberal and neoliberal economic ideas from a woman-centred perspective.
I then use this discussion to explore the limitations of some initiatives that
claim to 'empower' girls and women in the global south.

The changing nature of capitalism

Like patriarchy, capitalism has come to seem natural, but it is important
to recognise that it is a man-made and possibly transitory part of human
history. At the most basic and abstract level, it can be understood as an
economic system based on private ownership, the competitive pursuit

of profit as an end in itself, the use of money as the abstract measure of value and wealth, and the employment of wage labourers rather than serfs or slaves. It necessarily involves exploitation in the sense that profit can be made only if workers are paid less than the full value of what they produce. Since the mid-eighteenth century, when industrial capitalism was taking hold in western Europe, this drive to make profit has produced extraordinarily rapid innovation and growth. This was vividly described by Karl Marx and Friedrich Engels in the *Communist Manifesto* of 1848:

> Subjection of nature's forces to man, machinery, steam naviga-tion, railways, electric telegraphs, clearing of whole continents for cultivation, canalisation of rivers, whole populations conjured out of the ground – what earlier century had even a presentiment that such productive forces slumbered in the lap of social labour? (1848/1967:126)

Since then, economic growth and technological change have continued, spreading throughout the world, so that today we effectively have one main global capitalist economy, albeit one often torn by national and ideological rivalries. China (now the world's second largest economy, after the US) remains an outlier, in that many big enterprises remain state-owned or state-controlled and there is a high degree of economic planning. However, it is also a key player in the international economy, investing overseas and competing with private companies for market share and profits; in this sense, it is probably best described as 'state capitalist'.

The spread of capitalism has brought about a dramatic rise in living standards for vast numbers of people. A key indicator of this is the increase in life expectancy, first in the early industrialising nations and then else-where: the global average life expectancy of a child at birth is now nearly seventy, more than double what it was in 1900. Recent decades have also seen a rapid fall in the number of people living in what the World Bank (2018a) describes as 'extreme poverty', from over a third in 1990 to around a tenth in 2015.

The benefits of capitalist growth have, however, never been evenly spread between countries. Capitalism's current global reach is itself the result of centuries of colonial and imperialist expansion that began with European 'discovery' of the Americas, continued with increased European sway in parts of Asia and reached its peak in the late nineteenth century, when a number of European powers carved up much of Africa amongst themselves. While direct control has now generally ended, the legacy of this period is very much alive, setting the terms for global trade and the distribution of global resources and wealth. Although there seems to have been some reduction of inequalities between countries in the last forty years, these remain vast, 'extreme poverty' is concentrated in South Asia and sub-Saharan Africa, and recent progress on reducing such poverty seems to be stalling or even going into reverse (World Bank, 2018b).

Meanwhile, 'moderate poverty' is increasing in many areas, and the World Bank finds that most of the world's poor now live in middle-income countries. The increase in poverty is increasingly visible even in wealthy countries such as the UK, where the number of people who are homeless or dependent on food banks has steadily grown over the last ten years (for more detailed discussion of the UK situation, see Chapter 6). As Tithi Bhattacharya vividly puts it:

> [the] devastation of working class neighbourhoods in the global north has left behind boarded buildings, pawnshops and empty stoops. In the global south it has created vast slums as the breeding ground for violence and want. (2015:18)

Throughout the world, such negative impacts have been disproportionately experienced by women.

As some people are growing poorer, others are growing much richer, and the past decades have seen a rise in 'extreme wealth', with a growing gulf between the top one per cent of the world's population and everyone else: at the beginning of 2018 the Credit Suisse Global Wealth Report found that just one per cent of adults owned 47 per cent of the world's wealth, and a year later the development charity Oxfam reported that just *26 individuals* now hold as much wealth as the poorest half of the world's population (Credit Suisse, 2018; Elliott, 2019). The vast majority of the world's super-rich are men (Wang, 2019). A high concentration of wealth clearly gives its holders access to many governments across the world; even when governments appear willing to tax the super-rich, the globally dispersed and often intangible nature of their wealth makes this extraordinarily difficult. There is also mounting evidence that inequality has harmful effects on well-being, even in wealthy societies and even for rich people in these societies; these effects include a steep rise in mental illness in all groups.

The extent of poverty and inequality is now officially a matter of concern to powerful international organisations including the World Bank, the World Economic Forum, the OECD, the United Nations, the IMF and the EU, which tend to see these as economic problems that may hold back growth and threaten social and political stability. These growing problems are not inevitable, but reflect changes in the regulatory role of states, the nature of capitalism itself and underlying economic ideology.

The role of capitalist states in regulating national economies, curtailing exploitation, or in using taxation to reduce inequality and provide welfare services, has fluctuated both between countries and over time in response to a complex range of factors, including the rise of democracy, the power of organised labour, the economic effects of war and recession, and ideological developments. By the Second World War, there was widespread agreement in western democracies that unrestrained free-market capitalism was too prone to crisis, and that states had a role to play in regulating the economy and meeting citizens' welfare needs. Since the 1980s, however, there has been a general rolling back of state involvement, although the extent of this varies significantly – most obviously between the still largely social democratic and relatively egalitarian Nordic states, where poverty rates are low, and the US, where both poverty levels and the gap between rich and poor are much higher.

Capitalism itself is not a stable system, and it has changed significantly over time. In particular, there has been a long-term shift from industrial to finance capitalism, a process which has accelerated in recent years. Today, betting on changes in the global stock market is much more lucrative than producing material goods, so that banks are primarily trading in financial assets rather than lending to businesses, and algorithmic trading on the stock exchange seems to represent a new form of 'digital capitalism'. These changes are linked to a shift from tangible to intangible assets in an economy increasingly based on ideas, brand names and communications technology, rather than the physical capital represented by the factories or machines of old (for example, Uber does not own a single vehicle; instead, its asset is an algorithm that links taxi drivers and passengers across the world: Haskel and Westlake, 2017). Meanwhile, the speeding-up of economic activity has become bound up with the growth of ever more complex just-in-time global supply chains, and digital communications technology has enabled a new form of capitalism to develop that transforms human experiences, preferences and activities into behavioural data that can be traded as 'prediction products' in 'behavioural futures markets'; this in turn means that 'Power was once identified with the ownership of the means of production, but it is now identified with ownership of the means of behavioural modification' (Zuboff, 2019:379).

All this has been accompanied by a shrinking of the industrial working class in western countries, which is increasingly being replaced by a 'precariat' of workers in insecure, irregular, badly paid and part-time employment. There has also been a global movement of women of all classes into paid employment, which in turn has generated a huge demand for paid domestic and caring work, which has become an international market.

The cumulative effect of these recent changes has been to speed up and increase capitalism's inherent instability and to intensify contradictory pressures within it. These include the need to depress wages to maintain profitability at the same time as wanting workers to buy more goods, the need to pursue growth and maintain competitive edge without destroying the planet in the process and the need for women to be in paid employment while also raising children, caring for others and running the home. The resulting economic fragility became very apparent in 2020, when the COVID-19 pandemic spread throughout the world and much of the global economy rapidly seized up.

As outlined in the next section, economic changes have been accompanied by a general shift in western economic thinking towards neoliberal principles. These principles have been used to justify policies by both states and international bodies such as the World Bank and IMF that include the privatisation of publicly owned assets, the imposition of austerity measures, restrictions on trade unions and the dismantling of protective workplace legislation.

Capitalist economic theory: from Adam Smith in 1776 to neoliberalism in the twenty-first century

In 1776, Adam Smith's *The Wealth of Nations* laid out the main principles of classic liberal economic theory, principles that met the needs of the newly emerging system of industrial capitalism. Smith's central claim was that individuals know best what is in their own self-interest, and that, if they can pursue this without state intervention, then the laws of supply and demand will act like a 'hidden hand' to ensure that goods are produced for those who want them. This means that the rational pursuit of self-interest is not anti-social, and therefore to be discouraged, but economically beneficial; as he famously said, 'It is not from the benevolence of the butcher, the brewer or the baker, that we expect our dinner, but from their regard to their own self interest' (quoted in Marçal, 2015:8). Although he said that governments would have to provide some public goods, such as street lighting or bridges, Smith generally argued strongly in favour of laissez-faire, that is, the idea that governments should intervene as little as possible in economic life. This meant that producers, buyers and sellers should be set free from state regulation and intervention, and enabled to trade without tariffs or barriers, for a free-market economy would regulate itself in the best interest of everyone.

There are a number of problems with this argument. First, in liberal economic terms, people 'demand' goods only if they can pay for them. They may want something, or even desperately need it, but hungry people without money will not generate a demand for bread: as Smith said, the baker does not bake out of the goodness of his heart (and if he does, he will soon go out of business). Second, the values of the individualistic, competitive, rational and self-interested 'economic man' of liberal economic theory are certainly not an exhaustive description of human character, behaviour and motivation, even in relation to conventionally defined economic matters. Third, the approach sees only monetary exchanges, completely forgetting all the work and services that are essential for the survival or prosperity of any society but which are not paid for. Such work is, of course, disproportionately done by women, but liberal economic theory does not generally acknowledge this. It is, therefore, not interested in the question posed by Katrine Marçal (2015) in the title of her book on feminist economics: *Who Cooked Adam Smith's Dinner?* (spoiler alert: for most of his life it was his mother).

Although liberal theory did not explore the economic significance of women's unpaid work in the home, it recognised the importance of family life and the values of care and compassion associated with it. However, rather than recognising and rewarding these as human qualities, it treated them as specifically female; this conveniently meant that, unlike the male baker in his shop, women in the home would do their work for love rather than money. This perspective also supported the view that women's 'special qualities' would be tainted and corrupted if they participated alongside men in politics or paid employment, and it fiercely rejected any suggestion that their loving family duties should be 'sullied' by any idea of payment – hence fierce opposition in the 1920s to attempts by the Independent MP and social reformer Eleanor Rathbone to introduce a 'family endowment' for mothers in the UK. Rathbone believed that this would both give mothers a degree of economic independence and alleviate the squalor and poverty that she had witnessed. Her opponents claimed to revere motherhood. However, these 'sentimentalists' as Rathbone called them, were also

shocked at the base suggestion that anything so sordid as remuneration, anything so prosaic as the adjustment of means to ends, should be introduced into the sacred institution of the family and applied to the profession of motherhood. (Rathbone, 1927:66)

Neoliberalism

The neoliberal theory that developed from the 1940s left no room for such 'sentimentality'. Most western economies had survived the great depression of the 1930s by adopting some version of the principles advocated by the British economist John Maynard Keynes, who argued that state intervention, particularly in the form of fiscal and monetary policies, and including welfare spending, could 'iron out' the booms and slumps to which capitalist economies are otherwise prone – in popular language, states could 'spend their way' out of recession. State spending obviously increased further during the Second World War. After it ended in 1945, Keynesian theory combined with the need to rebuild economies and political pressure for greater welfare provision to legitimise much higher levels of state planning and spending than before. Although this shift went less far in the US than in western Europe, the general principles of Roosevelt's 1930s 'New Deal', including the idea that the state had some welfare responsibilities, remained largely in place.

In this context, the new neoliberal ideas associated with theorists such as Friedrich Hayek, Milton Friedman, Gary Becker and the Chicago School of Economics not only provided a vigorous reassertion of the classic liberal principles of laissez-faire and free markets but extended them. Neoliberalism stressed the importance of individual independence and self-reliance rather than state dependency, it saw efficiency as a primary virtue, it agreed with Adam Smith that society would prosper only if individuals were allowed to pursue their own self-interest, and it argued that the wealth of the most successful would 'trickle down' to benefit ordinary workers. Unlike classic liberal theory, neoliberalism did not exclude the family or women from market values; rather, it extended the idea of rational decision-making into all areas of human life, so that when we decide whom to marry, whether to have children or who should do the housework, we are all calculating what is in our own self-interest. In other words, we all behave like 'economic man', there is no place for any messier values or emotions and every area of life is recast 'on a contemporary business model with financialisation at its heart' (Farris and Rottenberg, 2017:10).

By the early 1970s, neoliberalism had become part of mainstream economics, influencing politicians from the left as well as the right of politics; by the Reagan/Thatcher years of the 1980s it was firmly entrenched, and, although not uncontested, it has continued to dominate economic thinking in the opening decades of the twenty-first century. Neoliberal ideas about the need to free up economic competition and promote self-reliance have been used in many western countries to justify reductions in both tax and welfare spending, the privatisation of some state-run industries and services, and the outsourcing of provision in others. The International Monetary Fund and World Bank have imposed similar policies as conditions of loans to 'developing' countries, reducing the role of the state and increasing that of banks and big international corporations.

The dominance of neoliberal thinking was the product of decades of effort as, with the help of funding from extremely wealthy backers, its proponents established a transatlantic network of lobbyists, academics, journalists, activists and think tanks to develop and promote its key ideas throughout society (Monbiot, 2016, 2017). As Margaret Thatcher said in 1981, 'Economics are the method; the object is to change the heart and soul' (quoted in Marçal, 2015:143). One result of neoliberalism's success in winning many hearts and souls has been widespread acceptance of some very harsh policies.

In particular, the neoliberal view of human nature tells us that individuals are all responsible for their own decisions in life, that we get what we deserve and that we should not expect others to bail us out when things go wrong (although it does seem to make an exception for bankers). We should therefore educate our children to be self-sufficient and 'to "invest" in themselves so that they are a better and more marketable product than their neighbour' (Tronto, 2017:33). If we are winners, this is due to our own efforts (these apparently include choosing entrepreneurial and/or wealthy parents) and the state should not seek to redistribute our winnings. When Oxfam reported that FTSE 100 bosses earned on average

120 times more than the average employee, and advocated increasing taxation on their earnings, Mark Littlewood, director general at the Institute of Economic Affairs, therefore responded by saying

> Oxfam is promoting a race to the bottom. Richer people are already highly taxed people – reducing their wealth beyond a certain point won't lead to redistribution, it will destroy it to the benefit of no one. (Quoted in Elliott, 2018)

If, on the other hand, we fail to get even moderately rich, then we are losers in every sense and we have only ourselves to blame. As Judith Butler describes it, one logical outcome of this thinking is the 'shout of joy' that greeted US Congressman Ron Paul at a rally when he suggested that seriously ill people who 'cannot pay for health insurance, or "choose" not to pay, as he would put it, would simply have to die'. Such 'choice' is of course made in the context of a profoundly unequal society in which everything, including healthcare, is in principle for sale and driven by the need to increase profit, so that 'market rationality is deciding whose health and life should be protected and whose health and life should not' (Butler, 2015:12, 11).

This market rationality prizes the values of efficiency, cost-effectiveness and time-management that are believed to maximise output in the workplace, whether by producing graduates more cheaply by reducing the time it takes to get a degree or by outsourcing the running of prisons to the lowest bidder. It also extends these values to family life, suggesting that short periods of 'quality time' with children can be as good as longer, less focused periods, and that good organisation is the key to a good work–life balance. Thus Margaret Thatcher wrote in 1954 that, with efficient management, 'as well as being a housewife it is possible to put in eight hours work a day besides' and 'you can achieve as much in a day as you set out to achieve if you think ahead and get everything well organised'.

Neoliberal arguments have appealed to many other ambitious women, many of whom, unlike Thatcher, describe themselves as feminists. Many other feminists are of course highly critical, and some fear that feminism has been taken over by an ideology that is deeply opposed to the interests of most women. All of this fiercely debated, and I will return to the issue in the next chapter. At this stage, I will focus on two key interconnected problem with neoliberal theory: its stress on self-reliance and its narrow understanding of economic activity.

Neoliberalism and the myth of independence

For neoliberal thinkers, the ideal person is a hard-working, competitive, rational, profit-seeking, self-interested and self-reliant individual. He or she is a worker, not a 'shirker' or a 'benefits scrounger', and he or she will look after themselves rather than relying on others. Although they may have friends and family, they are essentially self-sufficient and independent. If at any time they need medical assistance or care, or if they lose their job, they will be covered by insurance or savings. In contrast, those who are dependent on others (the state, family, friends or charities) to meet their physical or financial needs are inferior, second-class citizens. And although lip service is sometimes paid to the self-sacrifice of those who provide care for others, they are generally regarded as disposable and economically unproductive – which is why they should be encouraged to 'get a job' if they are looking after people in their own family or a 'better job' if they are a poorly paid care worker.

In contrast to neoliberalism's imaginary care-free individual, in the real world we all need other people to care for us at some stage of our life. Everyone reading this book will have been nurtured in someone else's womb and then looked after when they were a baby, many will need care if they get ill or if they become old and frail, and many who seem perfectly independent will, like Adam Smith, depend on someone else to cook their dinner. Many will also want, need or simply enjoy human relationships based on reciprocity, friendship and/or love, in which the giving and receiving of care and attention is unmediated by money or calculations of self-advancement. Such needs are basic to the human condition and, as Katrine Marçal says:

> Regardless of the seductive elegance of mathematics, we can't get away from the fact that at its core economics is based on the human

body. Bodies that work, bodies that need care, bodies that create other bodies … Bodies that need help through many phases of life. And a society that can support them. (2015:73)

It is tempting to say that only a male-stream economist could think otherwise. However, as Joan Tronto has argued, neoliberalism not only assumes that humans are 'the kind of creatures who fit within … a market-driven world' but it also enforces practices that spread this assumption by promoting a positive moral image of the independent individual (2017:29; see also Nguyen et al., 2017). Such neoliberal practices include making benefits conditional on paid employment, even for parents of young children or those caring for their elderly parents; privatising care services so that they can function as profit-making enterprises; treating care receivers as customers or consumers, rather than as citizens claiming their rights; denying any sense of collective responsibility for the welfare of others; and, when it is convenient, exploiting moral notions of care and family responsibility, so that 'The discourse of care creates a veil over the wounds inflicted by precarity and crisis, while facilitating the unloading of responsibilities onto individuals and families' (Nguyen et al., 2017:2010). These practices have informed and framed the language of public debates around care and welfare entitlements; as Thatcher would have wanted, they thereby helped win hearts and souls to the neoliberal point of view. Neoliberal assumptions were, however, challenged by the 2020 COVID-19 crisis, which revealed the extent of human interdependence and the need for people to help each other, make sacrifices in the interests of the general good and set aside their short-term selfish interests. The accompanying shift in discourse was epitomised in the UK when Boris Johnson, who was self-isolating after being tested positive for the virus (and who was later treated in an NHS intensive care unit), explicitly refuted Thatcher's famous claim that 'There's no such thing as society. There are individual men and women and their families' with the declaration that 'There really is such a thing as society' (quoted in PA Media, 2020).

Who cares (and cooks and cleans)?

Against neoliberal orthodoxy, feminist economists have argued for decades that looking after other people and their domestic needs is not a leisure activity but economically essential work, even when it is unpaid. They have therefore campaigned to have this 'women's work' recognised. Here Marilyn Waring's 1988 book *If Women Counted* has been particularly influential, and it contributed to a successful international campaign for time-use surveys to be carried out so that the value of unpaid work could be measured. This was unanimously agreed to by the 189 countries that signed up to the 'Platform for Action' that resulted from the United Nations World Conference on Women in Beijing in 1995.

Waring has since said that she fears that that time-use studies can only see women's work in terms of the measurable, monetary values of 'an individualised and commodified free market society' (Dobel with Walsh, 2014:135), and I have argued (2007, 2008) that the studies can never fully capture the ceaseless nature of many caring responsibilities. Nevertheless, they provide clear evidence that unpaid work is both an important and a largely female area of economic activity: a 2018 study for the International Labour Organization, which drew on time-use data from 64 countries, reported that unpaid care constitutes 9 per cent of global GDP, that three-quarters of this work is done by women, that there is no country in which it is shared equally with men and that any movement to equality is 'glacial'. (Addati et al., 2018:xxvii). The study also noted that there are 249 million women and 132 million men in the global *paid* care workforce; this represents 11.5 per cent of total global employment, and 19.3 per cent of global female employment.

In general, neoliberal economists have not been greatly interested in the social and economic implications of either women's unpaid work or the global shift towards paid care. This gives them a distorted view of economic activity that fails to understand that figures for economic growth are misleadingly high when, as in the Nordic countries, many women start being paid for work that was previously provided within households 'for free' (Aslaksen and Koren, 2014). They are also unable to anticipate the difficulties created when state-provided care is replaced by private profit-making companies, producing a clash of values and a predictable inability to provide decent care by adequately trained and paid workers at the same time as making a profit. The results can be seen in the UK, as private equity-owned care home chains collapse (Sodha, 2017) and more than a thousand nurseries and childminders have gone out of business since 2015 (Ferguson, 2017). Further limitations in dominant economic understanding became very clear in 2020, as measures taken to combat the spread of COVID-19 ran into difficulties when schools were closed at the same time as women workers were urgently needed to provide health services and their 'unskilled' work as hospital cleaners and care workers was suddenly understood to be critically important.

Women: saviours of the global capitalist economy?

As I said in my Introduction, the movement of women into paid employment and the elimination of gender inequality are now officially recognised by international bodies as important and desirable goals. As with ending poverty and inequality more generally, these bodies promote gender equality because of its beneficial effects on economic growth; from this perspective, what is good for women is also good for the economy. This approach wants to improve women's education so as to bring them into the global market economy as paid workers, entrepreneurs and consumers, and it claims to empower women by giving them economic independence. From this perspective, it is simply sound business sense to invest in and use the talents of women as well as men, with the added bonuses that women are thought more likely than men to use their education and earnings to benefit their whole family, the presence of more women business leaders may reduce excessive risk-taking and welfare costs can be cut if women, including lone mothers of young children, are in paid employment. It is also widely believed that educating women in the global south will help reduce the fertility rate – which has long been a key goal of US development policy.

Such thinking has been endorsed and supported by a number of global corporations. For example, the Ford Foundation has long financed feminist campaigns to empower women and end discrimination, first in the US and then globally; in 2004 the Nike Foundation established Girl Effect to harness 'the unique potential of adolescent girls to end poverty for themselves and the world' (www.girleffect.org); in 2008 Goldman Sachs began the 10,000 Women Global Initiative to 'foster economic growth by providing women entrepreneurs around the world with a business and management education, mentoring and networking, and access to capital' (www.goldmansachs.com/citizenship/10000women); and, by 2017, Unilever's Shakti Amma project, set up in 2001 to create a network of women in India to sell its products and improve community health in low-income rural areas, had nearly 75,000 such microentrepreneurs, thereby 'creating new opportunities for women while strengthening our business' (www.unilever.com/sustainable-living/enhancing-livelihoods/opportunities-for-women/expanding-opportunities-in-our-retail-value-chain). And in 2018, Ivanka Trump helped start the Women Entrepreneurs Finance Initiative, a fund administered by the World Bank with the goal of generating $1.6 billion in capital for female entrepreneurs in 'developing' countries.

So much for the theory. In practice, employment prospects for women in most of the world are often very limited. For women employed by transnational corporations in call centres or assembly lines in the global south, their pay may provide some economic independence, but this is often at the level of bare survival, and they are attractive to global corporations precisely because their labour is so cheap. Such corporations include Nike, whose aims in its Girl Effect project are at odds with the appalling working conditions in its Cambodian factories, where women on short-term contracts work 60-hour weeks in temperatures of 37°C (McVeigh, 2017); Nike has also been accused of gender discrimination in a US workplace (Helmore, 2018), and at the beginning of 2019 it was being investigated by EU officials over allegations of tax avoidance (Guardian staff and Reuters, 2019). A similar clash of values occurred when it was revealed that T-shirts designed to raise money for the British charity

Comic Relief's 'gender justice' campaign were being made in a factory in Bangladesh where the mainly female workers were paid just 35 pence an hour; the factory also supplied clothing to well-known UK companies including Tesco, Mothercare and M&S (Murphy, 2019).

In terms of the logic of the capitalist economy, such findings may be unfortunate, but they make hard-headed economic sense: if a company such as Nike unilaterally improved wages and conditions of employment, it would have to pass on its increased costs to its customers, thereby losing its competitive market edge and reducing its profitability. As Hester Eisenstein wryly notes, such considerations suggest that the education provided to the women entrepreneurs in the Goldman Sachs initiative might include teaching them 'how to run such companies even more cheaply, efficiently, and ruthlessly' (2017:47).

Micro-credit projects, through which very poor women are given small loans to start up small businesses, have also had mixed results. These projects have been widely seen as a particularly effective way of enabling women to turn their traditional skills into money. However, problems have arisen from traditional assumptions around gender roles, with men unwilling to forgo their authority within households and communities (here it is important to remember that such attitudes are not confined to developing or poor societies). In this context, women's new role can 'fuel competition, resentment or conflict', and they often lack real control over their earnings or investment decisions (Peterson, 2012:22). Other critics say that the approach substitutes individual initiative for more collective planning and resources, and that, because women have to pay off loans and the interest on their loans, they are really working for the banks rather than themselves; Susan Watkins concludes that, in general, 'evidence of any emancipatory effect for poor women is thin' (2018:53; for a more positive assessment, see International Labour Organization, undated). Related criticisms have been made of Unilever's Shakti Amma project with its micro-entrepreneurs. However, Elisabeth Prügl argues that, although these criticisms have validity, the reality may be more nuanced, and that women's reported increased income and self-confidence may be part of a process of change whereby 'narrow forms of empowerment may proliferate new meanings and unintended effects' (2015:624).

A key problem underlying many development projects and corporate initiatives aimed at women and girls is that these create unrealistic and individualised solutions to structural problems – most obviously in the Nike slogan about 'the unique potential of adolescent girls to end poverty for themselves and the world', cited above. As Katherine Moeller says, this solution 'positions Black and Brown girls as disproportionately respons- ible for solving the structural conditions and problems of poverty created by histories of exploitation in capitalist development', at the same time as 'absolving corporations and other institutions of their roles in producing and perpetuating it' (2018:137; 63). It also increases girls' and women's burdens rather than 'empowering' them precisely because it assumes and exploits existing gendered responsibilities: it imagines that women who are enabled through education to secure good employment will be able to provide financial support for their families, but it forgets that these women were not previously idle, and that they are unlikely to find that their traditional family duties magically disappear or that they will now be done by a willing brother or spouse. And of course, in racist patriarchal societies, black and brown girls will face particular difficulties in securing good employment.

As Moeller shows from her extensive ethnographic research on Nike's Girl Effect project, corporate intervention also constructs a particular image of the recipients of its largesse as 'simultaneously a universalized victim in need of saving and "the answer" to solving the problems of development and growth' (2018:12). She reports that, in an 18-month Nike training project in Rio de Janeiro, the recruitment poster said simply 'Female sex, 16–24 years old, and interested in entering the labor market or becoming an entrepreneur' (2018:128). In reality, however, its organis- ers were looking for girls who were black or brown, poor (but not too poor, not street children), who had the time to attend the classes, who had the money to pay their fares and who were neither pregnant nor already mothers. Perhaps unsurprisingly, the project recruited only 70 girls, instead of the hoped for 100, and it had little success in finding them the kind of administrative jobs it had trained them for (many had joined the programme with high aspirations; the majority got insecure, low-wage jobs in businesses such as telecommunications centres and supermarkets, and they were not informed about further educational possibilities). As Moeller comments, corporate sponsors were not giving these girls the same opportunities that they would like their own children to have; they were, however, expecting them to change the world.

Meanwhile, many women in poor areas of the world seek employment in wealthier countries, and the remittances they send home can be a significant contribution both to their family and, on a larger scale, to some national economies: by 2016, women were around half of all migrants, responsible for about half of the estimated US$601 billion in global remittances (although their wages are generally lower than men's, they generally send a higher percentage home: UN Women, 2017). These women are entering employment markets that are already structured by both gender and race, and in which their migrant status makes them triply disadvantaged. While there are many individual exceptions and important national variations, migrant women's employment is concentrated in low-paid sectors, particularly in hospitality (often as cleaners or waitresses), in care work and in domestic services, where the 'maid trade' has become a global industry. Some, particularly in the informal domestic and care sector, are undocumented workers; such workers are particularly vulnerable to exploitation. Other women come to richer countries as mail-order brides for men who 'want a wife they can control, and count on the vulnerability of those who depend on them for their stay in the country' (Federici, 2012:73). Many work in the sex industry, which generates global profits conservatively estimated at nearly US$28 billion (Magnusson, 2015). Others sell their bodies in different ways, and there is a growing baby-market for adoptions and surrogacy in a world in which, as V. Spike Peterson says, 'Infants, human organs, sexualized bodies, intimate caring, sensual pleasures, and spiritual salvation are all for sale' (2003:78).

The exploitation of women workers in or from the global south has mixed effects on women born in the west. Many can benefit from the availability of cheap consumer goods, forgetting that 'while we glory in "retail therapy" the women making our jeans pay for our choices' (Redfern and Aune, 2010:30) and that, as Nazma Akter, a Bangladeshi labour rights activist, says, 'When clothes are cheap, women are cheap' (quoted by Pankhurst, 2018). However, when western women are in competition with cheaper overseas workers, their wages too will be depressed; they are also at risk of losing their job if their employer moves production or services to a more profitable location where labour is cheaper. Western women are also competing in a domestic employment market that is increasingly reliant on temporary and/or part-time staff. Although some women welcome flexible employment, such work is often insecure, unpredictable and without the legal protections and benefits of full-time work.

Some provisional conclusions

In general, neoliberal principles favour loosening any constraints on today's global capitalism. The result is to favour the rich over the poor, men over women, and western women over those in the rest of the world. Neoliberalism also sees economic growth as the solution to poverty and inequality, without considering the damaging effects on workers who are trapped on a work-to-spend treadmill and who also have family responsibilities. Even more importantly, it does not address the catastrophic consequences of economic growth for the climate and the environment; these are likely to include poverty and misery on an unprecedented scale. And in 2020, governments that had adopted neoliberal policies and insisted on the need to 'balance the books' found themselves with run-down health services and punitive welfare systems that were quite inadequate in the face of the COVID-19 crisis, and that failed to meet the needs of the disproportionately female health and social care workforce.

All this makes neoliberal thinking an unlikely source of feminist ideas. Nevertheless, 'neoliberal feminism' has become an important strand of twenty-first century feminism. This is the focus of the next chapter.

6

Liberalism, neoliberalism and feminism: contradictions and concerns

T HE PREVIOUS CHAPTER addressed the male-centric nature of liberal and neoliberal economic theory and practice. This chapter focuses more directly on the implications for feminist politics. I start by looking briefly at some of the most visible forms of feminism in the west and their roots in liberal ideas around equal rights. I then address neoliberalism's alleged 'seduction' of feminism and the consequences of this. In the final section I use the UK as a case study to argue that the incompatibilities between feminism and neoliberalism help explain why Theresa May, a self-declared feminist, did more harm than good to most women during her time as Home Secretary and Prime Minister.

Fashionable feminisms

In the first decade of the twenty-first century, feminism was widely seen as out-of-date and irrelevant in most western countries. However, the next ten years saw it becoming much more visible and even fashionable, as a new generation of confident young women asserted their rights to live and enjoy their lives without constraint and new kinds of feminist activism emerged: as outlined in my Introduction, these include the #MeToo movement, mass demonstrations by women against Donald Trump and the growth of an international women's strike movement. These developments seem to offer grounds for optimism to those who hope feminism will move in a more radical, collective and socialist direction. Other developments, however, seem more negative or double-edged.

In particular, although feminism's association with a long list of glamorous celebrities has made it relatively easy for young western women to identify themselves as feminists and it can encourage them to engage with serious political issues, it can also reduce feminism to a glossy lifestyle choice for women with disposable incomes and a well developed sense of entitlement. Such feminism is well illustrated by a couple of lines from an edition of the fashion magazine *Elle*, which told its readers to 'be happy, confident and proud to call yourself a feminist today', in the knowledge that if you 'give a woman the right accessories ... she can conquer the world' (December 2014:195, 14). The flip side of this message seems to suggest that without the 'right accessories', a woman might as well give up. As R. Claire Snyder (2008) says, this kind of lifestyle feminism also seems to say that anything women choose to do represents an empowering feminist assertion of choice and independence – whether 'feeling good' involves buying lots of expensive clothes, engaging in sado-masochistic sex games or having surgery for breast enlargement, while Angela McRobbie regrets the replacement of earlier feminism 'by aggressive individualism, by a hedonistic female phallicism in the field of sexuality, and by obsession with consumer culture' (McRobbie, 2009:5).

It is of course good if feminism helps individual women feel better about themselves. However, consumer culture is an essential part of the capitalist economy, which thrives on the creation of insecurities that advertisers tell us can be overcome if we spend enough money on correcting an open-ended and ever-changing list of 'faults' with our female bodies. As Jessa Crispin robustly asserts, feminism can be much more than 'just another self-help system' in a world in which we should all be aspiring to 'wealth, comfort, and firm buttocks', and in which 'choices' are often manufactured by 'a system that measures success by money, that values consumerism and competition, [and] that devalues compassion and community' (Crispin, 2017:17, xiv, 88). According to the values of such a system, individuals should put themselves first and make their own future, rather than relying on anyone else or working together to achieve common goals. In this ideological context, even the #MeToo movement risks losing its sense of collectivism and solidarity, becoming instead a solipsistic 'look at ME' expression of individual experience, leaving little space for any sense of feminism as a collective endeavour that aims to expose and end structural inequalities or injustices.

Liberal origins and subsequent developments

The individualistic tendencies within western feminism reflect its origins in liberal, equal-rights theories. Women's legal and political rights were not easily won, and demanding them remains radical for any group that has been denied them. However, their meaning in practice is often limited by narrowly middle-class, male-based liberal assumptions that run into a number of interconnected difficulties when they are applied to women and used to frame feminist demands.

Like the liberal economic theory discussed in Chapter 5, liberal political theory has rested on a view of people as competitive, self-interested individuals who need rights to defend themselves against everyone else. Although it can recognise that societies need love and care, it has treated this as a matter for the female, domestic sphere that has little relevance for public life. The result has often been a focus on legal and political rather than economic or social rights, on equality of opportunity rather than outcomes and on the needs of individuals rather than groups. Even when it recognises that some groups experience discrimination or disadvantage, this competitive view of rights is unable to conceptualise the cross-cutting, intersectional nature of different forms of privilege and oppression. For example, it has framed the debates around the rights and needs of trans and cis women in an unhelpfully combative way that sets one group against another in a zero-sum game and fails to see shared interests and common goals.

Again like liberal economic theory, liberal political theory has generally been hostile to state intervention, unless this is necessary to defend life and property. In the past, this suspicion of state power has made liberals reluctant to use it to protect women from domestic abuse, promote workplace opportunities for women or redistribute economic resources in women's favour. Such theory has also tended to see sexual violence in terms of individual acts by 'bad men', rather than as a reflection of entrenched male power and a misogynistic culture (see Chapters 1 and 2).

Further problems have arisen from the man-made terms on which equal rights have been granted, and liberalism's inability to see or question the biased nature of these terms. As discussed in Chapter 2, patriarchy is underpinned by the assumption that men are 'normal', and that if women are in any way 'different' this is a sign of inferiority that they must overcome – in other words, women have increasingly been allowed to play the same game as men, but according to rules and definitions of 'merit' that have been already set. From this dominant perspective, women's ability to give birth, or their greater willingness to look after other people, are signs of weakness that limit their ability to compete, and maternity leave is a form of special treatment that discriminates against men. In the US, this meant that laws against sex discrimination were used to make it illegal for insurance policies or employment contracts to provide for maternity leave. After a series of legal battles in the 1970s, the law was reinterpreted to allow such cover, so long as 'pregnant persons' were not treated more favourably than other people with 'temporary disabilities'.

The liberal focus on women's rights in the public sphere has often reflected the class and race privileges of prominent feminists, who have equated liberation with freedom from domestic work, forgetting that employment often involves exploitation and tedium rather than fulfilment. This elite orientation was epitomised when Betty Friedan, founder of the National Organization for Women (see Chapter 1), advised unfulfilled housewives that they should find paid employment even if they had to spend most of their wages on a 'cleaning woman' (1963/1968:303) – failing to consider that the cleaner herself had needs and that these were unlikely to be met by cleaning another woman's bathroom. Despite, or in reaction to, the emergence of more radical and socialist feminisms during the 1970s, this kind of feminism re-emerged in the 1990s in the guise of 'power feminism', associated with writers such as Naomi Wolf (1993) in the US and Natasha Walter (1998) in the UK. Jettisoning talk of patriarchy and structural oppression, these writers argued that the key feminist battles had been won, that women should stop thinking of themselves as victims and that they should focus on taking advantage of the opportunities now open to them.

Since then, widespread talk about breaking the 'glass ceiling' in politics and employment has continued to focus on elite women rather than those who are multiply disadvantaged. Although some argue that powerful women will act for the benefit of other women, this has tended to mean mentoring other ambitious women rather than concern for those who are particularly exploited: as Crispin says:

> A woman CEO can proudly stand up and proclaim her belief in feminism – after all, it got her to this position of power – while still outsourcing her company's labor to factories where women and children work in slave-like conditions … and while paying her female employees disproportionately low salaries. (2017:20–1)

However, while they stressed the power of individual women to make the most of their lives, Wolf and Walter had been more ready than earlier liberal feminists to acknowledge the need for workplaces to change in order to take family responsibilities into account; they were also more likely to recognise the political significance of coercive sex or harassment and the need to act against it. These changes have become widely accepted, indicating a shift beyond liberalism that begins to challenge the idea of male 'normality' and acknowledges the interconnections between private and public life.

Since the late 1980s, related developments have occurred in more academic liberal feminist theory, producing what Ruth Abbey describes as 'the return of feminist liberalism' (2011: book title). This feminist liberalism rejects competitive individualism, and it reconceptualises liberal ideas of individual rights to define domestic violence, rape, female genital mutilation and forced marriage as violations of human rights, rather than marginalising them as 'women's issues'. It departs in important ways from free-market liberal economic theory, and wants states to become involved in making employment more compatible with caring responsibilities for both men and women; it also rejects the idea that individual self-fulfilment is the key feminist goal. However, it largely fails to address the overall power structures and vested interests within which feminist demands are made and received. It also neglects the critical importance of economic and social rights, without which legal rights can have little meaning.

Neoliberalism: the 'seducer' of feminism?

Some feminist critics of 'fashionable feminism' see this as part of a more general takeover of feminism by neoliberal ideology. To recap points made in Chapter 5: this ideology extends the liberal values of the competitive marketplace into all areas of life, including the family and personal relationships. It endorses a cost-benefit approach to life, which sees people as responsible for themselves but not for others; individuals should therefore calculate what is in their own self-interest and act accordingly. Such calculation leaves no place for liberal values of equality and justice, let alone socialist or feminist ideas of solidarity, social welfare, compassion or care. It also rules out discrimination based on irrational prejudice or traditional ideas, and it actively encourages women to enter the workforce. And it has been used to justify extremely harsh social and economic programmes, with devastating effects around the world.

This thinking can seem in tune with some kinds of 'go-getting' power feminism, and a number of left-leaning feminists believe that it has produced a damaging new form of 'neoliberal feminism'. They argue that this is particularly dangerous, not simply because it is *associated* with exploitative, unjust and anti-women policies but because it represents a takeover of feminism, which is now being used to *justify* these policies. Although the details of their critiques vary, the arguments of these writers overlap and are perhaps best summed up in the title of Hester Eisenstein's 2009 book: *Feminism Seduced: How Global Elites Use Women's Labor and Ideas to Exploit the World*. This section assesses these criticisms, focusing in particular on neoliberal feminist ideas about human rights and rationality.

Neoliberalism and human rights

At the 1995 United Nations Women's Conference in Beijing, Hillary Clinton famously proclaimed that 'human rights are women's rights, and women's rights are human rights'. Her powerful statement went beyond calls for formal legal equality with men to identify the linked problems of poverty, exclusion and violence experienced by many women around the world; here she included those in the US unable to afford healthcare or childcare and struggling to raise children on the minimum wage.

However, Clinton had nothing to say about challenging the global economic forces that impoverish so many men as well as women. Feminist critics label her a 'faux feminist' who endorses neoliberal ideas and ignores the structural sources of poverty and violence, and whose political track record reflects the interests of the corporate and financial interests that have funded her and Bill Clinton's political campaigns, rather than the needs of poor women. In particular, a collection of essays by American feminists, published in 2016 at a point when Clinton seemed set to become the first female US president, criticises what the introductory chapter describes as the 'harsh, capitalist, warmongering, punitive, and compassion-free policies to which she has devoted her career' (Featherstone and Frost, 2016:25). These policies include her support for Bill Clinton's welfare reforms which effectively removed the welfare safety net from impoverished families in the name of encouraging responsibility and ending 'dependency' (Piven and Block, 2018).

More generally, Silvia Federici argues that international bodies, including the UN, have paid lip service to the cause of women's rights because this 'channel[s] the politics of women's liberation within a frame compatible with the needs and plans of international capital and the developing neoliberal agenda' (2012:98). From this perspective, the kind of glossy projects to 'empower' women through education, micro-finance and employment in the global south that I described in Chapter 5 can look more like 'a depressing example of neo-liberal co-optation' than 'an inspiring example of feminist activism and democratic innovation' (Squires, 2007:51). Similarly, the new expectation that women should be in the paid labour market is presented as a triumph for feminism that recognises women's right to work. However, it is also a convenient way of legitimising increased exploitation in western workplaces, where a single wage is no longer sufficient to support a family, and it can be used to justify cutting welfare benefits for those who have 'irresponsibly' failed to secure adequate employment. In addition, the idea that work is liberating helps neoliberal feminists to overlook the 'profound contradiction' that arises as they 'urge Muslim and non-western migrant women to liberate themselves while channelling them towards the very sphere (domestic, low paying, and precarious jobs) from which the feminist movement had historically tried to liberate women' (Farris and Rottenberg, 2017:10).

While feminist ideas may be used by powerful economic interests, it seems at first sight fanciful to see this as a deliberate strategy of co-optation. However, Susan Watkins shows that by the 1970s some feminist organisations were receiving high levels of funding from US-based corporate sponsors, amongst which the Ford Foundation was pre-eminent. At first, these sponsors used liberal, anti-discrimination arguments to deliberately promote a 'safe' form of feminism: this would include women in existing structures rather than dismantling them, help women combine their family role with a career rather than attacking the nuclear family and provide them with equal opportunities in an unequal system. This funding meant that favoured forms of feminism were well financed and that former militants were transformed into salaried officials for whom 'fear of losing their livelihood led to growing conservatism and self-censorship'. By the 1990s, sponsors were pushing neoliberal arguments that explicitly focused on the ways in which feminist-friendly policies could benefit corporations rather than women. One result, Watkins argues, was that '[o]nce the verbiage was peeled away', the operative clauses of the Platform for Action that resulted from the Beijing conference amounted to 'women's integration into the existing global-capitalist order, underpinned by coercion' (2018:22–3, 24, 43).

Related problems of co-optation can arise when issues such as female genital mutilation (FGM), forced marriage or forced veiling are reframed as violations of human rights. On the plus side, this can help them get taken more seriously and sympathetically by official, male-dominated national and international organisations than if they are seen as 'women's issues' or if they are described as forms of patriarchal oppression (points made by Okin, 2000 and Walby, 2011). However, campaigns on these issues by western women on behalf of 'others' can also distract attention from economic exploitation and from problematic aspects of western culture, including a 'beauty' industry that promotes unnecessary procedures that include genital cosmetic surgery. Feminist campaigns can also be co-opted to justify both the pursuit of western economic and political interests and the racist agenda of far-right political groups.

Such co-optation was particularly clear in the build-up to the American invasion of Afghanistan in 2001, when the US government suddenly 'discovered' that women were being denied even basic rights; the invasion could therefore be portrayed as 'the greatest pageant of mass liberation since the fight for suffrage' (*Time* magazine, quoted in Watkins, 2018:47). It also underlay Donald Trump's portrayal of Mexican immigrants as rapists, from whom he was defending American women. In the US itself, long-standing fears around black sexuality have helped justify the mass incarceration of black men (NAACP, 2019), diverting attention from the lack of support services for survivors of violence or the need to address either the issues of education, poverty and unemployment that increase women's vulnerability, or the lack of positive opportunities for young black men. Meanwhile in Europe, far-right and racist groups have been able to use legitimate feminist concerns about the violation of women's rights to fuel anti-Islamic feeling and demonise Muslim culture as a whole, while ignoring widespread misogynistic abuse in other sections of society (Farris, 2017).

Neoliberalism and rationality

Neoliberal rationality has no time for old-fashioned prejudices that prevent the most talented individuals being appointed or promoted, and in principle it can readily accept that a more diverse workforce, particularly at senior levels, may produce better results. Businesses can therefore present a progressive, feminist face when introducing equal-opportunities policies, even though any benefits for women are only a side-effect of the overarching goal of profit maximisation. Meanwhile, neoliberal feminists insist that women should invest in themselves, plan all areas of their lives and fight their own corner. From this perspective, women have no reason to feel guilty if they focus on their career and employ less well-paid women to take care of their family and domestic responsibilities, because their own ability to pay is a product of their hard work and good decisions, while domestic workers are a 'whole other class of women ... not fully responsibilized and thus exploitable and disposable' (Rottenberg, 2018:20, 18).

Neoliberalism's stress on rational decision-making is epitomised by Sheryl Sandberg, chief operating officer at Facebook and author of the internationally best-selling book *Lean In: Women, Work and the Will to Lead* (2013), which argued that capitalism, as well as women, would benefit from gender equality and that ambitious women must learn to 'lean in' to the corporate table. Sandberg recognises that sexism in the employment market remains widespread, but she insists that women must stop seeing themselves as victims and take control of their own lives. She has been supported by many other prominent US feminists, including Gloria Steinem and Naomi Wolf; Oprah Winfrey has called her 'the new voice of revolutionary feminism' (quoted in hooks, 2013), and Jo Swinson, the former leader of the British Liberal Democrats, describes *Lean In* as 'brilliant' (2019:52). Sandberg's ideas are echoed in publications by other high-profile women in the US, most notably Ivanka Trump's 2017 *Women Who Work*, and former Fox anchorwoman Megyn Kelly's *Settle for More* (2016) (for a critical overview of these and related publications, see Rottenberg, 2018).

Sandberg tells women that if they want to succeed they must apply hard-headed logic to their personal life as well as their employment. They should therefore choose a partner who is willing to do his share of work in the home:

> When looking for a life partner, my advice to women is date all of them: the bad boys, the cool boys, the commitment-phobic boys, the crazy boys. But do not marry them. The things that make the

bad boys sexy do not make them good husbands. When it comes time to settle down, find someone who wants an equal partner. Someone who thinks women should be smart, opinionated and ambitious. Someone who values fairness and expects or, even better, wants to do his share in the home. These men exist and, trust me, over time, nothing is sexier. (2013:115–16)

For Sandberg, such men are leading the way to a 'truly equal world ... one where women ran half our countries and companies and men ran half our homes' (2013:7). However, women may find that men like this are in short supply, and that most other men rationally decide *against* giving up their patriarchal privileges, preferring instead a wife who prioritises her husband's domestic and career needs. They may also find that their life plans are unpredictably disrupted by events outside their control. Sandberg herself became a single parent in 2015 after the sudden, unexpected death of her husband; in a post on her personal Facebook page a year later, she said that she had failed to understand how difficult life is without a supportive partner, and 'how hard it is to succeed at work when you are overwhelmed at home' (www.facebook.com/sheryl/posts/10156819553860177).

Nevertheless, Catherine Rottenberg has found that young women in the US seem to be behaving as Sandberg advised, and applying rational cost-benefit analysis to their personal life. She cites as evidence the 'hook up' culture on US campuses, where many aspiring young women are looking for fun rather than a serious relationship that might hold back their career; that is, they are seeing themselves as 'human capital that must "self-invest" in order to enhance their portfolio value' (2018:96). Rottenberg also finds that these young women have not abandoned the idea of having a family, but that they see this as something for the future. Some are able to forward-plan by taking advantage of developments in reproductive technology: in a bid to attract and retain more female staff, Facebook and Apple now offer egg-freezing facilities to their employees. Meanwhile, they can follow the advice of Ivanka Trump to deploy 'savvy self-investment and entrepreneurial strategies of self-care' to enhance their human capital (quoted in Rottenberg, 2018:143).

If it is rational for women to pursue work–life balance, it may also be rational for companies to provide conditions of employment to support them, because this can be a way of attracting and retaining talented staff. It therefore leads to increased productivity and, by reducing stresses in the home, helps avoid the cost to employers and the wider society of family breakdown. Such employment conditions include providing parental leave and allowing employees, men as well as women, to work reduced or flexible hours without loss of seniority. Because the results are good for individuals, families and the economy, neoliberal logic suggests that, if some companies are short-sightedly unwilling to provide family-friendly employment, then governments will have to enforce this through legislation. In accordance with this logic, David Cameron, then the leader of the British Conservative Party, told its 2008 conference:

> It's because I want to strengthen families that I support flexible working. To those who say this is some intolerable burden on business, I say 'wrong'. Business pays the costs of family breakdown in taxes – and isn't it right that everyone, including business, should play their part in making Britain a more family-friendly country? Do you know what, if we don't change these antiquated business practices then women, half the talent of the country, are just put off from joining the workforce.

Cameron also swung his party into line with the other major UK parties by agreeing that the government should help working parents with their childcare costs. Again, this can be logically defended in terms of promoting economic growth; it was also clearly a result of *political* logic in that measures to address the real needs of working parents are likely to be popular with many voters. The idea of an expansion of nursery education that was privately run but financially supported by the state also seemed to open up new profit-making opportunities for entrepreneurs.

Such state intervention sits uneasily with neoliberalism's belief in rolling back the state, and the US, which lacks a mainstream socialist or collectivist tradition, has been much more resistant to such measures. Indeed, the US remains the only advanced industrial society with *no* statutory right to any form of paid maternity, parental or family leave (although in 1993 Bill Clinton introduced the right to twelve weeks' unpaid leave for parents when a baby is born or adopted). However, even here there has been some shift in attitudes, so that, when Sandberg started to call on Facebook for paid maternity and parental leave and for state assistance with childcare costs, this was in line with ideas that were gaining support, even in the Republican Party: influenced by his daughter Ivanka, Donald Trump's 2016 presidential campaign included promises of help with childcare and eldercare costs and six weeks of paid leave for new mothers, and his 2019 budget proposals included some limited suggestions on these issues (and he even learned to talk about parental rather than mothers' leave).

These sketchy ideas, which do not include details as to how they might be implemented, did not reflect a newly discovered concern for women's welfare. As with Cameron, they have been based on hard-headed calculations: in this case, around the falling birth rate, the relatively low rates of female participation in the workplace and a fear that the economic strains faced by parents are impeding economic growth (Keith, 2019). Emily Peck has commented that, in the context of Trump's other budget proposals for welfare cuts and an end to climate change research, his family-friendly ideas effectively meant that 'parents get the promise of six weeks off in exchange for diminished benefits over their child's life, plus a wrecked planet for when the kids are grown up' (Peck, 2019). Nevertheless, they represent a shift in public debate that pushes it in the direction of some long-standing feminist demands and shows at least a glimmering of the understanding that when women are not in the workplace they may in fact be doing important unpaid work.

Has neoliberal feminism really taken over?

Feminism has always been a broad church, frequently riven by deep ideological conflicts and, as I have said, liberal feminism has long been the default setting for western feminism. In this context, some feminist writers who reject neoliberalism also argue that those who dislike recent developments are indulging in nostalgia for an imagined past that also overlooks much that is happening in the present (Prügl, 2015). Catherine Eschle and Bice Maiguashca further claim that critics of neoliberal feminism such as Hester Eisenstein, Nancy Fraser and Angela McRobbie are 'disciplining feminism from an assumed position of authority and in accordance with their own purposes'; this purpose, they say, involves promoting a brand of socialist feminism that rejects the idea that some reforms within the existing system can 'be part and parcel of a better feminist future' or that a wide range of feminist activities can be seen as progressive. Rather than a simplistic 'good girl/bad girl' approach to contemporary feminism, Eschle and Maiguashca therefore call for a more nuanced analysis that can evaluate feminist activities and ideas without dismissing most of these out of hand (2014:640, 648; 2018).

In response to criticism, Eisenstein (2017) has defended her position, arguing that there used to be much wider questioning of the whole capitalist system by feminists, often within an explicitly Marxist framework, than there is today. However, as I show in the next chapter, the twenty-first century has seen significant developments in Marxist feminist theory. There has also been a surge of highly heterogeneous feminist activism around the world. Far from representing a takeover by neoliberal feminism, some of this is a direct reaction against harsh neoliberal policies, particularly the insistence on austerity cuts. For example, as I discussed in Chapter 3, grassroots intersectional, anti-austerity coalitions of women are emerging in the UK, while many women have been active in attempts to push the Labour Party in a more socialist and feminist direction, and austerity cuts in Europe have 'revitalized civil society and feminist struggles and alliances to defend social justice, equality, and democracy' (Kantola and Lombardo, 2017:269). More generally, the rise of visible poverty in some western countries makes the kind of 'fashionable feminism' that I described earlier seem self-indulgent; as the UK feminist Laurie Penny has said:

The young women of today know far better than their slightly older sisters who came of age in the listless 1990s ... How bloody important it is to talk about power, and class, and work, and love, race and poverty and gender identity. (2014:10)

In short, neoliberalism has not taken over feminism; it has, however, provoked feminist resistance.

This is not to deny that neoliberal thinking has had a widespread impact on mainststream feminist ideas, particularly in the US. However, even here Senator Bernie Sanders, a self-described democratic socialist, has managed to put his more egalitarian economic ideas on the mainstream political table. In practice, many left-wing men have a bad track record on 'women's issues' and a decidedly patriarchal view of gender roles and 'appropriate' behaviour. However, Sanders's proposals for a green new deal, greater workplace and union rights and a higher minimum wage would have disproportionately benefited poor women. He also has a long track record of advocating universal childcare for young children, and his 'Medicare for All' proposals covered full access to reproductive healthcare, including abortion. In early 2020, at a time when he was still in the race to become the Democratic Party's presidential candidate, Nancy Fraser and Liza Featherstone therefore argued that, unlike those feminists who were interested only in 'male/female parity within the privileged classes', Sanders was holding out a promise of 'gender equality organized for the benefit of the 99 per cent'; from their socialist feminist perspective, he was the 'true feminist choice'. By this time he was also not a lone socialist voice, and a number of women elected to Congress in 2018, of whom Alexandria Ocasio-Cortez is probably the most well known, have pushed an agenda that is both feminist and decidedly left-wing by previous US standards.

It is also important to remember that neoliberalism is not some monolithic, internally consistent ideology. Rather, as I hope to have shown, it is full of contradictions at all levels. These include contradictions between its demand for women to be in the workplace and the assumption that they will continue to take care of the home; between the rationally calculated self-interests of women and those of the men they would like as life partners; between the beliefs that businesses should be free from state intervention and that they should be required to provide family-friendly conditions of employment; between the insistence that people should take responsibility for their own decisions and the recognition that they may need state support for their childcare expenses; and between economic rationality and the need to attract voters.

These contradictions mean that neoliberal rationality can lead in unexpected directions, not all of which are negative. Thus Elisabeth Prügl has looked at some corporate interventions based on the idea that empowering women makes good business sense, and finds that this does not necessarily involve the co-optation of women; rather, in some cases it can 'open up spaces for change from the bottom' and 'provide openings to challenge oppressive power relations' (2015:627). More generally, the fact that such influential neoliberal feminists as Sandberg and Ivanka Trump are advocating family-friendly employment and support for childcare costs should surely be welcomed; it might even be seen as a feminist success, reflecting both a response to the very real needs of 'ordinary people' and a shift in public opinion that itself partly reflects the long-term impact of feminist ideas. Sandberg's argument that men must play a greater domestic role can also be seen as a welcome rejection of the normality of men's behaviour, and a recognition that gender equality requires that they too must change. Meanwhile, even though Donald Trump's statements about parental leave and support for childcare costs may be empty rhetoric, they raise expectations of a substantive follow-through, and he risks losing electoral support if this is not delivered. Taken together, these shifts have the potential to move in more positive directions, and they could be interpreted as evidence that feminist concerns are becoming mainstream rather than that feminism has been taken over.

In practice, however, it is difficult to reconcile these ideas with either the shorter-term economic imperatives of neoliberal capitalism or the collective interests of the 'successful' men who are currently privileged by the patriarchal assumptions that exempt them from domestic responsibilities and genuinely equal competition. As outlined in the previous section, other underlying difficulties make it unlikely that neoliberal feminists will make changes that benefit the majority of women. The next section uses the UK as a case study to illustrate and explore some of the contradictions of neoliberal feminism.

Neoliberal feminism in practice: the case of the British Conservative Party

Margaret Thatcher never described herself as a feminist. When she became the first female leader of the Conservative Party in 1975, it was largely a party of both social conservatism and neoliberal economics: that is, it combined traditional views about sexual behaviour, gender roles and the importance of the family with neoliberal ideas around free markets, privatisation, low taxation, free competition and individual responsibility. This combination appeared to involve a contradiction between an emotional attachment to an idealised and increasingly outdated picture of female-centred family life, and an economic logic that welcomed equal competition between women and men in the public sphere as a way of ensuring that women's talents were not 'wasted'. However, by the 1990s, some 'free-market feminists' were claiming that traditional family values could be combined with economic logic. For example, David Conway argued that free markets have 'a natural tendency towards the formation and continuance of strong traditional two-parent families' (1998:9); this meant that, although the economy would benefit if women could compete equally with men, this must not mean any 'special treatment' for women, such as maternity leave or state-funded childcare. By this period, both traditional and neoliberal values of personal responsibility were also being used to make a distinction between the 'deserving' and 'undeserving' poor, and to portray 'unmarried mothers' as both a symptom and a source of general moral decline.

In contrast, the Labour Party, which won the 1997 election with a landslide, recognised that families had changed. Rather than encouraging women to stay at home, it promised more family-friendly employment and affordable childcare; it also emphasised other issues that women voters said were important to them, particularly the health service and education. The party's claim to be about women as well as men was embodied in a dramatic rise in its number of female MPs, from 37 in 1992 to 101 in 1997 – an increase made possible by the 'all-women shortlists' policy, adopted in 1993, which required Labour candidates in fifty per cent of safe and winnable seats to be women. In the same year, just 13 Conservative women MPs were elected.

The 'New Labour' governments from 1997 to 2010 did not represent a clean break with neoliberal policies. Retaining the neoliberal rhetoric of competition, efficiency, responsibility and consumer choice, the party leaders made little or no attempt to reverse the privatisation of previously nationalised industries, to introduce more progressive taxation or to tackle the power of finance capital, and their focus on equality of opportunity rather than outcomes ignored the growing gulf between rich and poor. In addition, the stress on accountability and cost-effectiveness in public services involved a narrow, 'time is money' rationality that often ran counter to good-quality provision, especially in caring services, while Labour's work and welfare policies were fundamentally flawed by their failure to see the social and economic importance of women's unpaid work. There was also a tension between the hierarchical, top-down nature of the Labour Party in this period, and the anti-hierarchical principles of many grassroots feminist groups (Bashevkin, 2000; Bryson and Deery, 2011; Bryson and Fisher, eds, 2011).

Nevertheless, the party also moved far enough away from neoliberal principles to introduce interventionist measures that benefited many women. These included better maternity leave, the first ever (unpaid) paternity leave, support for childcare and parenting (particularly through Sure Start Children's Centres), the national minimum wage, stronger anti-discrimination legislation and new laws on domestic violence. By the time it won the 2005 election, the Labour Party had reversed the traditional gender gap in voting behaviour (which had seen women more likely than men to vote Conservative, and less likely to vote Labour); this trend was particularly strong amongst young women. In contrast, the Conservatives seemed generally out of touch with the new realities of many people's lives, and they still had only 17 female MPs.

A few steps forward for women

Labour's third consecutive electoral victory strengthened the arguments that some Conservative women throughout the party were already making: that their party's neglect of gender issues and its failure to select women candidates in winnable seats was not only wrong in itself but also electorally disastrous. Such thinking led Theresa May (then in the Shadow Cabinet) and Baroness Anne Jenkin to found Women2Win, a group aimed at increasing the number of Conservative women MPs, which soon helped ensure the election of a new and younger leader, David Cameron, who promised both a new form of 'compassionate Conservatism' that would step back from the harsh logic of neoliberalism, and a general 'feminisation' of the party that would integrate women and their concerns into it (for an assessment, see Childs and Campbell, 2018).

Many of the women involved in Women2Win described themselves as feminists; these included May, who famously wore the Fawcett Society's 'This is what a feminist looks like' T-shirt in 2006. They made links with feminist networks, organisations and experts outside the party to develop ideas and understanding around what women voters wanted, how more Conservative women could be encouraged to stand for election and what changes the party could make to ensure that more were selected as candidates in winnable seats. The group's thinking involved the recognition that women had different life experiences from men, that women as a group had been disadvantaged or discriminated against and that they should support each other in bringing about change. However, it also insisted that if women wanted to be seen as equals they must be seen as *individuals*, competing on merit, rather than expecting any kind of special treatment.

In line with these ideas, May and Cameron rejected the idea of quotas or Labour's policy of all-women shortlists. However, for a short period Cameron introduced an 'A-list' of priority candidates. Together with encouragement, mentoring and training for potential candidates from Women2Win, this helped increase the number of Conservative women

MPs to 87 (24 per cent of the party's total) after the December 2019 general election. Of course, not all Conservative women MPs saw themselves as feminists, but Harriet Harman, a vocal feminist who has been a Labour MP since 1982, said in 2018 that there had been

> a dramatic change in the nature of Conservative women MPs. We have now got feminists on the Tory side, who are very different from the doughty tweedy matrons of the past. These MPs are more modern, and people that we, as Labour women, can work cross-party with. (Quoted in Asthana, 2018)

The increase in and changing type of women candidates and MPs was accompanied by a shift in policy concerns and priorities that brought the Conservatives more in line with the other main parties. By 2010, it recognised that sexual and domestic violence were serious political issues that required state action; it agreed that it should work towards ending gender-based discrimination and the gender pay gap; it accepted that working parents might need help with childcare costs; it wanted parents to be able to work more flexible hours if they chose to; and it no longer opposed either the minimum wage or unpaid paternity leave (Cameron himself took the two weeks' paternity leave that Labour had introduced and his party had previously opposed).

The 2010 election resulted in a Conservative-led coalition with the Liberal Democrats, whose inclusion in government strengthened its support for 'women-friendly' policies, including greater financial support for the childcare costs of working parents and the introduction of shared parental leave. Some lower-earning women also benefited when the tax threshold was raised, and state pensioners, the majority of whom are women, had the value of their pension protected.

May was now Home Secretary and, in addition to supporting and encouraging such party policies, she did important work on issues around domestic violence, which she continued into her premiership (2016–19). In particular, the 2019 Domestic Abuse Bill recognised 'coercive control', which can be both emotional and financial, as a criminal offence alongside physical abuse. Writing in the *Guardian* in 2018, May also said that she wanted to enable courts to intervene earlier in cases of domestic violence and that 'It is critical that people fleeing violent partners have a safe place to go. I am committed to delivering a sustainable funding model for refuges so that there is no postcode lottery.' In 2015, she introduced the Modern Slavery Act to tackle what she described as 'the great human rights issue of our time'; this resulted in a steep rise in both cases reported and successful convictions (Schraer, 2019). She also spoke out forcefully on the issue of FGM, and introduced a national prevention strategy along with legislation to enable parents to be prosecuted if they fail to prevent their daughter from being cut (Topping, 2014).

More steps back

While some Conservative politicians may have cynically endorsed 'women-friendly' policies as a means of attracting women's votes, May's commitment seemed genuine enough. However, any positive effects pale into insignificance in the light of other policies that she either supported or introduced as Home Secretary (2010–16) and Prime Minister (2016–19); overall, the governments that she and Cameron led had an overwhelmingly negative impact on the lives of many women, particularly those who are poor and/or black or minority ethnic. Here two policy areas were critical: May's determination to deliver Cameron's election promise to reduce immigration, and the imposition of austerity measures.

By 2012, the first of these produced May's notorious 'hostile environment' policy, which became enshrined in the Immigration Acts of 2014 and 2016. Designed to deter and remove illegal immigrants, the policy often effectively means 'deport first, appeal later', and landlords, banks and NHS workers are required to check on the immigration status of potential tenants, customers and patients. Setting aside the question of whether a drastic reduction in immigration is desirable, it is clear that the whole idea of a 'hostile environment' stokes racism and can make it difficult for BAME UK citizens to access services, while many legitimate asylum seekers and workers have been caused appalling and unnecessary suffering, and many people who have a right to remain in the UK have been wrongly classified as illegal immigrants.

The 'hostile environment' policy creates particular difficulties for those women whose claims for asylum involve intimate and sensitive experiences around sexual abuse and rape that are difficult to articulate, let alone explain to impatient immigration officials. It also undermines May's aim of combating domestic violence, FGM and modern slavery, as some women fear that they will be deported if they try to escape or report their situation. Others are unable to provide their passports or the documentary evidence that would prove their right to remain, as these have been taken by their partners or the traffickers who control them. And in 2015, a Channel 4 investigation into conditions in the Yarl's Wood women's detention centre led Yvette Cooper, then Shadow Home Secretary, to accuse May of allowing the 'state-sponsored abuse of women' (Mason, 2015).

May's promises to women were further undermined by her consistent support for the punitive austerity measures introduced from 2010 by the Conservative Chancellor of the Exchequer, George Osborne. These involved changes to the tax and benefits system that abandoned any ideas of 'compassionate Conservatism' or women-friendly policies and pushed many individuals and families into poverty and destitution. Women were particularly badly affected; indeed figures from the House of Commons library indicating that, by 2020, 81 per cent of the cumulative negative impact of the changes would have fallen on them, with BAME women particularly badly affected (Women's Budget Group, 2016; Women's Budget Group and the Runnymede Trust, 2017).

Many women faced further hardships as central government funding for local councils was reduced by nearly fifty per cent between 2010/11 and 2017/18, with further reductions to follow. This inevitably produced job cuts and a reduction in key services, resulting in what Heather Wakefield describes as a 'triple whammy' of damaging effects for women, who are disproportionately likely to use services, to be employed by local authorities and to have to fill the gaps when services are cut. Cuts included provision for adult social care that in 2019 left 1.4 million people without the care they need, and the closure of around a thousand Sure Start children's centres between 2010 and 2018 (Pearson, 2019; Wakefield, 2019).

Local authority cuts have also made a nonsense of May's promised support for women who are experiencing domestic violence. Over 75 per cent of England's local authorities reduced their spending on domestic violence refuges by nearly a quarter between 2010 and 2017, 17 per cent of specialist gender-based violence refuges in England closed during the same period and by 2018 a third of all women referred to refuges were being turned away – an average of 155 women and 103 children a day (Reis, 2018). By early 2020, this figure was even higher (Women's Aid, 2020), leaving the sector unable to meet the needs of many desperate women as cases of abuse rose during the COVID-19 lockdown. May's stated commitment to helping abused women was further undermined when her resignation honours list included a knighthood for the former cricketer Geoffrey Boycott, despite his earlier conviction for domestic assault (Wolfe-Robinson, 2019).

The problems facing abused women have been further increased by the introduction of Universal Credit, ostensibly intended to simplify the benefits system and make it easier for people to work, but widely experienced as punitive, stigmatising and deliberately difficult to access. Because benefits are consolidated into one payment that is usually made into one bank account, it makes women more vulnerable to the economic abuse that May had tried to make a criminal offence (although women can in theory ask for credit to be paid into more than one account, it will obviously be very hard for someone to do this if they are already in an abusive relationship). And because Universal Credit does not provide immediate access to benefits it also makes it very difficult for a woman to leave her partner without being pushed into unmanageable debt. The conditions attached to the receipt of Universal Credit also mean that a woman will face sanctions if she turns down a job that is near her ex-partner's home, or if he makes malicious allegations about her entitlements.

Although working parents were promised that they would be supported by 15 hours of free childcare, this has fallen short of expectations, partly because it is particularly difficult to match with the shifting needs of those with irregular working hours, and partly because inadequate funding means that, as I said in Chapter 5, many nurseries have simply gone out of business. Meanwhile, new restrictions that limit child benefits and tax credits to the first two children in a family have involved the humiliating exemption that has become known as the 'rape clause': this requires a woman to fill in a lengthy form to show that her third child was conceived without her consent; over five hundred women in the 2018–19 financial year were able to show this (Davidson, 2019).

As early as 2010, the Women's Budget Group's analysis of the cumulative effect of austerity measures concluded that the cuts 'represent an immense reduction in the standard of living and financial independence of millions of women, and a reversal in progress made towards gender equality' (Women's Budget Group, 2010, 1–2). This view was confirmed in 2018 in a report by Philip Alston, the UN's 'special rapporteur' on extreme poverty and human rights, who investigated conditions in the UK. Alston not only condemned 'punitive, mean-spirited, and often callous' austerity policies but also highlighted the disproportionate effects on women, arguing that 'If you got a group of misogynists in a room and said how can we make this system work for men and not for women they would not have come up with too many ideas that are not already in place' (Alston, 2018; Booth and Butler, 2018) Or as the comedian Bridget Christie put it in 2015:

> If May's 'This is what a feminist looks like' T-shirt were to list all the negative things she had done or supported on the back, starting with 'I axed the health in pregnancy grant. I closed Sure Start centres' it would have to be much longer than the front; in fact, her T-shirt would resemble a tailcoat.

Underlying problems

The damage that Conservative Party policies have done to so many women is presumably not deliberate but collateral, while May's failure to deliver much that is positive for women is not simply a reflection of the personal failings of a woman wearing a duplicitously double-sided item of clothing (see above). Rather, it reflects both the limitations of liberal and neoliberal feminism and the contradictions that both involve: as Beatrix Campbell wrote in her 1987 study of the 'iron ladies' of the Conservative Party, 'Can Conservatives be feminists? The answer is yes, of course ... [but] their feminism is rooted in liberalism and ... tends to end where contemporary feminism starts: with investigating and organizing against the *social system* of sexual oppression, and mapping the connection between class and sex' (1987:200; see also Bryson and Heppell, 2010).

The fact that May's key claim to feminist success is better political representation for Conservative women reflects the elite-oriented focus of her feminism, which finds it easier to accommodate the needs of relatively privileged and aspirational women than those who are disadvantaged. The limited nature of even this success also reflects the difficulties of achieving change by focusing on the needs of women as individuals rather than by recognising that structural problems may require more positive action, including the use of quotas. A focus on the logical desirability of equal competition also loses sight of the opposing interests of the men who are likely to be displaced, and who do not experience gender equality as a win-win game. As Joni Lovenduski has argued, genuine political equality between women and men would also require a 'paradigm shift' to rewrite and redesign political rules, roles and institutions; this, she says, is unlikely to be achieved in the face of 'deep-rooted political masculinity' (2019:31).

The 'family-friendly' workplace policies and finance for childcare that May supported when Home Secretary are of course welcome, although these were limited and delivered less than they promised. However, because Cameron justified these primarily in financial terms, rather than because they would benefit women; this implies that they should logically be dropped if businesses do not benefit. Such short-term financial logic has already been used to justify the cuts to local council funding that led to the closure of Sure Start centres, overriding longer-term (and ultimately probably cost-saving), social good. The broader attacks on social welfare that May supported also reflect neoliberal ideas of personal responsibility that blame those who cannot support themselves for their own situation, even when this is clearly out of their control. As with liberal and neoliberal thinking in general, this logic is underpinned by an inability to see that people can contribute to society, even when they are not in paid employment – most obviously when they are bringing up the next generation of citizens and workers; as I said earlier, this view has also characterised Labour Party policies.

Later developments

By the late 2010s, some liberal or neoliberal feminists, including Jo Swinson (the leader of the Liberal Democrats for a few months in 2019) were showing much greater awareness of sexism as a system of oppression, the interconnected nature of public and private inequalities and their intersection with other dimensions of inequality. Swinson set out her ideas in *Equal Power, Gender Equality and How to Achieve It*, in which she describes feminism as

> a movement to create a world free of gender prejudice, stereotypes and discrimination, a world where the entrenched bias of the default male is painstakingly unpicked, and a world where power that is currently concentrated in the hands of the rich, white men is spread and shared – and not just with rich, white women. (2019:340)

At first sight, this looks like an important step that goes well beyond the elitist, neoliberal feminism of May or Hillary Clinton. However, Swinson's awareness of class issues was limited by her failure to investigate the economic causes of exploitation and growing inequality, or to question why the financial economy should be prioritised while household work is ignored; here she might benefit from reading some of the work on social reproduction discussed in the next chapter. Any ideas that Swinson had on combating 'entrenched economic disadvantage' (2019:345) were also undermined by her political record as a member of Cameron's coalition cabinet who voted in favour of austerity measures. Although she saw the need for legislation on issues such as parental leave, her liberalism led her to believe that 'the power of generating public debate and the gentle pressure of government on an issue [are] often more effective in driving change quickly' (2019:119) (here she cited positive responses from the advertising industry in relation to issues she helped raise around body image, although the observable changes are minimal). All this means that, although Swinson's feminist ideas seem much more considered than May's, they too soon run up against liberal and neoliberal assumptions that generally offer little more than upbeat and often individualistic solutions and do not consider whether there might be a need for more radical economic change.

Although Boris Johnson too has described himself as a feminist, this has never been reflected in his political priorities, while his language and personal behaviour have often been decidedly sexist, as well as racist and homophobic (Bienkov, 2019; Toksvig, 2019). As I said in the previous chapter, in early 2020 the COVID-19 crisis led him to use language that stepped back from neoliberal individualism, and the government committed vast sums of money in an effort to save the economy and meet the financial needs of companies and laid-off workers. However, Johnson and his government seemed to take the perspective of men with steady jobs, adequate housing and few caring responsibilities as the starting-point for their decisions. If, instead, they had taken an imaginative leap, and started with the needs of a low-paid woman worker in insecure employment, living in a small flat with several small children and a controlling and potentially abusive partner, they might have taken immediate steps to limit the potentially damaging effects of the lockdown. They might, for example, have: tried to ensure that packed lunches were sent to all school pupils entitled to free school dinners; offered to cover costs for hotel owners willing to help meet the predictable rise in demand for places in domestic violence refuges; taken action to support households without the internet access needed to claim benefits or enable children to do their schoolwork; and immediately opened up golf courses and the grounds of private schools to relieve pressure on parks (rather than closing some of the latter because too many people were using them). They might also have recognised that women (not only doctors and nurses but also care workers and hospital cleaners) are in the front line against the virus, and that many of these women are badly paid, and/or migrant workers: 77 per cent of those in high-exposure jobs are women, and over a third earn only poverty-level wages (Booth, 2020; Women's Budget Group, 2020). These women are also often the primary carers for children and other family members.

In contrast to the government's failure, many women's groups demanded action on these issues from the start (see for example Fawcett, 2020); rather than setting aside their feminism to focus on the immediate health crisis, they have shown that this is in fact a feminist issue that depends on women's paid and unpaid work and that cannot be addressed adequately if women's voices are silenced. The crisis also produced a host of grassroots initiatives, often led by women, to meet the needs of vulnerable people in their community, and it is became rapidly clear that getting through the crisis and addressing the needs of women as well as men needed to involve thinking outside the 'what's in it for ME?' mindset of neoliberal ideology.

Conclusions

Taking the UK as a case study confirms that it is relatively easy for neo-liberal feminists to take on the rhetoric of 'safe' feminist issues, particularly equal opportunities for ambitious women and the need to protect women from violence, but that they are unlikely to provide the economic resources and support that that effective solutions would require. As I said in earlier sections, feminist calls for more family-friendly employment conditions and assistance with childcare costs are increasingly being supported by some business leaders and politicians, who see them as making sound business sense. Such gains are, however, provisional, they are liable to be withdrawn if they are not shown to be cost-effective and they are massively outweighed by the negative impact of other neoliberal economic policies, which treat issues of justice and equality as secondary to the rational calculation of financial expediency and the short-term pursuit of profit. Neoliberalism also fails to join the dots between apparently separate problems or to recognise the economic and social importance of women's traditionally unpaid work.

Framing issues through a neoliberal lens does little to meet the needs of more than an elite minority of women. The next chapter considers whether a Marxist feminist lens might be any more helpful.

7

Marxist feminism: reframing the issues

I N CHAPTERS 5 and 6, I argued that the liberal and neoliberal ideas that dominate western economic thinking today cannot provide the basis for the kind of feminist politics that will benefit the majority of women. I rejected the assumption that we are essentially competitive, self-sufficient individuals and that we can and should rationally calculate and pursue our own self-interest in all areas of life. I also criticised neoliberal feminism's failure to understand the importance of 'women's work', its focus on high-achieving women and its apparent willingness to sacrifice everything to the short-term demands of profit and economic growth.

This chapter considers whether recent feminist attempts to use Marxist concepts to understand and address feminist issues can be more helpful. At first sight, it seems odd to turn to a Victorian patriarch for inspiration, and Marxist theory has, like liberal theory, generally ignored or sidelined women's needs and experiences. Nevertheless, since the late nineteenth century, some feminists have argued that it can provide a powerful analytic tool that should inform feminist politics, and Marxist feminism has been a significant strand within western feminism since the 1960s.

Recent developments transform traditional Marxism's understanding of human history and its focus on the 'working class' and the workplace as the sources of socialist struggle and change. Echoing Marçal's question 'Who cooked Adam Smith's dinner?' (see Chapter 5), the writers and activists discussed in this chapter are asking 'who produces the workers?' – that is, who gives birth, rears and feeds children, who educates them and who takes care of adult workers' emotional, nutritional and domestic needs so that they can continue to work effectively? They argue that all those who take part in the necessary activities that 'producing workers' involves are part of the working class, and that class struggles for a better society are not confined to the paid workplace. They also seek to show that patriarchy is inextricably bound up with the economic logic of capitalism; some further argue that increased tensions between capitalism's need for women to contribute to both production and the creation and maintenance of a healthy workforce are now generating a deep-seated crisis that threatens the stability of global capitalism itself.

These theoretical developments are sometimes expressed in quite technical language that can seem off-puttingly difficult to many readers. However, they can also provide important insights with very practical implications. My aim here is to pull out key arguments and ideas while avoiding unnecessary jargon, and to make difficult concepts more accessible. The chapter therefore opens with a brief discussion of some central terms and ideas, before tracing the evolution of today's arguments and their implications for feminist politics.

The basics: classic Marxism and the 'women's question'

In 1903, Clara Zetkin, a leading left-wing member of Germany's Social Democratic Party, wrote that '[Marx's] materialist concept of history has not supplied us with any ready-made formulas concerning the women's question, yet it has done something much more important: it has given us the correct unerring method to comprehend that question' (in Foner, 1984:93). Simply put, this Marxist method saw man as a productive animal, using his mind and his body to take advantage of the natural resources around him and to develop the tools and technologies that make human societies possible. From this perspective, history is not primarily about military battles, the actions of political leaders or the development of new ideas. Rather, it is driven by changes in how we produce, so that, over time, increasingly sophisticated tools and technologies enable the development of increasingly complex forms of social organisation, along with supporting systems of law, politics and beliefs.

Marx said that the shift from one way of producing to another and from one kind of society to another was seldom smooth; indeed it was likely to involve violent revolution, as a ruling group whose power was based on outmoded ways of producing would resist the claims of an emerging class and a new socio-economic and political order. Marx was particularly interested in understanding how capitalism had arisen out of its origins in feudalism, and in identifying the internal contradictions that, he believed, would lead to its collapse. He famously saw the next stage of human history in terms of revolution by the propertyless proletariat, leading to new forms of social organisation that would no longer involve exploitation and that would, eventually, be based on the socialist principle of 'from each according to his ability; to each according to his needs'.

Many subsequent male socialist theorists have rejected both Marx's specific predictions about the future overthrow of capitalism and a simplistic interpretation of his theory that reduces the whole of human life to economic or technological developments. Nevertheless, many others have taken his underlying materialist conception of history as the starting-point for the analysis of how existing societies function and how they might be changed, directing our attention towards the economic foundations of social and political life and the class interests that these involve (see for example the following, who take Marx's basic premises in a range of different directions: Cohen, 1978; Callinicos, 2003; Hobsbawm, 2011; Harvey, 2018; Varoufakis, 2018).

Marx himself did not apply his ideas to the analysis of women's situation, but his colleague Friedrich Engels attempted to do so. In *The Origin of the Family, Private Property and the State* (1884), Engels argued that, although women had been subordinated by men for most of human history, this was neither natural nor inevitable. Rather, he said, women's subordination began only when early developments in production enabled

187

some men to acquire private wealth which they wanted to pass to sons they knew to be their own; to do this, they had to control women. Engels further argued that this motivation would no longer exist in a future communist society, in which private ownership had been abolished, and that the economic basis of women's subordination was already ending in working-class families, as working men did not own property and their wives often had their own earnings.

Engels's attempt to give women's subordination a history and to link this to wider socio-economic developments fed into a growing belief amongst some late nineteenth-century socialists that feminist and socialist struggles were linked, and that real improvements in women's lives could be achieved only through a working-class struggle to overthrow the existing economic system. However, few later feminists have accepted Engels's arguments in full (see my discussion in Bryson, 2016).

A key set of problems arise from Engels's attempt to reduce everything to a narrow economic cause. In particular, he failed to see that the subordination of women extended to family and personal life: he dismissed domestic violence in his supposedly equal working-class families as 'a leftover piece of the brutality towards women that has become deep-rooted since the introduction of monogamy' (1884/1973:83), and he had nothing to say about the ways in which working men benefited from women's work in the home. However, some other leading Marxist men recognised the harsh impact of domestic drudgery on working women's lives: in 1878, the leading German socialist August Bebel described how a wife 'sits up and sews and patches deep into the night ... she must work like a dray-horse; for her there is no rest or recreation' (1878/1904:6), while Lenin wrote of the need to root out the male 'slave-owner's point of view' (1907/1977:115). Trotsky went even further, arguing that eliminating such domestic slavery was an essential precondition for a communist society:

> From the enslavement of women grew prejudices and superstitions which shaped the children of the new generation ... Freeing the

mother means cutting the last umbilical cord linking the people with the dark and superstitious past. (1924–25/ 1970:34–5)

However, none of these men made these issues a political priority; most simply seemed to assume that they would somehow solve themselves in a future socialist society.

In contrast, Alexandra Kollontai, appointed by Lenin as Commissar (Minister) of Social Welfare in Russia in 2017 and as head of the women's department (Zhenotdel) in 1920, placed women and their concerns at the centre of her politics. She extended Trotsky's ideas to argue that the development of communist morality must also involve ending the idea of possessiveness in family and sexual relationships: in particular, she believed that communal childcare would extend women's maternal love to all the children in society and teach a new generation 'to value the beauties of solidarity and sociability, and become accustomed to looking at the world through the prism of the collective and not through his own selfish ego' (quoted in Stites, 1978:267). During her brief period in political office, she therefore took steps to introduce state childcare, as well as collective laundries and eating facilities; she also tried to involve women in organising the services that they needed, she gave married women full legal independence, she legalised abortion and she established the principle of equal pay. In practice, however, the circumstances of post-revolutionary confusion, followed by the period of 'war communism' (when the country was fighting for its very survival, famine was widespread and the economy was in ruins) meant that collective provision of childcare and domestic services was basic and unwelcoming, while material conditions for most women, as for most men, deteriorated sharply. After 1923, Kollontai's views were officially declared erroneous in the Soviet Union, where any notion of either feminism or socialism as a source of freedom and equality soon disappeared. Nevertheless, her awareness of the interlinked nature of private and public life and the impossibility of transforming one without the other remains highly relevant today.

Meanwhile, some male socialists were overtly dismissive of women's concerns, some were positively hostile and many prominent female campaigners, including Zetkin, were subject to cruel sexist jokes from their male colleagues. However, Marxist women did not yet have a way of conceptualising the sexist behaviour of socialist men, and most went along with the official line that issues of class were much more important than those of gender. Zetkin accordingly rejected the idea that socialist women might form alliances with middle-class feminists who were campaigning for women's right to education, decent employment and the vote; even Kollontai failed to acknowledge any potential conflicts of interest between working-class men and women.

The argument that socialists must always prioritise class interests recurred throughout the twentieth century, often promoted by socialist men who argued that 'women's issues' were a bourgeois distraction from more important concerns and that they would automatically be resolved 'after the revolution'. These men often also seemed to assume that the role of women in left-wing organisations was primarily to service their domestic and sexual needs; their sexist attitudes and behaviour helped provoke the development of second-wave feminism in the 1960s (see Chapters 1 and 2).

As women in this period started to share their experiences, they developed a new form of analysis that linked the 'bad behaviour' of individual left-wing men to the deep-seated and general privileging of men's interests in a society that was patriarchal as well as capitalist. In this context, some socialist feminists refused to deny the existence and effects of power relationships between women and men in left-wing organisations, or to choose between the interests of their sex and those of their class. Instead, they sought to understand the interconnections between capitalism and patriarchy; as part of this endeavour, they also attempted to extend Marxist economic analysis beyond a narrow focus on men's activities to include what is now often called *social reproduction*.

Social reproduction

The starting-point for this new analysis remains the classic Marxist idea that societies have a real, material base, and that effective political strategies need to understand both the constraints and the possibilities that arise from changes at this level. However, the approach differs from classic Marxism in expanding the notion of the material base to include 'social reproduction' as well as conventionally defined economic production (Bhattacharya, 2017; Bhattacharya (ed.), 2017). It starts by making 'women's work' visible, and it also goes further in analysing the relationship between the two kinds of work and the implications for the socioeconomic system as a whole.

The concept of 'social reproduction' has been defined in a number of ways, and it overlaps with what some writers have referred to as 'the reproduction of labour power' (Vogel, 1983), 'sex affective production' (Ferguson, 1989) or '(re)production' (Bryson, 2004). I use it here to encompass all of the domestic, procreative and caring activities and relationships that are needed to reproduce and maintain the workforce at a socially acceptable level on a daily and generational basis – in other words, the life-making, life-sustaining work without which society could not survive, let alone flourish. As Tithi Bhattacharya says, the COVID-19 crisis made the importance of such work dramatically clear:

> under lockdown, nobody is saying, 'We need stockbrokers and investment bankers! Let's keep those services open!' They are saying, 'Let's keep nurses working, cleaners working, garbage removal services open, food production ongoing.' Food, fuel, shelter, cleaning: these are the 'essential services'. (2020)

The activities and relationships involved in social reproduction can be organised in a wide range of ways, and they are bound up with the wider socio-economic and physical environment, including access to clean water, food, education and housing. The concept's origin in Marxist theory tells us that the organisation of social reproduction need not involve the subordination of women, as power relationships between women and men are historically produced, rather than based in nature. It also reminds us that genuine social change cannot be achieved simply because we want it, and that political opportunities can be both constrained and created by their material environment. However, as with patriarchy, debates around social reproduction need to be handled with care, and I argue that it is important not to see all forms of oppression and inequality simply as products of the capitalist economy with which they are entangled.

Domestic labour

Some important pioneering ideas about the economic importance of housework had been developed in the 1930s by women in the American Communist Party. Mary Inman (a white woman) identified oppression in the family and sexual relationships (which she referred to as 'male domination under class rule'), and she extended Marxist economic categories to argue that the 'labour power' of working men is maintained and reproduced by women's domestic labour. This means that, if housewives agitate and organise for changes in their working conditions, this is just as valid a form of anti-capitalist class struggle as a strike by factory workers (Shaffer, 1979; Weigland, 2001). As discussed in Chapter 3, some black American communist women argued in the same period that the most exploited workers were not those in the factories but black domestic women workers, whose experiences and activism should therefore be the starting-point for working-class resistance to capitalist exploitation. Although these ideas were soon forgotten and they have only quite recently been rediscovered, other women have made related arguments over the years.

In particular, the so-called 'domestic labour debate' of the 1970s sought to use Marxist concepts and terminology to understand how women's unpaid work within the home served the interests of the capitalist economy. Although at times this seemed like 'an obscure exercise in Marxist pedantry' of little interest to most women (Vogel, 1983:21), the debate played an important role in exposing the sex-specific oppression of women for a new generation of left-wing feminist women and in linking the analyses of patriarchy and capitalism. In political terms, the debate also popularised the idea that 'Woman is the slave of a wage-slave, and her slavery ensures the slavery of her man' (Selma James, quoted in Malos, 1980:178). It also fed into the international 'Wages for Housework' campaign, which demanded that the capitalist state pay for the unwaged work that sustains it (Dalla Costa, 1973; Malos, 1980; Federici, 2012). This campaign had little immediate political impact in western nations, but it was linked to the successful international campaign to measure women's work through time-use studies, discussed in Chapter 5. As Maria Mies (1998) has argued, the insight that capitalism depends upon and exploits women's unpaid domestic labour can also usefully be extended to analyse the ways in which other forms of unpaid work, including subsistence agriculture (producing food and other goods for immediate use rather than sale), are linked to the processes of international capital accumulation.

Although it was not much discussed at the time, a Marxist feminist perspective also reminds us that changes in the material conditions in which domestic labour is performed can have an impact on gender roles. Family size, access to decent housing and the availability of electricity, clean water and household appliances all reduce the time needed for basic household tasks, in principle releasing women from the kind of ceaseless toil described by Bebel (see previous section). Even today, basic household tasks in much of the world can be back-breaking and enormously time-consuming. By the time of the 1970s domestic labour debate they still involved quite hard work for many women in western societies including the UK, where disposable nappies were only just coming on the market, automatic washing machines and freezers were luxury items, there were few convenience foods and, for most people, eating out was a very rare treat.

Even in wealthy countries, many poor women still struggle to keep their families clean and fed in insanitary, overcrowded accommodation. However, many others are able to use labour-saving equipment to reduce the time spent on household tasks, many also outsource some of this work by buying ready meals and eating out and some employ cleaners (usually other women). This makes it possible, if not always easy, for many women to spend more hours in paid employment. However, some women's liberation from household chores can mean the exploitation of others, either as badly paid workers in the food-processing and hospitality sectors or as directly paid domestic staff. Marxist feminists argue that, whoever does it, this work is an integral part of the capitalist economy and that it must be taken into account, both when analysing economic activity and when campaigning for change. As the women in the American Communist Party said nearly a hundred years ago, this means that anti-capitalist action can be taken by women working in domestic settings, whether paid or unpaid. Some writers and activists today therefore support the idea of an international women's strike that would include both paid and unpaid domestic workers (see Chapter 8).

Meanwhile, we need to remember that, despite recent changes in some families, men's relative exemption from household chores both gives them an advantage in the employment market and means that, as Heidi Hartmann said in 1979, many men still 'have a higher standard of living than women in terms of luxury consumption, leisure time and personalised services' (Hartmann, 1979/1986:9). This means that men in all classes can have at least a short-term material interest in maintaining the current gender division of labour.

Reproduction

By the 1980s, some Marxist feminists were extending their analysis well beyond housework. For Lise Vogel, the source of women's oppression lay in their childbearing role, which necessarily reduces their economic productivity, and leads to both the gender division of labour and women's economic dependency on men. In *Marxism and the Oppression of Women* (first published in 1983 and reissued in 2014), she argued that these had become institutionalised under capitalism, as home and work became increasingly separate and working-class men received a 'family wage' to support their less economically productive wives. She concluded both that working-class women do experience sex-specific oppression and that they are oppressed by capitalism rather than by working-class men. She further argued that this oppression would be ended in a socialist society in which economic activity would be directed at meeting human needs, rather than driven by the endless pursuit of profit. Vogel usefully highlighted capitalism's need for women's reproductive labour. However, her original analysis generalised from the experiences of white, male-headed western families with secure employment; since then, the increased numbers of lone-parent families and the decline of the family wage in most western countries have made the details of her argument less relevant. Vogel's analysis was also too reductionist, overlooking the sexist and oppressive behaviour of many working-class and/or socialist men, and their interest in continuing a gender division of labour from which they benefited. Because she saw patriarchy as the product of class society, rather than having an independent history, Vogel was on the 'unified system' side of debates amongst Marxist feminists as to whether capitalism and patriarchy constitute one fused system of 'capitalist patriarchy' or whether, although clearly entangled, they are analytically distinct.

Although Vogel recognised that biological reproduction can be socially organised in a range of different ways, she treated the biological 'facts' involved as unproblematically constant, rather than seeing that they too have a history that may be at times independent, or partially independent, from developments in production. In contrast, Mary O'Brien argued in 1981 that the early discovery by men of their role in procreation and the more recent development of effective contraception mark key turning points in human history and relationships between the sexes: the former gave men a motive to control women, so that they could know which children they had fathered, and the latter potentially allows women to control their own fertility. Since then, the rapid development of new reproductive technologies, including in-vitro fertilisation (IVF) and egg freezing, have combined with changes around sexuality and family structure in many countries to mean that a single woman, a lesbian couple, a post-menopausal woman or a trans man can all now give birth.

We have not, however, reached the stage imagined by Shulamith Firestone in 1970. In *The Dialectic of Sex*, she famously predicted that artificial reproduction outside the womb would soon be possible, and that, although men would try to use reproductive technology against women, this had the potential to finally liberate women from the basic source of their oppression: that is, their childbearing role. Firestone (who never had children) saw childbirth as a purely negative experience, and she argued that women could seize control of reproductive technology in the context of a wider proletarian revolution. These views have not been accepted by many feminists. Nevertheless, the understanding that biological reproduction has a history, and that technological developments in this area could be used either to benefit or to oppress women, remains important.

In practice, new developments can represent new sources of profit, exploitation and control rather than liberation. For example, the wombs of impoverished women can now be 'rented' by wealthy couples who want their own genetic child, while some IT firms, including Apple and Facebook, are offering free egg-freezing services to female employees, so that they can postpone pregnancy and devote their most productive years to the company (Fraser, 2016). Seeking to ensure that new technologies are used to benefit rather than exploit people is therefore a key issue for feminists, as is access to safe, affordable contraception and abortion and the general right for women to make their own reproductive and sexual decisions. Efforts to change practices and ideas in these areas can be as important as attempts to change conditions of paid employment; they should therefore be seen as basic material demands, as well as cultural, ideological or political struggles.

Care

As discussed in Chapters 5 and 6, care too is an essential precondition for any kind of economic activity; until recently, it had been invisible to neoliberal economists, but the COVID-19 pandemic made its importance much more clear. Many Marxist feminists today argue that care is therefore a key part of the material basis of society, and that it has its own history. In this context, some writers are analysing the shifting boundaries between love, care and work in a world in which the reach of profit-making is extending into all areas of life and care is increasingly part of the global market economy. Some are concluding not only that the commodification of care is having damaging effects on individuals and their families (after all, when did human misery ever stand in the way of profit?), but that it is also bound up with a crisis in the entire global capitalist system.

Much of the care of children, elderly people and others who are unable to look after themselves remains an informal activity provided by family members, friends and others in the wider community, who are often a source of emotional as well as physical support. Caring for others is also disproportionately the responsibility of women. However, the provision of such informal care is increasingly under stress from a number of sources. Most obviously, women all over the world are more involved in the labour market than ever before, sometimes through choice, sometimes through necessity and sometimes as a condition of welfare support. Many have to work long days, or they may have to juggle several part-time jobs with unpredictable working hours. In many countries, including the UK, older people who might have looked after their own aged parents or their grandchildren are expected to retire at an increasingly late age; in other countries, younger family members who emigrate to find employment overseas may have to leave their own children behind. Although many states have developed measures to support employees with caring responsibilities, including parental or family leave, free or subsidised childcare provision and day centres or residential homes for elderly people, these fall short of what is needed, even in the Nordic countries, which have the most generous welfare systems. Such support is, moreover, often being withdrawn as a part of austerity and structural adjustment programmes and in line with the neoliberal focus on individual self-reliance discussed in Chapters 5 and 6.

From a neoliberal perspective, the solution is of course to shift from care provided by family or state to the market economy, where care services can provide new opportunities for profit. There are however a number of problems with this 'solution'. These problems seem invisible to neoliberal economists, but a Marxist analysis that understands the profit-driven and necessarily exploitative and 'uncaring' nature of free market capitalism throws them into sharp relief.

First, as I pointed out in Chapter 5, the profitability of the sector is difficult to sustain. Ownership of care homes for elderly and/or disabled people in the UK has largely shifted from local councils to private ownership, fewer people are receiving state help with the costs of care and the largest for-profit chains are increasingly in debt to private equity companies. These are looking for a swift return on their investment and charging extremely high interest rates; some chains are now on the brink of financial collapse. Similarly, nurseries for young children are increasingly privately owned by large chains as part of international businesses, and some are facing further financial difficulties as an inadequately funded government scheme for more free childcare is failing to cover the costs involved. This raises the danger both of closures and of the establishment of a two-tier service, with only a few families able to afford good-quality care. This has clear implications for the effective 'production' of the next generation of workers and citizens.

Second, paid care work under current conditions often involves particularly high levels of exploitation. In a patriarchal world in which 'women's work' has little value, care work has always been poorly paid and today it is increasingly done by migrant women workers. This has led to the development of complex 'care chains' between and within the global south and north, so that, while some are able to 'outsource' their traditional responsibilities, others are leaving their children on the other side of the world. Combined with low pay and often stressful working conditions, this means that changes in care provision 'both reflect and contribute to global inequalities' (Yeandle et al., 2017:6). Even employers who would like to treat their staff well find it increasingly difficult to make any profit without capping pay, increasing workloads and/or providing a poorer standard of care.

At first sight, exploitation is less clear-cut when a care worker is directly employed by another woman as a nanny or cleaner, as her employer is not driven by the same need to maximise profits or expand their enterprise as a private company. Nevertheless, it remains in her employer's economic interest to extract as much work out of her for the lowest possible wage. Some female employers will be 'generous', but the realities of the gender pay gap means that in many cases they too will be short of money and that they will necessarily seek to minimise their care costs. As a study of migrant care workers in London argues:

> both sets of women are caught in a bigger game whose rules they have not written – one of global inequality in which wages earned as a nanny abroad outstrip those of a middle-class professional in one's own country, in which the gap between the rich and poorer nations is widening ... and in which two wages are often needed to maintain a household in the contemporary world. (Datta et al., 2006:9)

A third problem with the neoliberal solution to the problem of care stems from the clash of values involved when the provision of care is reduced to a source of profit. Care is an inherently relational activity and, if it is to be done well, it cannot be reduced to a check-list of tasks to be performed as quickly as possible. Today, however, it is becoming much like this, both when it is paid for and when it is done by family members in the time they have left from their paid employment. Despite the neoliberal insistence that we should be driven by calculated self-interest, family care is still widely expected to be motivated by love and duty (even if it also involves resentment and hostility). This means that, when it is subject to the logic of efficiency and time management, this can feel uncomfortably like the 'McDonaldisation of love' (Boyd, 2002:466, quoting Anne Manne). It is also of course traditionally seen as the responsibility of women, who often experience far more guilt than men if they outsource it to someone else; it is perhaps unsurprising that a large UK study found that working mothers of small children were by far the most stressed group in the country (Doward, 2019). Good paid care too needs a flexible, open-ended approach that allows more time than a calculation of cost-efficiency might at first sight suggest; such time is, however, incompatible with profit maximisation, and therefore seldom available.

Social reproduction: a crisis in global capitalism?

Once we understand that domestic work, biological reproduction and care are essential foundations for conventionally defined economic activity, we can see that difficulties in these areas pose problems for the entire capitalist economic system, within which production is just one subsystem (Fraser, 2016). As Nancy Fraser says, we can also see how the organisation of social reproduction as a whole is bound up with the subordination or oppression of women:

> [the] gendered, hierarchical division between 'production' and 'reproduction' is a defining structure of capitalist society and a deep source of the gender asymmetries hard-wired in it. There can be no 'emancipation of women' so long as this structure remains intact. (2015)

This division is not only oppressive, it is also increasingly unsustainable. Although for a short while in western societies the 'male breadwinner' model might have seemed to solve capitalism's need for both productive and reproductive labour, this 'solution' was short-lived. Today, capitalist production's accelerated drive to accumulation is creating a series of tensions that may be building up to crisis level. In 2011, I saw these as a series of 'emerging contradictions' between conditions of production and reproduction:

> between capitalism's need to exploit women's traditional skills and attributes in the labor market and its need for their unpaid work in the family; between the profit motive and the provision of care; and between the human need to be valued for ourselves and the drive to commodify all human relationships. (Bryson, 2011:72)

The problem is one not simply for the individuals who are most directly affected but for the sustainability of the system as a whole, as capitalist markets can only meet those human needs that can generate a profit; when these needs can no longer be satisfied through women's unpaid labour they are therefore liable to go unmet. Thus Fraser argues that capitalist production 'free rides on social reproduction … yet its orientation to endless accumulation threatens to destabilize these very conditions of its possibility' (2014:70–71) and that 'No society that systematically undermines social reproduction can endure for long. Today, however, a new form of capitalist society is doing just that' (2016:99). From this perspective, capitalism cannot continue as it is, so 'the question is not whether this capitalism will be transformed, but how, by whom and in whose interests' (2015).

Bhattacharya sees what is happening as deliberate class warfare against the global working class that aims to break union power in the workplace while also attacking key areas of social reproduction by privatising social services and welfare and imposing punitive policies in the global south that drive up the price of basic necessities:

> By systematically privatizing previously socialized resources, reducing the quality of services, capital *aimed* to make the work of daily regeneration more vulnerable and precarious while simultaneously unloading the entire responsibility and discourse of reproduction onto individual families. (2015:17, emphasis added)

This sounds overly conspiratorial. Capitalists may deliberately destroy union power, but they do not, on the whole, *aim* to destroy the conditions of their own existence, whether this be the reproduction of the workforce or a habitable environment. However, because they are driven by the remorseless, abstract logic of capitalism to sacrifice everything to the endless pursuit of profit this is indeed frequently what they *do*.

We are also seeing a major clash within capitalism between its neoliberal values, which need women as well as men in the workplace and will (at least in theory) rationally recruit on a gender-blind notion of merit, and men's patriarchal self-interest in retaining both their traditionally superior economic position and their relative exemption from household chores. There is also a very different clash of values, as the importance of education, love, care and the protection of the environment are rhetorically acknowledged or even celebrated, while they remain economically invisible and often impossible to realise in practice. Ideas of long-term interests and collective responsibilities also persist to challenge the rigour of neoliberal logic: for example, caring for elderly people and others who will never be productive workers is not economically rational, but workers are unlikely to accept that their life should end when they retire or if they become disabled; meanwhile, most will want their own parents to be properly looked after when they get old. The continuing strength of these collective and caring values was clear during the 2020 COVID-19 crisis, when most people accepted major disruption to their normal life in the interest of the public good, and many actively reached out to assist vulnerable members of their community – even as corporate 'vulture capitalists' moved in to exploit the situation (Klein, 2020; see also Klein, 2007, 2017; Loewenstein, 2013).

All these fissures, discontinuities and contradictions weaken the apparently overwhelming power of global capitalism, and open up spaces to reassert the importance of non-economic values and take action to challenge conditions of social reproduction. For Fraser,

> What is required, above all, is to overcome financialized capitalism's rapacious subjugation of reproduction to production – but this time without sacrificing either emancipation or social protection. (2016:117)

Taking this down to earth, she and her fellow writers see this as involving a range of actions that include the unionisation of migrant cleaning workers (Shalmy, 2018), new forms of strike action by women (Arruzza et al., 2018) and campaigns for decent housing, education, clean water, the financial recognition of caring work, and women's right to make their own reproductive decisions.

Marxism and feminism: insights and limitations

Feminists have been able to draw on Marxist ideas to reach a number of interconnected conclusions that I find largely convincing: that because capitalist societies exploit women's reproductive labour they depend upon the oppression of women; that meaningful sex equality for the majority of women will therefore not be achieved without major economic change; that the analysis of social reproduction is not some kind of optional extra if we want to understand how economies and societies function; that the organisation of social reproduction is historically specific; that it can therefore be challenged and changed; that such change cannot be achieved at will, but only when particular material conditions have developed; and that such conditions are already developing in the globalised capitalist economy.

However, we cannot simply reduce women's situation to the needs of capitalism. While the subordination of reproduction to production involves the economic subordination of women to men, and capitalism 'mobilizes patriarchy in its quest for profit' (Colley, 2015:175), this does not mean that capitalism *causes* patriarchy in all its multidimensional, ubiquitous and interconnected manifestations, or that, if capitalism were magically overthrown, patriarchal power would disappear. Any causal link between capitalism and particular non-economic aspects of gendered oppression, such as sexual violence, is also unclear. I am not saying that there is no connection: for example, as I indicated in Chapter 1, sexual violence can be an expression of male entitlement by economically dominant men, or an expression of resentment by men at the real or perceived loss of this power. Such arguments are, however, somewhat tenuous, and it is unclear why or whether men's sense of sexual and domestic entitlement would disappear in a different economic system, along with their more general position as the standard of what it means to be human. In this context, it is worth noting that very few socialist men seem to be participating in the debates around social reproduction, suggesting that they see this as a form of 'women's work', an abstract version of 'you make the tea, while I make the revolution'. It is also important to note that left-wing movements and parties are not immune to sexually predatory men; although such men are increasingly called to account, some members still see feminist attempts to challenge bad behaviour as a divisive distraction from more 'important' issues (National Committee of the US Freedom Socialist Party, 2013; Penny, 2014:87; Perraudin, 2019).

I have no wish to resurrect the old dual versus unified systems debate, and I agree with Cinzia Arruzza (2013) that gender and class are so intertwined in capitalist production and power relations that it is probably not helpful to discuss which comes first. From this open-ended perspective, we can at least agree that patriarchy is extremely useful for capitalism, that many men reap a patriarchal dividend that is not available to similarly situated women and that we cannot effectively oppose patriarchy, or some particular aspects of patriarchy, without understanding its role in today's capitalist system. Conversely, effective opposition to capitalism can take place in the arena of social reproduction as well as in the workplace, and socialist feminists need to foreground gender issues: we can never assume that if we take care of capitalism, patriarchy will take care of itself.

Conclusions

As Marx said, capitalism has been a progressive stage in human history, and it has now created the material preconditions for a society in which we could control our own fertility, eliminate poverty and be liberated from ceaseless drudgery. At the same time, the exploitation of human labour to produce profit lies at its heart, and capitalism has always generated immense suffering as well as wealth. Today, the continued and increasingly rapid growth that finance capital requires is increasing exploitation and inequality, while threatening both the natural world and the conditions of its own reproduction. Capitalism is also deeply entangled with patriarchy, in terms of both material practices and rewards and the more general privileging of men's interests and perspectives, even as its 'gender-blind' economic rationality sometimes points in other directions. As this and the preceding two chapters have shown, its damaging effects are now hitting the poorest women particularly hard.

Of course, global finance capital remains enormously powerful, and the mindset promoted and sustained by neoliberal economic theory means that even apparently minor and moderate calls for reform are likely to generate strong opposition at local, national and international levels. At the same time, its emerging contradictions are making it highly vulnerable to disruption. The political implications of this are discussed further in the next chapter.

8

Why feminists should logically be socialists (and vice versa)

S O FAR, I have argued that patriarchy is built into all societies, that it is entangled with other dimensions of structural oppression and that it cannot be successfully challenged on an individual, case by case basis, but requires collective actions and solutions. I have also addressed the fact that gender-based inequalities and exploitation are also clearly much more acute in some societies than in others, and experienced very differently by different groups of women. In this context, I have drawn on intersectional analysis to argue that, if feminism is to do more than enable a handful of women to join existing elites, its starting-point should be those who are multiply disadvantaged rather than those who are relatively privileged. I have also rejected the kind of either/or binary thinking that obscures complexity and shuts down discussion. Beyond this, I have argued that any real improvement in most women's lives would challenge the economic logic of short-term profitability that drives global capitalism to exploit the vulnerable and devastate the planet. And I have argued that this same logic is generating another capitalist crisis, as the focus on making money and drawing women into the labour market forgets the economic necessity of the unpaid work that they have traditionally done, and risks leaving basic human needs unmet.

All of this seems to point to some kind of collectivist, socialist solution. By this, I most definitely do not mean the kind of repressive, undemocratic state socialism associated with the former Soviet Union and other eastern bloc states or with contemporary China. Nor am I attempting to provide a strict definition of this highly contested term. Instead, I am taking a minimalist approach, treating socialism as an ideology that is broadly based on democratic and egalitarian principles of economic and social justice; these principles are linked to the belief that societies should be organised for the benefit of the many, not the few, and this will require both restrictions on the operations of free market economies and positive interventions to promote equality and welfare. These interventions should not, however, simply be imposed by governments from above. Instead, they should be part of a wider process of democratic decision-making and involvement at all levels of society that links local communities and workplaces to regional, national and international decision-making bodies. What this means in practice is of course also highly contested. Here I am again taking a minimalist approach, advocating as a relatively realistic starting-point something closer to Nordic social democracy than the more market-driven economy of the US.

In the first section of this chapter, I expand upon the affinities between socialist and feminist goals and ways of thinking. The second section traces the development of socialist feminist ideas from the late eighteenth century, showing both that socialism and feminism can learn from each other's principles and perspectives, and that neither a feminist nor a socialist movement can deliver its promises without the other. I then explore the practical implications for western societies in the context of twenty-first century developments in feminist politics, including the experience of Nordic countries.

Feminism and socialism: socialism and feminism

In this section, I step back from immediate political debates to identify the underlying commonalities between many forms of feminism and socialism. My arguments here are based on the assumption that non-socialist feminists do not want to drive women into poverty (even if their focus is on elite women), and that most socialists agree with the principle that a good society should address the needs and interests of women as well as men (even if they have tended to forget this in practice).

Feminists and socialists both believe that there is much that is wrong with existing societies. They also believe that the injustices and inequalities they see are neither natural nor inevitable, and that we can and should work together to make a better world. This means that feminism and socialism are both inherently optimistic. For many, this optimism is based on the understanding that we are not essentially solitary and independent creatures (our prolonged period of dependency on others in infancy and our need to co-operate if we are to meet our material needs both rule this out), and that human nature is not exclusively and always selfish and competitive. Many feminists and socialists further believe that societies can be organised to encourage the human qualities of co-operation, care and compassion, while reining in the competitive, self-centred pursuit of short-term gain.

Socialism and feminism also share egalitarian principles that extend beyond formal legal and political equality to wider social and economic areas of life. Here they focus on equality of outcomes as well as opportunities, and advocate a system in which rewards are more equally and equitably distributed; there is mounting evidence that this would improve the welfare of rich as well as poor people (Wilkinson and Pickett, 2009, 2018). In other words, the goal of feminists and socialists is not to provide opportunities that will enable a few women or working-class people to join existing elites within a hierarchical, competitive society in which most men and women can only be losers, and many will live in poverty. Rather, it is to challenge the nature and extent of existing inequalities, the distribution of rewards and the principles that underpin them.

For some socialists, the ultimate ideal society is one based on the classic principle of 'from each according to their ability, to each according to their needs'. From a feminist perspective, these contributions and needs include giving and receiving love and care as well as material goods, so that in an ideal society those who spend time caring for others would no longer be economically penalised and made financially dependent. This means that, even if women continued to provide more care than men, heterosexual relationships would no longer be distorted by economic considerations: here Kristen Ghodsee argues that the benefits for women of living in socialist societies, even the kind of repressive state socialism that formerly existed in the Soviet Union and eastern Europe, include 'better sex', as this can be freely chosen by economically independent women rather than tainted by the need to find a man to support them (Ghodsee, 2018:book title).

In reality of course, the ultimate socialist-feminist/feminist-socialist society is not on the immediate political horizon anywhere in the world. It is, however, feasible for wealthy countries such as the UK and US to aim for a sizeable reduction in economic inequalities, so that the extremes of wealth described in Chapter 4 are curbed and poverty is reduced; these countries could also place the health, care and welfare of citizens at the centre of policy-making. Such countries can also take steps to recognise and reduce their role in creating and sustaining global inequalities and exploitation, including their continuing responsibility for climate change. And working to eliminate poverty logically involves looking at the underlying economic system, which in turn implies challenging unregulated market capitalism and the neoliberal ideology that supports it. Any reduction in poverty would disproportionately benefit women; the poorest groups of women, who include many trans and migrant women, would benefit most.

Most strands of socialist theory and practice involve some kind of collective thinking that goes beyond individuals and their families to look at shared social needs and class interests; this often involves an emphasis on comradeship and working-class unity. Feminists too are thinking collectively whenever they identify gendered inequalities in power and economic rewards or, as in the #MeToo movement, discover the patterned nature of apparently separate or individual bad experiences at the hands of men. When inequalities and injustices are widely shared and embedded in society, it is not enough to exhort individuals to fight their own corner; recognising this is a necessary first step towards finding solutions.

While socialism and feminism have often seemed to represent separate strands of radical thought, there is a long history of socialist feminist ideas that has included contributions by men as well as women. The next section provides a brief outline of this often overlooked tradition before returning to the recent developments in Marxist feminist analysis that I discussed in Chapter 7.

Feminist socialism/socialist feminism: a brief history

The so-called utopian socialists of the late eighteenth and early nineteenth centuries represent an important starting-point for the argument that the goals of socialism and the emancipation of women are interdependent. The most famous of these early socialists, who believed that a better society could be brought about by reason and persuasion rather than revolution, are Robert Owen, Charles Fourier and Henri de St Simon, but the most sustained socialist analysis of women's oppression was provided by Anna Wheeler and William Thompson in their 1824 *Appeal of One Half of the Human Race, Women, Against the Pretensions of the Other Half, Men, to Retain Them in Political and Thence Civil and Domestic Slavery* (although jointly written, this was published under Thompson's name only). These early socialists differed on many details, but they all largely agreed that a free, egalitarian and socialist society could succeed only if relationships between the sexes were also based on freedom and equality rather than ownership and dependency, and that conventional family life was a source of selfish individualism that was incompatible with socialist co-operation and would therefore have to be transformed. Conversely, they also argued that this transformation of personal and family life would be possible only in a more equal society, in which relationships could be freely chosen, rather than based on dependency and possession.

By the beginning of the twentieth century, related ideas were being developed by some socialist women such as Sylvia Pankhurst, who combined militant campaigning for women's suffrage with active involvement in socialist organisations and practical work with women in the slums of London's East End. Unlike her mother and her older sister (Emmeline and Christabel Pankhurst), she refused to prioritise votes for women over full adult suffrage, she saw the vote as a means to social and economic reform rather than an end in itself, and she insisted that working men were both potential allies and fellow victims of exploitation. Many socialist men at the time agreed with feminist goals in principle, and some leading members of the Labour Party, including Keir Hardie and George Lansbury, were highly supportive of the women's suffrage campaign. However, discriminatory practices and traditional assumptions about gender roles generally went unchallenged. These assumptions were memorably captured by Hannah Mitchell, a working-class socialist and suffrage campaigner from the north of England, who complained that

> I soon found that a lot of the Socialist talk about freedom was only talk, and these Socialist young men expected Sunday dinners and huge teas with home-made cakes, potted meat and pies, exactly like their reactionary fellows. (Mitchell, 1977:96)

Meanwhile, as discussed in Chapter 7, most Marxist socialists in Germany and Russia marginalised or ignored 'women's issues'. Alexandra Kollontai provided a notable exception. Her belief that public and private morality were interdependent, so that equal domestic and personal relationships both required and enabled co-operative and egalitarian economic arrangements, echoes the ideas of the utopian socialists; it also anticipates much more recent socialist feminist approaches.

The arguments discussed so far in this necessarily brief and selective history indicate not simply that it would be nice if socialist men were to take women into account, but that socialism will not be possible without the morality that equal relationships can provide – or, to put it another way, if relationships between the sexes are based on exploitation, oppression or inequality, then the moral foundations that a co-operative and inclusive socialist society requires will not be there. Much of this can sound like wishful thinking, but, as discussed in Chapter 6 in relation to the rise of neoliberalism, the capturing of hearts and minds is an important aspect of political struggle and the mindset that allows one kind of oppressive relationship, whether this be based on race, class, religion, social orientation or gender, is unlikely to successfully eliminate others.

Later developments

The recent Marxist feminist theory that I discussed in Chapter 7 provides more tangible reasons for socialists to listen to feminists and for feminists to listen to socialists. To summarise my earlier arguments: contrary to the assumptions of most male-stream socialists, the 'productive' work traditionally associated with men is not the only or primary form of economic activity, for it depends on the important life-giving and life-sustaining work of 'social reproduction' (biological reproduction, domestic work and care) traditionally associated with women. Today, social reproduction is increasingly under pressure as the competitive, individualistic logic of neoliberalism dominates all areas of life, and human needs that cannot generate profit go unmet (see Chapters 5, 6 and 7). These developments are contrary to the interests of both women and men and threaten the functioning of social and economic life. If essential social and care needs cannot be met by the market, and if the work involved is to be properly recognised, rewarded and redistributed, a more socialist, collective approach seems inevitable, with an increase in state funding or good-quality provision and the widespread introduction of much shorter and more flexible working hours for men as well as women. The unpalatable alternatives are the increased exploitation of an underpaid subgroup, mainly female and often involving migrant workers (which displaces the care deficit to the workers' own families and/or country of origin), or unsustainable levels of stress and neglect for all except the very rich.

Here again socialism and feminism seem to point in the same direction, as both recognise the reality of human interdependence and the consequent need for value systems based on solidarity, co-operation and the collective good rather than individual satisfaction and the pursuit of short-term profit. The importance of such non-capitalist values was highlighted by the COVID-19 pandemic, as individuals were asked to make enormous financial sacrifices, to surrender taken-for-granted freedoms and, in the case of many key workers, to risk their lives in the interests of the wider society.

The need for collective thinking and increased public spending is also indicated by feminist analyses of sexual violence and predatory behaviour, discussed in Chapters 1 and 2. This leads beyond awareness of individual experiences to link male violence to the wider power structures of patriarchal societies, including men's economic power in both the workplace and the home: while ill-treatment of women can be bound up with wealthy men's sense of entitlement, it can also reflect other men's frustration at the loss of privileges that they have been taught to expect. It is also clear that protecting women from violence involves more than making this illegal; at the very least, it requires providing adequate funding for women's refuges and rape crisis centres. As discussed in Chapter 4, solutions to practical problems around what are currently framed as the conflicting needs of trans and cis women also require increased public support: for example, if there were sufficient well-funded refuges that could offer a safe, private space to any woman who needed it, disputes around trans women's right to access these refuges would be less acute. Interventions in the global economy are of course also required if the increasingly devastating impact of climate change is to be halted or reversed.

Feminist politics and socialism in the twenty-first century

In the Introduction, I outlined some of the many kinds of feminist activity that have developed in recent years. Feminists today are addressing a wide range of issues that include gendered violence across public and private life; women's poverty and the gender pay gap; the need to value and support women's paid and unpaid care work; and women's under-representation in political and economic elites. Some forms of feminist activism focus on a particular issue; others understand that injustices of gender are interconnected, both with each other and with other forms of injustice, particularly those of race and class; some also carry their feminist activism into campaigns against militarisation or environmental destruction.

Feminist political methods are similarly diverse, ranging from the very local to the global, from academic research to mass demonstrations, from workplace campaigns to corporate initiatives and from lobbying parliaments to working with asylum seekers. Some feminist groups focus on specific groups of women, such as migrants, while some try to include women from all backgrounds. Some are deliberately non-hierarchical, and some are conventionally organised. Some feminists work in women-only groups, and many work with men in trade unions, political parties or direct-action campaigns.

While some kinds of feminist activism can loosely be described as socialist, others are not socialist in any way; indeed, some are strongly anti-socialist. In particular, as discussed in Chapter 6, the kind of neoliberal feminism promoted by women such as Sheryl Sandberg and Ivanka Trump is primarily concerned with enabling more women to become 'successful', rather than trying to improve the situation of those in more lowly positions, and it focuses on securing equal pay and bonuses for high-flying women rather than eliminating poverty. Basically, such feminism wants the same, unequal world, but with more women in elite positions. It argues that this will be good for profitability and growth, forgetting that there are other human values and ignoring the devastating environmental consequences of this growth for the planet.

In stark contrast, the recent growth of the international feminist strike movement seems to open up exciting new possibilities, and in 2019 Arruzza, Bhattacharya and Fraser argued that this represents 'a new global feminist movement that may gain sufficient force to disrupt existing alliances and redraw the political map' and that demonstrates 'the power of those whose paid and unpaid work sustains the world' (2019:6, 7). The strike movement seems genuinely global, rather than western-led, and in the following year the call to strike, which was initiated by the Asia Pacific Forum on Women, Law and Development (https://apwld.org), was supported by over a million women from 59 countries (https://wom ensglobalstrike.com). The movement is organised from below rather than top-down. It is decidedly anti-capitalist, and, although women in different countries prioritise different issues, there is a general focus on gendered violence and on the need to properly value women's work, both paid and unpaid. Camille Barbagallo (2020), one of the strike organisers in the UK, finds that the movement 'provides the intellectual and political organising space to ... return our struggles to the streets and out of the framework of lobbying or of policy or of being "smart business women getting ahead"'.

In the context of both the rising influence of neoliberal feminism and the growing feminist strike movement, Arruzza, Bhattacharya and Fraser argue that we are at a fork in the road:

> One path leads to a scorched planet where human life is immiserated, if it remains possible at all. The other points to the sort of world that has always figured in humanity's dreams: one whose wealth and natural resources are shared by all, where equality and freedom are premises, not aspirations. What makes the choice so pressing is the disappearance of any middle way. (2018:114)

Hester Eisenstein makes the related point that

> it is only in a broad alliance of left forces with the collective force of women in social movements, from the Zapista women in Chiapas to the MST in Brazil, to welfare activists and the Black Lives Matter movement in the United States, among many other groupings, that there is any hope of stopping or slowing the capitalist juggernaut that is leading the world to near certain economic, and indeed ecological, disaster. (2017:49)

I agree with the above writers that feminist goals cannot be met in societies driven by neoliberal values, and that these values are threatening the entire planet. However, I do not think that our choices are quite as stark as they suggest, or that reforms 'within the system' cannot make a difference. First, I do not think that all the ideas of neoliberal feminism should be dismissed out of hand. As I said in Chapter 6, such feminism sometimes reaches surprisingly radical conclusions, calling for changes that many socialist feminists have been advocating for years. In particular, both Sandberg and (to a lesser extent) Ivanka Trump are challenging the patriarchal rules of the game by saying that men as well as women should be active parents, conditions of employment should change to recognise workers' family responsibilities and the state may have to help with childcare and eldercare costs; Sandberg is also showing awareness of the dire financial situation faced by many mothers in the US. In practice, it seems highly unlikely that widespread changes to workplace practices or adequate state support for caring responsibilities would be introduced by Republican administrations in the US or Conservative administrations in the UK. Nevertheless, the ground is shifting, expectations have been raised and some transformative ideas are becoming almost mainstream. This means that when neoliberal feminists fail to deliver what they promise (as they will, because their promises will not be compatible with profit), those whose expectations have been disappointed may turn in more radical directions: as the nineteenth-century French historian Alexis de Tocqueville observed, revolutions are more often the product of minor improvements and rising hopes than of total immiseration.

This suggests that socialist feminists should support Sandberg and Trump's call for more family-friendly employment as 'transitional demands': that is, demands that fall far short of what we really want but that can be pushed further (for example, if the state is to provide good childcare, it will, logically, have to employ qualified workers, and such workers will be entitled to be properly paid). Attempts to realise these transitional demands will also demonstrate the inability of states to deliver what people need without more radical change. Similar considerations apply at a global level: as I said in my Introduction, there has been a shift in the official position of the major national and international economic and political organisations, which are now publicly committed to the goal of gender equality. Even if this commitment is motivated by the belief that this will be a source of profit, it gives feminists a degree of leverage: as Cynthia Enloe says, bad practices persist, but at least 'both UN and member state officials now have to spend more energy and political currency trying to explain away their complicity with efforts to sustain patriarchy' (2017:57).

My second reason for supporting campaigns for moderate reforms is that these can have life-changing effects. To give one example: Angela

Rayner was a teenage single mother with no qualifications and little idea of how to care for her baby when the 1997 Labour government introduced the first of over 3,500 Sure Start centres, aimed at giving all children the best possible start by supporting and encouraging their parents. Rayner is now a leading Labour MP, and she has frequently spoken about how the programme transformed her life. (After Labour lost the 2010 election, the policy was abandoned; by 2019, over one thousand centres had been closed). More generally, we need to remember that the austerity measures that were introduced in response to the 2008 financial crisis, and that have had particularly damaging effects on the poorest women (see Chapters 5 and 6), were not inevitable. Rather, they were an ideologically motivated choice, through which a banking crisis caused by reckless speculation and irresponsible lending was presented as a consequence of government over-spending on welfare and public services. These policies can therefore be challenged and reversed, and even relatively minor improvements are important for those most immediately affected.

The above examples show that, when feminists say that we have to choose between system overthrow or more moderate change, they are creating a false dichotomy and taking a luxury position that most people simply cannot afford. Of course any reforms will often be opposed by powerful national and/or international vested interests, and it is important that some feminists confront these; but reforms can sometimes succeed, they are important in themselves and they can also lead to further progressive change.

My third, connected, reason for disagreeing with the above writers is that states are not simply instruments of patriarchy and/or capitalist class rule, and state power is not some monolithic entity that must be bypassed, overthrown or captured by feminist anti-capitalists to prevent it blocking meaningful change. Rather, state power and political processes are fractured, dynamic and context-dependent, and policy outcomes are never simply in the interests of patriarchy or capitalism (apart from anything else, patriarchy and capitalism are themselves full of internal contradictions and conflicting interests). In this context, many socialists and feminists can agree that they should work both 'in and against' the state, in tandem with wider forms of political activism and participation. These can both provide support for feminists in political office and call them to account.

This leads to my final point: in many countries feminists are in a new position – that is, we are no longer simply outsiders. It is not just that there are more women in powerful political positions but that there are more *feminist* women, including *socialist feminist* women, and also some socialist feminist men. The next section considers what policies we might want these feminist politicians to pursue.

Feminist policies

The policy proposals that I discuss here are primarily applicable to western democracies such as the UK. However, they are inevitably bound up with their wider global context, including the climate emergency and the COVID-19 pandemic, and the underlying principles will hopefully have wider relevance. They are informed by intersectional analysis (see Chapter 3), which indicates that the starting-point for feminist policies should be the most disadvantaged women in society; these women should, as far as possible, be active participants in policy-making.

The underlying policy areas that I identify as particularly important for feminists cluster around work, care, welfare and the relationships between them. As I have argued in previous chapters, feminist perspectives move beyond conventional, male-stream, economic and political thinking to highlight the critical importance of care and the need to see this as a form of work. This work is the basis for our economy and our society; it is also a public good for which we have a collective responsibility (Lynch et al., 2009). Caring work and responsibilities should therefore be recognised, supported, rewarded and more equitably distributed. This in turn requires an open-ended set of policies; some of these already exist or are being developed, while others involve longer-term, blue-skies thinking and would involve a radical change in mindset.

Most obviously, workplaces need to be organised around the assumption that 'normal' employees are likely to have family or community responsibilities: measures here include paid family leave (perhaps with periods of parental leave specifically allocated to fathers), flexible working, much shorter working hours and better protection for workers in the 'gig economy'. These measures would have to be legally enforceable entitlements, so that good employers are not undercut. Retailers would also be required to scrutinise their supply chains to ensure that overseas suppliers were providing decent conditions of employment.

The starting-point for policies around paid care provision, both for children and for adults, should be that the goal is accessible, good-quality care for all who need it. This means employing well-trained, properly paid staff, and it is highly unlikely to be profitable; it should not be treated as a money-making opportunity and it should therefore be publicly funded or provided. Meanwhile, those who spend their time looking after other people without pay should not have to sacrifice their economic independence or live in poverty; measures here might include a payment to family carers that is at least as high as any minimum wage (which in turn should be a genuinely 'living wage'), or it might be linked to the introduction of some kind of 'universal basic income' (Schultz, 2017). These measures in turn would be linked to a right to 'universal basic services', including healthcare, social care, housing, transport and internet access. In 2019, the idea of such universal entitlements seemed like fantasy; by early 2020, when the COVID-19 pandemic revealed the gaping hole in many countries' welfare systems, it was rising up the mainstream political agenda (Lansley, 2020; Wignaraja and Horvath, 2020).

Recognising the value of the work traditionally done by women would help reduce the gender pay gap, while encouraging men to take family leave and work shorter hours would reduce the competitive advantage that their current domestic absenteeism often gives them in the workplace. Economically independent women would have more choices in life, including alternatives to living in an abusive relationship, while greater involvement of men in childcare would also challenge gender stereotypes, and help free boys from 'the small, hard cage' of traditional masculinity in which they are so often imprisoned (Adichie, 2014:26). Measures to promote gender equality in the workplace should also be made more effective for women who face more than one form of discrimination; existing legislation, which in the UK and EU countries outlaws workplace discrimination in relation to a number of 'protected characteristics', including gender, should therefore be extended to include class and to recognise the effects of multiple discrimination (see Chapter 3). Other policy areas such as transport or the rights of disabled people may not seem overtly feminist issues, but they are certainly gendered; an intersectional feminist perspective is needed if the distinctive needs of different groups of women are to be taken into account.

Some of the above measures would be costly, and they would be paid for by a package of redistributive taxes. Although such taxes would be opposed by many, they are garnering support – indeed, by 2019 a growing number of billionaires, including Bill Gates, Warren Buffet and George Soros, were calling for higher taxation on their wealth (Coudriet, 2019). Ideally, extreme wealth would be tackled globally, perhaps by taxes on financial transactions (the so-called Tobin tax), or some kind of global wealth tax, as advocated by Thomas Piketty (2014) or through multinational agreement on ways to impose a digital sales tax on companies such as Amazon and Facebook. Because economic inequality is gendered, any redistribution of wealth or income would be to the advantage of most women.

The above proposals fall far short of a comprehensive challenge to capitalism. Nevertheless, they challenge the values that underpin it, and they expose its inability to understand non-monetary motivations or relationships. This can make them seem dangerously radical in countries where neoliberal assumptions seem simply 'common sense', and they would probably be rejected on sight by many people in the UK. However, other policies that were widely seen as extreme a generation ago – such giving men a right to paternity leave – are now treated as 'common sense'. Many of them are also already in place in the Nordic countries.

Lessons from the north

As I said in the Introduction, Denmark, Finland, Iceland, Norway and Sweden appear to be the most gender-equal group of countries in the world. As discussed below, important problems remain. However, a combination of social democratic and feminist principles has helped develop a set of interconnected policies that have improved many women's lives at home and in the workplace; they have also helped achieve high levels of political representation for feminist women; this means that women are well placed both to defend existing gains and to push for further change.

Social democratic ideas dominated Nordic politics for most of the twentieth century; although now challenged, they remain strong. Social democratic principles do not directly seek to overthrow capitalism, but they challenge its nature. In particular, they push governments to actively pursue greater social and economic equality, and they argue that strong welfare states are to everyone's benefit, so that relatively high levels of taxation are justified in societies in which everyone contributes and everyone gains. Feminists have extended these principles to push for policies that treat care as a key foundation of economic and social life; these policies are also based on the understanding that gender equality in politics and the workplace requires greater equality in the home.

The result has been a wide range of policies in relation to childcare, education, political representation, employment and welfare provision specifically designed to challenge gender inequalities in public and private life. These include employment conditions that recognise the family responsibilities of men as well as women, and state provision or funding for childcare. Beyond this, policies vary, and Nordic feminists are engaged in ongoing debates around issues such as the long-term impact of providing a state-funded income to parents who want to care for their small children at home (because this is largely taken up by women, it reduces their future career prospects, and it may make it easier for some migrant men from more patriarchal cultures to confine their wives to a domestic role), and whether policies should actively encourage men to do more as fathers (by reserving part of parental leave to them on a 'use it or lose it' basis) or treat this as a private matter for parents to decide (Ellingsaeter, 2014). There are also national policy differences around sex work, with ongoing debates as to the effects of the policies adopted in Sweden, Norway and

Iceland, which have criminalised men who buy sex rather than the women who sell it. While some feminists see this as a model to adopt elsewhere (Murphy, 2013; Topping, 2013), the evidence that the policy has had positive effects on attitudes or the extent of the sex trade is unclear, and many reports indicate that, as the trade has been driven underground, the lives and livelihoods of sex workers have been put in increased danger, sex trafficking has increased and trafficked women are likely to be immediately deported rather than offered support (Skilbrei and Holmström, 2013; Kingston and Thomas, 2019; Mac and Smith, 2018).

In general, Nordic policies have produced some important political, cultural and socio-economic changes, but this does not mean that patriarchy has been overthrown. As elsewhere, migrant women and those from a non-western background face particular problems and remain marginalised. Domestic and/or sexual violence against women remains a widespread problem, with rates amongst the highest in the EU (Wemrell et al., 2019). Women in general still do more domestic work than men; there is a significant gender pay gap; and the employment market remains significantly gendered, with men and women tending to work in different sectors and women workers concentrated at lower levels – indeed, Nordic women are less likely to be in the top employment positions than those in the rest of Europe or the US (Sanandaji, 2016). Nevertheless, because class equality has also been a key objective of Nordic policy, the gap between rich and poor is much less than in the UK or the US, and the relative absence of women in top managerial roles is more than balanced by the much lower number who are living in poverty (Nieuwenhuis and Maldonado, 2018). Moreover, because paid working hours are generally much shorter than elsewhere, both women and men have a better balance between paid work and the rest of their life, and the pursuit of a career need not mean that parents hardly see their children.

The first decades of the twenty-first century have put the long-established principles of Nordic social democracy on the defensive, as more centrist parties have broken the social democratic parties' monopoly of power and promoted neoliberal ideas around individualism, self-responsibility, workers' right to keep more of their own earnings and a reduction in the role of the state (Wiggen, 2017; Rydgren and Meiden, 2019). Far-right and anti-immigrant parties have also grown rapidly. In this context, the continuing pursuit of gender equality cannot be taken for granted – indeed, it is increasingly being justified in neoliberal terms as a way of increasing prosperity and economic growth, rather than as an end in itself (see for example, Nordic Council of Ministers, 2018a). The parties of the extreme right are virulently anti-feminist. However, as elsewhere, they employ feminist ideas to demonise all non-western migrant men for their real or imagined rejection of gender equality and their 'barbaric' treatment of women. This makes it harder to meet the needs of migrant women, which can include protection from members of their own community (Wemrell et al., 2019). In response, some anti-racist feminists from a wide range of backgrounds are opposing right-wing ideas and actively giving voice to migrant women, arguing that their safety is under greater threat from right-wing Nordic racists than from migrant men (Sager and Mulinari, 2018). More generally, because feminist women are now well represented in decision-making bodies, they can act to defend or extend existing 'women-friendly' policies, while also understanding the diversity of women's experiences.

Feminists in other countries cannot simply import Nordic policies, but they can learn from them – from their problems as well as their successes. At the very least, they offer a practical alternative to neoliberalism and a step in a more egalitarian direction; although the Nordic gender glass may be half-empty, it is generally much fuller than elsewhere in the world (for a balanced appraisal that reaches this conclusion, see Lister, 2009; for statistical information, see Nordic Council of Ministers, 2015, 2018b).

Which way now?

There is nothing 'natural' or eternal about the capitalist economic system or its values. We saw in Chapters 5 and 6 that it has changed its nature over the years, and today it faces deep challenges. The most fundamental of these is the climate crisis. As Naomi Klein has said, tackling this requires public investment, job creation, regulation, and higher taxes, so that 'To admit that the climate crisis is real is to admit the end of the neoliberal project' (2017:8). Such an admission requires political leaders to hold their economic theories up to the light – and, if they do so, they will discover that they are so full of holes that nothing of substance is left. When this admission is combined with a shift in mindset that the COVID-19 pandemic could help inspire, some might then realise that we cannot sustain an economic system that is unable to see work unless it is paid, has no way of understanding that growth is not necessarily good and that chooses to imagine human beings as essentially competitive individuals, rather than as potentially co-operative people who are (or at the very least have been) dependent on someone else's care. At this point, some might just come up with ideas that are more in line with socialist feminist values: values which have not simply been drawn up by 'great men' while someone else cooks their dinner, but which reflect the contributions, experiences and needs of half the world's population.

These values can be promoted and defended in many ways. As I have said, I do not believe we are at a fork in the feminist road, for there are many routes to a more equal society that recognises the value of co-operation and care, and that does not reduce human society to the competitive pursuit of economic gain, regardless of the consequences. We may however be at some kind of tipping point, and different forms of feminist activism can be seen as complementary rather than in competition with each other, often with cumulative effects. The existence of multiple forms of activism also guards against the danger that those who have reached positions of power and influence are sucked into conventional ways of thinking, that they assume they have all the answers and/or that they try to act *for* other women rather than *with* them. Instead, they should remember the message of intersectional theory: that, if we focus on the most privileged women, society as a whole can stay much the same; but if our starting-point is those who are multiply deprived, then the whole system will have to change.

Beyond this, feminists will inevitably continue to disagree over their priorities, their methods and the kinds of change they want. Here it is important to see the value of difference, and not let disagreements escalate into divisions that set feminists against each other, and lose sight of more important shared goals. Above all, we need to remember that, in the words of the late Jo Cox (a young Labour woman MP, who was murdered in 2016), 'we are far more united and have far more in common with each other than things that divide us.'

Conclusions

FEMINISTS ARE EVERYWHERE – from refugee camps to parliaments, from picket lines to academic conferences and from playgrounds to the United Nations. Some are now in the corridors of power, others are shouting loudly in the streets, and many are working quietly in their homes, their workplaces, their schools and their neighbourhoods. Digital technology means that feminist actions and ideas in one part of the world can spread rapidly, and that feminists can draw inspiration and strength from one another; it also means that many women can easily access a ready-made feminist language that makes sense of their own experiences, helps them recognise the oppressive nature of some forms of male behaviour, and enables them to recognise and challenge apparently unrelated aspects of male power.

Although feminists certainly do not rule the world, feminism has become a powerful political force, one that is increasingly difficult for political and economic leaders to ignore. At the same time, most of these leaders recognise only the most limited forms of feminism, and, although they may support some feminist goals, they will do so only if they think this will be profitable and not too disruptive.

I have argued throughout this book that feminist aims should be broad and inclusive, and that they need to go far beyond the pursuit of equality on terms that men have already set. These existing terms reflect the assumptions of the man-made economic, social and political theories that dominate public discussion; policies based upon them cannot deliver what most feminists want. These policies are also in danger of destroying the planet.

The long-term goal of inclusive feminism should be a world that understands both the diversity of human experiences and the underlying human need for care. In a more inclusive version of an old socialist ideal, such a world would be governed by the principle of 'from each according to their ability; to each according to their needs'.

Meanwhile, the steps we take on this journey are as important as the final destination, and they should always be treated as such. They will often be taken in alliance with socialist men; they must always include the most disadvantaged women; they will never be taken entirely alone.

References

WHEN TWO DATES are given for a publication, the earlier refers to the original edition; page references are always to the later edition.

Abbey, R. (2011) *The Return of Feminist Liberalism* (Durham: Acumen).

Abbey, R. (ed.) (2013) *Feminist Interpretations of John Rawls* (Durham: The Pennsylvania University Press).

Addati, L., U. Cattaneo, V. Esquival and I. Valarino (2018) *Care Work and Care Jobs for the Future of Decent Work* (Geneva: International Labour Office).

Adewunmi, B. (2012) 'What the Girls spat on Twitter tells us about feminism', *Guardian*, 8 October.

Adichie, C.N. (2014) *We Should All Be Feminists* (London: Fourth Estate).

Adichie, C.N. (2018) 'This could be the beginning of a revolution', interviewed by L. Allardice, *Guardian*, 28 April.

Ahmed, S. (2015) 'Sexism – A Problem with a Name', *New Formations*, 86, 3–13.

Ainsworth, C. (2015) 'Sex Redefined', *Nature News*, 518:7539, 288–91.

Alcoff, L. (2007) 'Fraser on Redistribution, Recognition, and Identity', *European Journal of Political Theory*, 6:3, 255–65.

All Party Parliamentary Group on Sex Equality (2018) *Invisible Women* (London: Young Women's Trust and The Fawcett Society).

Alston, P. (2018) *Statement on Visit to the United Kingdom* (United Nations Human Rights, Office of the High Commissioner). www.ohchr.org/EN/NewsEvents/Pages/DisplayNews.aspx?NewsID=23881&LangID=E, accessed 30 January 2020.

Arruzza, C. (2013) *Dangerous Liaisons: The Marriages and Divorces of Marxism and Feminism* (London: The Merlin Press).

References

Arruzza, C., T. Bhattacharya and N. Fraser (2018) 'Notes for a Feminist Manifesto', *New Left Review*, 114, 113–34.

Arruzza, C., T. Bhattacharya and N. Fraser (2019) *Feminism for the 99%* (London: Verso).

Aslaksen, J. and C. Koren (2014) 'Reflections on Unpaid Household Work, Economic Growth, and Consumption Possibilities', in M. Bjornholt and A. McKay (eds), *Counting on Marilyn Waring: New Advances in Feminist Economics*, second edition (Bradford, Ont.: Demeter Press).

Asthana, A. (2018) 'Harriet Harman hails the rise of "Tory feminist" MPs', *Guardian*, 6 March.

Ball, P. (2020) 'Coronavirus hits men harder. Here's what scientists know about it', *Guardian*, 17 April.

Barbagallo, C. (2020) interviewed by Helen Chapman 'International Women's Day: Why we strike'. Verso blog, 6 March, www.versobooks.com/blogs/4584-international-women-s-day-why-we-strike, accessed 15 April 2020.

Barker, M.-J. and A. Iantaffi (2019) *Life Isn't Binary: On Being Both, Beyond, and In-Between* (London and Philadelphia: Jessica Kingsley Publishers).

Bashevkin, S. (2000) 'From Tough Times to Better Times: Feminism, Public Policy, and New Labour Politics in Britain', *International Political Science Review*, 21:4, 407–24.

Bassel, L. and A. Emejulu (2017) *Minority Women and Austerity: Survival and Resistance in France and Britain* (Bristol: Policy Press).

Bassel, L. and A. Emejulu (2019) 'The Whitewashing of Austerity Britain', *Red Pepper*, Spring, 22–4.

Bates, L. (2014) *Everyday Sexism* (London: Simon and Schuster).

BBC Reality Fact Check (2018) 'How many transgender inmates are there?', *BBC News*, 13 August.

Beard, M. (2017) *Women and Power: A Manifesto* (London: Profile Books Ltd).

Bebel, A. (1904) *Woman under Socialism*, translated by D. de Leon (New York: New York Labour Press).

Bell, D. and R. Klein (eds) (1996) *Radically Speaking: Feminism Reclaimed* (London: Zed Books).

Berthezène, C. and J. Gottlieb (eds) (2018) *Rethinking Right-Wing Women: Gender and the Conservative Party, 1880s to the Present* (Manchester: Manchester University Press).

Bhandar, B. and D. da Silva (2013) 'White Feminist Fatigue Syndrome: A Reply to Nancy Fraser', *Critical Legal Thinking*, 21 October. http://criticallegalthinking.com, accessed 29 December 2019.

Bhattacharya, T. (2015) 'How Not to Skip Class: Social Reproduction of Labor and the Global Working Class', *Viewpoint Magazine*, 31 October. www.viewpointmag. com, accessed 8 January 2020.

Bhattacharya, T. (2017) 'Introduction: Mapping Social Reproduction Theory', in T. Bhattacharya (ed.), *Social Reproduction Theory* (London: Pluto Press).

Bhattacharya, T. (ed.) (2017) *Social Reproduction Theory* (London: Pluto Press).

Bhattacharya, T. (2020) 'Social Reproduction and the Pandemic', interviewed by Sarah Jaffe, *Dissent*, 2 April. www.dissentmagazine.org/online, accessed 15 April 2020.

Bienkov, A. (2019) 'Boris Johnson called gay men "tank-topped bumboys" and black people "piccaninnies" with "watermelon smiles"', *Business Insider*, 22 November. www.businessinsider.com, accessed 13 April 2020.

Bilge, S. (2013) 'Intersectionality Undone: Saving Intersectionality from Feminist Intersectionality Studies', *Du Bois Review*, 10:2, 405–24.

Bindel, J. (2004) 'Gender benders, beware', *Guardian*, 31 January.

Bindel, J. (2007) 'My trans mission', *Guardian*, 1 October.

Bittman, M. (2004) 'Parenting and Employment: What Time-Use Surveys Show', in N. Folbre and M. Bittman (eds), *Family Time: The Social Organization of Childcare* (London and New York: Routledge).

Bjornholt, M. and A. McKay (eds) *Counting on Marilyn Waring: New Advances in Feminist Economics*, second edition (Bradford, Ont.: Demeter Press).

Black Women's Blueprint (2011/2016) 'An Open Letter from Black Women to the Slutwalk', *Gender and Society*, 30:1, 9–13.

Blumberg, R. (1991) *Gender, Family and Economy: The Triple Overlap* (London: Sage Publications).

Booth, R. (2020) 'Low-paid women in UK at "high risk" of coronavirus exposure', *Guardian*, 29 March.

Booth, R. and P. Butler (2018) 'UK austerity has inflicted "great misery" on citizens, UN says', *Guardian*, 16 November.

Boyd, E. (2002) '"Being there." Mothers who Stay at Home, Gender and Time', *Women's Studies International Forum*, 25:4, 463–70.

Brownmiller, S. (1977) *Against Our Will* (Harmondsworth: Penguin).

Bryson, V. (2000) 'Perspectives on Gender Equality: Challenging the Terms of Debate', in J. Browne (ed.), *The Future of Gender* (Cambridge: Cambridge University Press).

Bryson, V. (2004) 'Marxism and Feminism: Can the "unhappy marriage" Be Saved?', *Journal of Political Ideologies*, 9:1, 13–30.

Bryson, V. (2007) *Gender and the Politics of Time* (Bristol: The Policy Press).

Bryson, V. (2008) 'Time-Use Studies: A Potentially Feminist Tool?', *International Feminist Journal of Politics*, 10:2, 135–53.

References

Bryson, V. (2011) 'Sexuality: The Contradictions of Love and Work', in A. Jonasdottir, V. Bryson and K. Jones (eds), *Sexuality, Gender and Power: Intersectional and Transnational Perspectives* (New York and Abingdon: Routledge).

Bryson, V. (2016) *Feminist Political Theory* (London: Palgrave).

Bryson, V. and R. Deery, (2011) 'Social Justice and Time: The Impact of Public Sector Reform on the Work of Midwives in the National Health Service', in V. Bryson and P. Fisher (eds), *Redefining Social Justice: New Labour, Rhetoric and Reality* (Manchester: Manchester University Press).

Bryson, V. and P. Fisher (eds) (2011) *Redefining Social Justice: New Labour, Rhetoric and Reality* (Manchester: Manchester University Press).

Bryson, V. and T. Heppell (2010) 'Conservatism and Feminism: The Case of the British Conservative Party', *Journal of Political Ideologies*, 15:1, 31–50.

Burchill, J. (2014) 'Don't you dare tell me to check my privilege', *Spectator*, 22 February.

Butler, J. (1990) *Gender Trouble: Feminism and the Subversion of Identity* (London: Routledge).

Butler, J. (1998) 'Merely Cultural', *New Left Review*, 227:33–44.

Butler, J. (2015) *Notes Toward a Performative Theory of Assembly* (Cambridge, Mass.: Harvard University Press).

Butterworth, B. (2020) 'Labour leadership election: Rebecca Long-Bailey, Lisa Nandy and Keir Starmer heckled as they back trans rights reforms', *Independent*, 20 February.

Callinicos, A. (2003) *An Anti-Capitalist Manifesto* (Cambridge: Polity Press).

Campbell, B. (1987) *The Iron Ladies. Why Do Women Vote Tory?* (Virago: London).

Campbell, B. (2013) *End of Equality: The Only Way Is Women's Liberation* (London: Seagull Books).

Carastathis, A. (2016) *Intersectionality: Origins, Contestations, Horizons* (Lincoln and London: University of Nebraska Press).

Carbin, M. and S. Edenheim (2013) 'The Intersectional Turn In Feminist Theory: A Dream of a Common Language?', *European Journal of Women's Studies*, 20:3, 233–48.

Carver, T. (1996) *Gender Is Not a Synonym for Women* (Boulder, Col.: Lynne Rienner Publishers, Inc.).

Chandler, S. (2019) 'Can we take back intersectionality?', *gal-dem*, 12 February. https//gal.dem.com, accessed 2 January 2020.

Childs, S. and R. Campbell (2018) 'The (feminised) Conservative Party', in C. Berthezène and J. Gottlieb (eds), *Rethinking Right-Wing Women: Gender and the Conservative Party, 1880s to the Present* (Manchester: Manchester University Press).

Christie, B. (2015) 'Feminists never have sex, and hate men opening doors for them, even into other dimensions', *Guardian*, 22 June.

Clinton, H. (1995) *Remarks to the UN 4th World Conference on Women*. americanrhetoric.com/speeches/hillaryclintonbeijingspeech.htm, accessed 7 January 2020.

Cockburn, C. (2015) 'Transversal Politics: A Practice of Peace', *Pacifist Feminism*, 22. www.icip-perlapau.cat/numero22/articles_centrals/article_central_1, accessed 7 July 2020.

Cohen, G. (1978) *Karl Marx's Theory of History: A Defence* (Oxford: Oxford University Press).

Colley, H. (2015) 'Labour-Power', in S. Mojab (ed.), *Marxism and Feminism* (London: Zed Books).

Collins, P. (1990/2000) *Black Feminist Thought* (New York and London: Routledge).

Collins, P. (1998) *Fighting Word: Black Women and the Search for Justice* (Minneapolis: University of Minnesota Press).

Collins, P. and S. Bilge (2016) *Intersectionality* (Cambridge: Polity Press).

Combahee River Collective (1983/2015) 'The Combahee River Collective Statement' (1977), in C. Moraga and G. Anzaldua (eds), *This Bridge Called My Back: Writings by Radical Women of Color* (Albany: State University of New York Press).

Connell, R. (2012) 'Transsexual Women and Feminist Thought: Toward New Understanding and New Politics', *Signs*, 37:4, 857–81.

Conway, D. (1998) *Free Market Feminism* (London: Institute for Economic Affairs).

Coole, D. (1993) *Women in Political Theory* (London: Harvester Wheatsheaf).

Cooper, J. (1988) *A Voice from the South*, with an 'Introduction' by M.H. Washington (New York and Oxford: Oxford University Press).

Cosslett, R. and H. Baxter (2012) 'In defense of Caitlin Moran and populist feminism', *New Statesman*, 22 October.

Coudriet, C. (2019 'These billionaires want the ultra-wealthy to pay more in taxes', *Forbes*, 15 October. www.forbes.com/sites/cartercoudriet/2019/10/15/billionaires-more-taxes-gates-buffett-bloomberg/#1af68ca77792, accessed 7 July 2020.

Credit Suisse (2018) *Global Wealth Report: 2018*. www.credit-suisse.com/about-us-news/en/articles/news-and-expertise/global-wealth-report-2018-us-and-china-in-the-lead-201810.html, accessed 7 January 2020.

Crenshaw, K. (1989/1998) 'Demarginalizing the Intersection of Race and Sex: A Black Feminist Critique of Antidiscrimination Doctrine, Feminist Theory, and Antiracist Politics', in A. Phillips (ed.), *Feminism and Politics* (Oxford: Oxford University Press).

Crenshaw, K. (1991) 'Mapping the Margins: Intersectionality, Identity Politics, and Violence Against Women of Color', *Stanford Law Review*, 43:6, 1241–99.

References

Crenshaw, K. (2011) 'Postscript', in H. Lutz, M. Vivar and L. Supik L. (eds), *Framing Intersectionality: Debates on a Multi-Faceted Concept in Gender Studies* (Farnham: Ashgate).

Crenshaw, K. (2016) 'The urgency of intersectionality', *TED Talk*, 14 November. www.ted.com/talks/kimberle_crenshaw_the_urgency_of_intersectionality?language=en, accessed 2 January 2020.

Crenshaw, K. (2018) 'What is intersectionality?', *Talk to National Association of Independent Schools*, 22 June. www.youtube.com/watch?v=ViDtnfQ9FHc, accessed 2 January 2020.

Criado-Perez, C. (2019) *Invisible Women: Exposing Data Bias in a World Designed for Men* (London: Chatto and Windus).

Crispin, J. (2017) *Why I Am Not a Feminist: A Feminist Manifesto* (London: Melville House).

Culhane, L. and A. Bazeley (2019) *Gender Stereotypes in Early Childhood – A Literature Review* (London: Fawcett Society). www.fawcettsociety.org.uk, accessed 29 December 2019.

Dahlgreen, W. (2016) 'Only 2% of young men feel completely masculine', *YouGov*, 13 May. www.yougov.co.uk, accessed 6 January 2020.

Dalla Costa, M. (1973) *The Power of Women and the Subversion of the Community* (Bristol: Falling Wall Press).

Daly, M. (1973) *Beyond God the Father* (Boston: Beacon Press).

Datta, K., C. Mcllwaine, Y. Evans, J. Herbert, J. May and J. Wills (2006) *Work, Care and Life among Low-Paid Migrant Workers in London: Towards a Migrant Ethic of Care* (London: Department of Geography, Queen Mary, University of London).

Davidman, S. (2010) 'Beyond Borders: Lived Experiences of Atypically Gendered Transsexual People', in S. Hines and T. Sanger (eds), *Transgender Identities* (New York and London: Routledge).

Davidson, G. (2019) 'Hundreds of women forced to claim "rape clause" exemption to receive child tax credits', *Scotsman*, 31 July.

Davis, A. (1982/1990) *Women, Race and Class* (London: Women's Press).

Davis, G. (2015) *Contesting Intersex: The Dubious Diagnosis* (New York and London: New York University Press).

Davis, H.F. (2017) *Beyond Trans. Does Gender Matter?* (New York: New York University Press).

Dawson, J. (2017) *The Gender Games: The Problem with Men and Women … From Someone Who Has Been Both* (London: Two Roads).

De Beauvoir, S. (1949/1972) *The Second Sex* (Harmondsworth: Penguin).

Diangelo, R. (2018) *White Fragility: Why It's so Hard for White People to Talk about Racism* (Boston: Beacon Press).

Dobel, R., with J. Walsh (2014) 'Narrative Trumps Numbers. Marilyn Waring in the World', in M. Bjornholt and A. McKay (eds), *Counting on Marilyn Waring: New Advances in Feminist Economics*, second edition (Bradford, Ont.: Demeter Press).

Donegan, M. (2018) '#MeToo and the rift within feminism', The Long Read, *Guardian*, 11 May.

Doward, J. (2019) 'Working mothers "up to 4 times more stressed"', *Observer*, 27 January.

Dreyfus, E. (2018) 'Global Internet Access Is Even Worse Than Dire Predictions Suggest'. *Wired*, www.wired.com, accessed 22 January.

Dzodan, F. (2011) 'My feminism will be intersectional or it will be bullshit', *tigerbeatdown*, 10 October. http://tigerbeatdown.com/2011/10/10/my-feminism-will-be-intersectional-or-it-will-be-bullshit, accessed 2 January 2020.

Eddo-Lodge, R. (2017) *Why I'm No Longer Talking to White People about Race* (London: Bloomsbury Circus).

EHRC (Equalities and Human Rights Commission) (2017) *Sexual Harassment and the Law: Guidance for Employers*. www.equalityhumanrights.com/en/publication-download/sexual-harassment-and-law-guidance-employers, accessed 29 December 2019.

EHRC (Equalities and Human Rights Commission) (2019) *Women's Rights and Gender Equality in 2018, Update Report*. www.equalityhumanrights.com/en/publication-download/womens-rights-and-gender-equality-2018-update-report, accessed 29 December 2019.

Eisenstein, H. (2009) *Feminism Seduced: How Global Elites Use Women's Labor and Ideas to Exploit the World* (Boulder, Colo.: Paradigm Publishers).

Eisenstein, H. (2017) 'Hegemonic Feminism, Neoliberalism and Womenomics: "Empowerment" instead of Liberation?', *New Formations*, 91, 35–49.

Eisenstein, H. (2018) 'Querying Intersectionality', *Science and Society*, 82:2, 248–61.

Eliot, P. (2010) *Debates in Transgender, Queer, and Feminist Theory* (Farnham: Ashgate).

Ellingsaeter, A. (2014) 'Nordic Earner-Carer Models – Why Stability and Instability?', *Journal of Social Policy*, 43:3, 555–74.

Elliott, L. (2018) 'Inequality gap widens as 42 people hold same wealth as 3.7bn poorest', *Guardian*, 22 January.

Elliott, L. (2019) 'World's 26 richest people own as much as poorest 50%, says Oxfam', *Guardian*, 21 January.

Engels, F. (1884/1978) *The Origin of the Family: Private Property and the State* (Peking: Foreign Languages Press).

Enloe, C. (2017) *The Big Push: Exposing and Challenging the Persistence of Patriarchy* (Oxford: Myriad Editions).

Eschle, C. and B. Maiguashca (2014) 'Reclaiming Feminist Futures: Co-opted Progressive Politics in a Neoliberal Age', *Political Studies*, 62:3, 634–51.

Eschle, C. and B. Maiguashca (2018) 'Theorising Feminist Organising in and against Neoliberalism: Beyond Co-Optation and Resistance?', *European Journal of Politics and Gender*, 1:2, 223–39.

Esping-Anderson, G. (1990) *The Three Worlds of Welfare Capitalism* (Cambridge: Polity Press).

Evans, Elizabeth (2015) *The Politics of Third Wave Feminisms: Neoliberalism, Intersectionality, and the State in Britain and the US* (Basingstoke: Palgrave Macmillan).

Fair Play for Women (2018) *Supporting Women in Domestic and Sexual Violence Services: Giving a Voice to Silenced Women: Evidence from Professionals and Survivors*. www.fairplayforwomen.com, accessed 6 January 2020.

Farris, S. (2017) *In the Name of Women's Rights: The Rise of Femonationalism* (Durham, NC: Duke University Press).

Farris, S. and C. Rottenberg (2017) 'Introduction: Righting Feminism', *New Formations*, 91, 5–15.

Fawcett Society (2018a) *#MeToo One Year On – What's Changed?*, October. www.fawcettsociety.org.uk/metoo-one-year, accessed 29 December 2019.

Fawcett Society (2018b) *Sex Discrimination Law Review: Final Report*, 23 January. www.fawcettsociety.org.uk/sex-discrimination-law-review-final-report, accessed 3 January 2020.

Fawcett Society (2019) *Q&A on Sex, Gender and Gender Identity*. www.fawcettsociety.org.uk, accessed 6 January 2020.

Fawcett Society (2020) *Coronavirus: Joint Call for Women's Visibility in UK Response*. www.fawcettsociety.org.uk/news/coronavirus-joint-call-womens-visibility-uk-response, accessed 20 April 2020.

Fawcett Society (undated) *Make Equality Law Fit for the Twenty First Century*. www.fawcettsociety.org.uk/make-equality-law-21st-century, accessed 3 January 2020.

Featherstone, L. (ed.) (2016) *False Choices: The Faux Feminism of Hillary Rodham Clinton* (London and Brooklyn: Verso).

Featherstone, L. and A. Frost (2016) 'Introduction', in L. Featherstone (ed.), *False Choices: The Faux Feminism of Hillary Rodham Clinton* (London and Brooklyn: Verso).

Federici, S. (2012) *Revolution at Point Zeto: Housework, Reproduction, and Feminist Struggle* (Oakland: PM Press).

Ferguson, A. (1989) *Blood at the Root* (London: Pandora Press).

Ferguson, D. (2017) 'A thousand nurseries close as free childcare scheme falters', *Guardian*, 18 November.

Fiani, C. and H. Han (2019) 'Navigating Identity: Experiences of Binary and Non-Binary Transgender and Gender Non-Conforming (TGNC) Adults', *International Journal of Transgenderism*, 20:2–3, 181–194.

Fine, C. (2017) *Testosterone Rex: Unmaking the Myths of Our Gendered Minds* (London: Icon Books).

Finlayson, L., K. Jenkins and R. Worsdale (2018) '"I'm not transphobic, but …":
A Feminist Case against the Feminist Case against Trans Inclusivity', 17 October. www.versobooks.com/blogs/4090-i-m-not-transphobic-but-a-feminist-case-agai nst-the-feminist-case-against-trans-inclusivity, accessed 6 January 2020.

Firestone, S. (1970/1979) *The Dialectic of Sex* (London: Women's Press).

Foley, B. (2018) 'Intersectionality: A Marxist Critique', *Science and Society*, 82:2, 269–75.

Foner, P. (1984) *Clara Zetkin: Selected Writings* (New York: International Publishers).

Fraser, N. (1998) 'Heterosexism, Misrecognition and Capitalism: A Response to Judith Butler', *New Left Review*, 228, 140–9.

Fraser, N. (2000) 'Rethinking Recognition' *New Left Review*, 3, 107–20.

Fraser, N. (2014) 'Behind Marx's Hidden Abode: For an Expanded Conception of Capitalism', *New Left Review*, 86, 55–72.

Fraser, N. (2015) 'A feminism where "lean in" means leaning on others', interviewed by Gary Gutting, *New Yorker*, 15 October.

Fraser, N. (2016) 'Contradictions of Capital and Care', *New Left Review*, 100, 99–117.

Fraser, N. (2020) 'Taking Care of Each Other Is Essential Work', interview by C. Chang, *Vice*, www.vice.com/en_us/article/jge39g/taking-care-of-each-other-is-essential-work, accessed 15 April 2020.

Fraser, N. and L. Featherstone (2020) 'Why Bernie is the true feminist choice', *Jacobin*, 10 February.

Fredman, S. (2016) *Intersectional Discrimination in EU Gender Equality and Non-Discrimination Law* (Brussels: European Commission).

Freedman, H. (2019) 'Sport can help clarify the trans debate', *Guardian*, 6 March.

Friedan, B. (1963/1986) *The Feminine Mystique* (Harmondsworth: Penguin Books).

Friedman, M., C. Rice and J. Rinaldi (2020) *Thickening Fat: Fat Bodies, Intersectionality and Social Justice* (Abingdon: Routledge).

Gender Critical Greens (2016) *Gender Is Not an Identity, It Is a Tool of Patriarchy: A Feminist View of Gender-Identity Politics*, 31 August. https://gendercriticalgreens.wordpress.com.

References

Ghodsee, K. (2018) *Why Women Have Better Sex under Socialism and Other Arguments for Economic Independence* (London: Bodley Head).

Gibbons, K. (2019) 'Gay groups clash over "homophobic policies"', *Times*, 26 October.

Gibbs, S. (2015) 'Women less likely to be shown ads for high-paid jobs on Google, study shows', *Guardian*, 8 July.

Giddings, P. (1984) *When and Where I Enter: The Impact of Black Women on Race and Sex in America* (New York: William Morrow and Company, Inc.).

Giminez, M. (2018) 'Intersectionality: Marxist Critical Observations', *Science and Society*, 82:2, 261–9.

Government Equalities Office (2018) *Trans People in the UK*. https://assets.publishing.service.gov.uk, accessed 6 January 2020.

Government Equalities Office (2019) *National LGBT Survey: Summary Report*. www.gov.uk/government/publications/national-lgbt-survey-summary-report/national-lgbt-survey-summary-report, accessed 6 January 2020.

Greed, C. (2019) 'Join the Queue: Including Women's Toilet Need in Public Space', *Sociological Review*, 67:4, 908–96.

Greer, G. (2018) *On Rape* (London: Bloomsbury Publishing).

Grierson, J. (2018) 'Hostile environment: anatomy of a policy disaster', *Guardian*, 27 August.

Griffith, E. (1984) *In Her Own Right: The Life of Elizabeth Cady Stanton* (New York and Oxford: Oxford University Press).

Guardian staff and Reuters (2019) 'EU investigating Nike's tax status in the Netherlands', *Guardian*, 10 January.

Guest Author (2019) 'McKinnon, Manchester and Bury Black Pudding', *Fair Play for Women*, 22 October. https://fairplayforwomen.com/mckinnon, accessed 6 January 2020.

Guobadia, O. (2018) 'Kimberlé Crenshaw and Lady Phyll talk intersectionality, solidarity, and self-care', 31 August. *Them.Us*, www.them.us/story/kimberle-crenshaw-lady-phyll-intersectionality, accessed 2 January 2020.

Halberstam, J. (2018) *Trans*A Quick and Quirky Account of Gender Variability* (Oakland, Calif.: University of California Press).

Hartmann, H. (1986) 'The Unhappy Marriage of Marxism and Feminism: Towards a More Progressive Union', in L. Sargent (ed.), *The Unhappy Marriage of Marxism and Feminism: A Debate on Class and Patriarchy* (London: Pluto Press).

Harvey, D. (2018) *Marx, Capital and the Madness of Economic Reason* (Oxford: Oxford University Press).

Haskel, J. and Westlake, S. (2017) *Capitalism without Capital: The Rise of the Intangible Economy* (Princeton: Princeton University Press).

Helmore, E. (2018) 'Nike hit with lawsuit from four women who allege gender discrimination', *Guardian*, 10 August.

Hepple, B. (2010) 'The New Single Equality Act in Britain', *Equal Rights Review*, 5, 11–24.

Hicks, M. (2018) 'Why tech's gender problem is nothing new', *Guardian*, 12 October.

Hines, S. (2013) *Gender Diversity, Recognition and Citizenship* (Basingstoke and New York: Palgrave Macmillan).

Hines, S. (2018) *Is Gender Fluid? A Primer for the Twenty First Century* (London: Thomas and Hudson).

Hines, S. (2019) 'The feminist frontier: on trans and feminism', *Journal of Gender Studies*, 28:2, 147–57.

Hobsbawm, E. (2011) *How to Change the World* (New Haven and London: Yale University Press).

hooks, b. (1981) *Ain't I a Woman: Black Women and Feminism* (Boston: South End Press).

hooks, b. (1984) *Feminist Theory: From Margin to Center* (Boston, Mass.: South End Press).

hooks, b. (2013) 'Dig Deep. Beyond Lean In', *The Feminist Wire*, 28 October. https://thefeministwire.com/2013/10/17973, accessed 7 January 2020.

Horowitz, D. (1998) *Betty Friedan and the Making of* The Feminine Mystique (Amherst: University of Massachusetts Press).

Howard League for Penal Reform (2014) *Commission on Sex in Prison. Coercive Sex in Prison. Briefing Paper 3* (London; Howard League).

Hull, G., P. Scott and B. Smith (eds) (1982) *All the Women Are White, All the Blacks Are Men, But Some of Us Are Brave* (New York: Feminist Press).

Hyman, C. (2019) 'One in 50 prisoners identifies as transgender amid concerns inmates are attempting to secure prison perks', *Telegraph*, 9 July.

International Labour Organization (undated) *Small Change, Big Changes: Women and Microfinance* (Geneva: International Labour Office). www.ilo.org/gender, accessed 7 January 2020.

Intersex Society of North America (undated) 'What Is Intersex?'. https://isna.org/faq/what_is_intersex, accessed 29 December 2019.

Iqbal, N. (2017) 'Munroe Bergdorf on the L'Oréal racism row', *Guardian*, 4 September.

Ishkanian, A. and A. Saavedra (2019) 'The Politics and Practices of Intersectional Prefiguration in Social Movements: The Case of Sisters Uncut', *Sociological Review*, 67:5, 985–1001.

Jeffreys, S. (2014a) *Gender Hurts: A Feminist Analysis of the Politics of Transgenderism* (London and New York: Routledge).

References

Jeffreys, S. (2014b) 'The Politics of the Toilet: A Feminist Response to the Campaign to "Degender" a Women's Space', *Women's Studies International Forum*, 45, 42–51.

Kantola, J. and E. Lombardo (2017) 'Gender and the Politics of the Econ Crisis in Europe', in J. Kantola and E. Lombardo (eds), *Gender and the Economic Crisis in Europe: Politics, Institutions and Intersectionality* (Basingstoke: Palgrave Macmillan).

Keith, T. (2019) 'White House and Ivanka Trump propose new spending on child care', *Nation Public Radio*, 10 March. www.npr.org/2019/03/10/701870547/exclusive-white-house-and-ivanka-trump-propose-new-spending-on-child-care, accessed 30 January 2020.

Kelly, J. (2018) 'Saying you're a feminist is not enough', interviewed by D. Aitkenhead, *Guardian*, 26 January.

Kelly, M. (2016) *Settle for More* (New York: Harper Collins).

Kennedy, M. (2017) 'Jenni Murray: trans women shouldn't call themselves "real women"', *Guardian*, 5 March.

Khan, M. (ed.) (2019) *It's Not About the Burqa: Muslim Women on Faith, Feminism, Sexuality and Race* (London: Picador).

Kingston, S. and T. Thomas (2019) 'No Model in Practice: A "Nordic Model" to Respond to Prostitution?', *Crime, Law and Social Change*, 71, 423–39.

Klein, N. (2007) *The Shock Doctrine* (London: Allen Lane).

Klein, N. (2017) *No Is Not Enough: Defeating the New Shock Politics* (London: Penguin).

Klein, N. (2020) 'Coronavirus capitalism – and how to end it', *Intercept*, 16 March. https://theintercept.com/2020/03/16/coronavirus-capitalism, accessed 7 July 2020.

Knox, T., L. Anderson and A. Heather (2019) 'Transwomen in elite women's sport – clarifying the nuances of our approach', posted on the *Journal of Medical Ethics Blog*, 12 August. https://blogs.bmj.com/medical-ethics/2019/08/12/transwomen-in-elite-womens-sport-clarifying-the-nuances-of-our-approach/, accessed 7 July 2020.

Krook, M. (2019) 'Global Feminist Collaborations and the Concept of Violence Against Women in Politics', *Journal of International Affairs*, 72:2, 77–94.

Krotoski, A. (2020) *The Digital Human. Series 19: Coercion*, BBC Radio 4, 30 March.

Lansley, S. (2020) 'The case for a universal basic income is stronger than ever', *Prospect*, 16 April. www.prospectmagazine.co.uk, accessed 19 April 2020.

Laws, I. (2013) 'Better Sex Education for Children Is Needed to Combat Dangers of Pornography', *British Medical Journal*, 23 September. https://doi.org/10.1136/bmj.f5764.

Lenin, V. (1907/1977) *On the Emancipation of Women* (Moscow: Progress Publishers).

Lester, C.N. (2017) *Trans Like Me: Conversations for All of Us* (New York: Seal Press).

Lewis, G. (2013) 'Unsafe Travel: Experiencing Intersectionality and Feminist Displacements', *Signs*, 38:4, 869–92.

Lewis, H. (2014) 'The uses and abuses of intersectionality', *New Statesman*, 20 February.

Lewis, H. (2016) *The Politics of Everybody: Feminism, Queer Theory and Marxism at the Intersection* (London: Zed Books).

Liberty (ed.) (2018) 'A Guide to the Hostile Environment'. www.libertyhumanrights. or.uk, accessed 2 January 2020.

Lister, R. (2003) *Citizenship. Feminist Perspectives* (Basingstoke: Macmillan).

Lister, R. (2009) 'A Nordic Nirvana?', *Social Politics: International Studies in Gender, State and Society*, 16:2, 342–78.

Loewenstein, A. (2013) *Profits of Doom: How Vulture Capitalism Is Swallowing the World* (Melbourne: Melbourne University Press).

Lombardo, E. and M. Verloo (2009) 'Institutionalizing Intersectionality in the European Union?', *International Feminist Journal of Politics*, 11:14, 478–95.

Lorde, A. (1984) *Sister Outsider: Essays and Speeches* (New York: Ten Speed Press).

Lovenduski, J. (2019) 'Feminist Reflections on Representative Democracy', in A. Gamble and T. Wright (eds), *Rethinking Democracy* (Chichester: John Wiley).

Lugones, M. (2010) 'Toward a Decolonial Feminism', *Hypatia*, 25:4, 742–59.

Lynch, K., J. Baker and M. Lyons (2009) *Affective Equality: Love, Care and Injustice* (Basingstoke: Palgrave Macmillan).

Mac, J. and M. Smith (2018) *Revolting Prostitutes: The Fight for Sex Workers' Rights* (London: Verso).

Mackay, F. (2015) *Radical Feminism. Feminist Activism in Movement* (Basingstoke: Palgrave Macmillan).

Magnusson, J. (2015) 'Financialization', in S. Mojab (ed.), *Marxism and Feminism* (London: Zed Books).

Malos, E. (1980) *The Politics of Housework* (London: Allison and Busby Ltd).

Mantilla, K. (2015) *Gender Talking: How Misogyny Went Viral* (Santa Barbara, Calif.: Praeger).

Marçal, K. (2015) *Who Cooked Adam Smith's Dinner?* (New York: Pegasus Books Ltd).

Marx, K. and F. Engels (1848/1967) *Manifesto of the Communist Party* (London: Allen and Unwin).

Mason, R. (2015) 'Theresa May "allowed state-sanctioned abuse of women" at Yarl's Wood', *Guardian*, 3 March.

Mason, R. (2019) 'Leadership rivals line up to declare themselves feminists', *Guardian*, 31 May.

May, T. (2018) 'Our bill will protect women from economic abuse too', *Guardian*, 8 March.

References

Mazzucato, M. (2020) 'The Covid-19 crisis is a chance to do capitalism differently', *Guardian*, 18 March.

McBee, T.P. (2018) *Amateur. A Reckoning with Gender, Identity and Masculinity* (Edinburgh: Canongate).

McBride (2018) *Tomorrow Will Be Different* (New York: Penguin).

McCall, B. (2019) 'Five staff resign at leading UK transgender youth clinic', *Medscape*, 12 April. www.medscape.com/viewarticle/911736, accessed 6 January 2020.

McDuffie, E. (2011) *Sojourning for Freedom: Black Women, American Communism, and the Making of Black Left Feminism* (Durham, NC: Duke University Press).

McRobbie, A. (2009) *The Aftermath of Feminism: Gender, Culture and Social Change* (London: Sage).

McVeigh, K. (2017) 'Cambodian female workers in Nike, Asics and Puma factories suffer mass faintings', *Guardian*, 25 June.

Mendes, K. (2015) *Slutwalk. Feminism, Activism and Media* (Basingstoke: Palgrave Macmillan).

Menon. N. (2012) *Seeing like a Feminist* (New Delhi: Zabaan and Penguin Books India).

Mies, M. (1998) *Capitalism and Accumulation on a World Scale: Women in the International Division of Labour* (London and New York: Zed Books).

Mill, J.S. (1869/1983) *The Subjection of Women* (London: Virago).

Millett, K. (1970/1985) *Sexual Politics* (London: Virago).

Mitchell, H. (1977) *The Hard Way Up* (London: Virago).

Mlambo-Ngcuka, P. (2018) 'Forward', in UN Women, *Annual Report, 2017–18*. http://cpnn-world.org/new/?p=13224, accessed 28 December 2019.

Moalem, S. (2020) *The Better Half: On the Genetic Superiority of Women* (New York: Farrar, Strauss and Giroux).

Moeller, K. (2018) *The Gender Effect: Capitalism, Feminism and the Corporate Politics of Development* (Oakland: University of California Press).

Mojab, S. (2015) 'Introduction: Marxism and Feminism', in S. Mojab (ed.), *Marxism and Feminism* (London: Zed Books).

Mojab, S. (ed.) (2015) *Marxism and Feminism* (London: Zed Books).

Monbiot, G. (2016) 'Neoliberalism: the ideology at the heart of all our problems', *Guardian*, 15 April.

Monbiot, G. (2017) 'Neoliberalism: the deep story that lies behind Donald Trump's triumph', *Guardian*, 14 November.

Monro, S. (2005) *Gender Politics* (London: Pluto Press).

Moraga, C. and G. Anzaldua (eds) (1983/2015) *This Bridge Called My Back: Writings by Radical Women of Color* (Albany: State University of New York Press).

Morgan, R. (1984) *Sisterhood Is Global. The International Women's Movement Anthology* (Harmondsworth: Penguin).

Murphy, M. (2013) 'The Nordic model is the only model that actually works', *Feminist Current*, 27 March. www.feministcurrent.com/2013/03/27/the-nordic-model-is-the-only-model-that-actually-works-duh-says-sweden, accessed 9 July 2020.

Murphy, S. (2019) 'Tesco, Mothercare and M&S use factory paying workers 35p an hour', *Guardian*, 21 January.

NAACP (2019) *Criminal Justice Fact Sheet.* www.naacp.org/criminal-justice-fact-sheet, accessed 7 January 2020.

Nash, J. (2014) 'Institutionalizing the Margins', *Social Texts*, 32:1, 45–65.

Nash, J. (2019) *Black Feminism Reimagined after Intersectionality* (Durham, NC, and London: Duke University Press).

National Committee of the US Freedom Socialist Party (2013) 'Feminism and the Crisis in the British SWP'. https://socialism.com/statement/feminism-and-the-crisis-in-the-british-swp/, accessed 15 April 2020.

Neuman, S. (2020) 'Global lockdowns resulting in "horrifying surge" in domestic violence, U.N. warns', 6 April. *NPR*, www.npr.org/sections/coronavirus-live-updates/2020/04/06/827908402/global-lockdowns-resulting-in-horrifying-surge-in-domestic-violence-u-n-warns?t=1586164291784, accessed 20 April 2020.

Nguyen, M., R. Zavoretti and J. Tronto (2017) 'Beyond the Global Care Chain: Boundaries, Insitutions and Ethics of Care', *Ethics and Social Welfare*, 11:3, 199–212.

Nieuwenhuis, R. and L. Maldonado (eds) (2018) *Single Parents in a Gendered Triple Bind* (Bristol: Policy Press).

Nordic Council of Ministers (2015) *Nordic Gender Equality in Figures.* www.norden.org/en/publication/nordic-gender-equality-figures-2015, accessed 27 January 2020.

Nordic Council of Ministers (2018a) *Summary of 'Is the Last Mile the Longest? Economic Gains from Gender Equality in Nordic Countries'.* www.norden.org/en/publication/summary-brief-last-mile-longest, accessed 26 January 2020.

Nordic Council of Ministers (2018b) *The Nordic Gender Effect at Work.* www.norden.org/en/publication/nordic-gender-effect-work, accessed 27 January 2020.

Norman, J. (2020) '"Key workers" are the unrecognised backbone of our economy. They deserve more', HUFFPOST, 20 March. www.huffingtonpost.co.uk/entry/coronavirus-economy-women-care-key-workers_uk_5e74d095c5b6f5b7c542bc34, accessed 7 July 2020.

O'Brien, M. (1981) *The Politics of Reproduction* (London: Routledge and Kegan Paul).

Oakley, A. (1972/2016) *Sex, Gender and Society* (Abingdon: Routledge).

Office for National Statistics (2018a) *Sexual Offending: Victimisation and the Path through the Criminal Justice System.* www.ons.gov.uk/peoplepopulationandcommunity/

crimeandjustice/articles/sexualoffendingvictimisationandthepaththroughthecrimi naljusticesystem/2018–12–13, accessed 28 December 2019.

Office for National Statistics (2018b) *Domestic Abuse in England and Wales: Year Ending March 2018*. www.ons.gov.uk/releases/domesticabuseinenglandandwales yearendingmarch2018, accessed 28 December 2019.

Office for National Statistics (2019) *Gender Pay Gap in the UK*. www.ons.gov.uk/em ploymentandlabourmarket/peopleinwork/earningsandworkinghours/bulletins/ genderpaygapintheuk/2019, accessed 28 December 2019.

Okin, S. (1990) *Justice, Gender and the Family* (New York: Basic Books).

Okin, S. (2000) 'Feminism, Women's Human Rights, and Cultural Differences', in U. Narayan and S. Harding (eds), *Decentering the Centre* (Bloomington and Indianapolis: Indiana University Press).

Okolosie, L. (2018) 'Emma Watson's willingness to face the truth about racism is refreshing', *Guardian*, 10 January.

Olchawski, J. (2016) *Sex Equality. State of the Nation 2016* (London: Fawcett).

Olufemi, L. (2020) *Feminism, Interrupted. Disrupting Power* (London: Pluto Press).

Onwuachi-Willig, A. (2018) 'What about #Ustoo?: The Invisibility of Race in the #Metoo Movement', *Yale Law Journal Forum*, 128, 18 June. www.yalelawjournal. org/forum/what-about-ustoo, accessed 29 December 2019.

Oppenheim, M. (2020) 'Coronavirus: domestic abuse victims can leave home to access help during lockdown, Priti Patel says', *Independent*, 30 March.

PA Media (2020) '"There is such a thing as society" says Boris Johnson from bunker', *Observer*, 29 March.

Painter, N. (1997) *Sojourner Truth: A Life, a Symbol* (New York: W.W. Norton & Company).

Pankhurst, H. (2018) 'The #MeToo movement needs to become a truly global phe-nomenon', *Guardian*, 10 May.

Parveen, N. (2018) 'Karen White: how "manipulative" transgender inmate attacked again', *Guardian*, 11 October.

Patil, V. (2013) 'From Patriarchy to Intersectionality': A Transnational Feminist Assessment of How Far We've Really Come', *Signs*, 38:4, 847–67.

Pearson, R. (2019) 'A Feminist Analysis of Neoliberalism and Austerity Policies in the UK', *Soundings*, 71, 28–39.

Peck, E. (2019) 'Trump's Parental Leave Proposal Is Pure Hypocrisy', *HuffPost US*. www.huffingtonpost.co.uk/entry/trump-paid-parental-leave, accessed 29 January 2020.

Penny, L. (2014) *Unspeakable Things: Sex, Lies and Revolution* (London: Bloomsbury).

Perraudin, F. (2019) 'Labour adopts new sexual harassment policy', *Guardian*, 5 March.

Perry, R. (1986) *The Celebrated Mary Astell* (Chicago and London: University of Chicago Press).

Peterson, V.S. (2003) *A Critical Rewriting of Global Political Economy: Integrating Reproductive, Productive and Virtual Economies* (London and New York: Routledge).

Peterson, V.S. (2012) 'Inequalities, Informalization and Feminist Quandaries', *International Feminist Journal of Politics*, 14:1, 5–35.

Photiou, A. (2017) 'Dawn Butler takes aim at the gender pay gap', *The Voice*, 17 September. www.voice-online.co.uk, accessed 20 January 2020.

Piketty, T. (2014) *Capital in the Twenty-First Century*, translated by A. Goldhammer (Cambridge, Mass.: Harvard University Press).

Piven, F. and F. Block (2018) 'Ending Poverty as We Know It', in L. Featherstone (ed.), *False Choices: The Faux Feminism of Hillary Rodham Clinton* (London and Brooklyn: Verso).

Prügl, E. (2015) 'Neoliberalising Feminism', *New Political Economy*, 20:4, 614–31.

Rathbone, E. (1927) *The Disinherited Family: A Plea for Direct Provision for the Costs of Child Maintenance through Family Allowances* (London: Allen and Unwin).

Rawls, J. (1971) *A Theory of Justice* (Oxford: Oxford University Press).

Raymond, J. (1979/1994) *The Transsexual Empire: The Making of the She-Male* (New York: Teachers College Press).

Redfern, C. and K. Aune (2010) *Reclaiming the F Word: The New Feminist Movement* (London and New York: Zed Books).

Reed, T. (2019) 'The Gender Recognition Act Discussion', *Gender Identity Research and Education Society*. www.gires.org.uk/the-gender-recognition-act-discussion-july-2019, accessed 6 January 2020.

Reis, S. (2018) *The Impact of Austerity on Women in the UK*. Women's Budget Group, www.wbg.org.uk, accessed 7 January 2020.

Rich, A. (1977) *Of Woman Born: Motherhood as Experience and Institution* (London: Virago).

Rippon, G. (2019) *The Gendered Brain* (London: Penguin).

Roiphe, K. (2018) 'The Other Whisper Network: How Twitter Feminism Is Bad for Women', *Harper's Magazine*, March. https://harpers.org/archive/2018/03/the-other-whisper-network-2, accessed 29 December 2019.

Rottenberg, C. (2018) *The Rise of Neoliberal Feminism* (Oxford: Oxford University Press).

Rowbottom, M. (2019) 'IAAF rule transgender female athletes must further reduce testosterone levels', *inside the games*, 15 October. www.insidethegames.biz/arti cles/1085978/iaaf-transgender-testosterone-levels, accessed 6 January 2020.

Russell, S. (2018) 'Intersectionality: A Young Scholar Responds', *Science and Society*, 82:2, 287–91.

Rydgren, J. and S. van der Meiden (2019) 'The Radical Right and the End of Swedish Exceptionalism', *European Political Science*, 18, 439–55. https://doi.org/10.1057/s41304-018-0159-6.

Sager, M. and D. Mulinari, (2018) 'Safety for Whom? Exploring Feminationalism and Care-Racism in Sweden', *Women's Studies International Forum*, 68, 149–56.

Salem, S. (2018) 'Intersectionality and Its Discontents: Intersectionality as Travelling Theory', *European Journal of Women's Studies*, 25:4, 403–18.

Sanandaji, N. (2016) *The Nordic Gender Equality Paradox* (Stockholm: Timbro).

Sandberg, S. (2013) *Lean In: Women, Work and the Will to Lead* (New York: Random House).

Saner, E. (2017) 'Is the patriarchy over?', *Guardian*, 31 December.

Schilt, K. (2006) 'Just One of the Guys? How Transmen Make Gender Visible at Work', *Gender and Society*, 20:4, 465–90.

Schilt, K. (2011) *Just One of the Guys?: Transgender Men and the Persistence of Gender Inequality* (Chicago and London: University of Chicago Press).

Schraer, R. (2019) 'Modern slavery: what has Theresa May done to tackle it?', BBC Reality Check, 11 June.

Schultz, P. (2017) 'Universal basic income in a feminist perspective and gender analysis', *Global Social Policy*, 17:1, 89–92.

Segal, L. (1987) *Is the Future Female? Troubled Thoughts on Contemporary Feminism* (London: Virago).

Serano, J. (2007) *Whipping Girl: A Transsexual Woman on Sexism and the Scapegoating of Feminists* (Emeryville, Calif.: Seal Press).

Serano, J. (2013) *Excluded: Making Feminist and Queer Movements More Inclusive* (Berkeley: Seal Press).

Serano, J. (2017) 'Transgender agendas, social contagion, peer pressure, and prevalence', 27 November. *Medium*, https://medium.com/@juliaserano/transgender-agendas-social-contagion-peer-pressure-and-prevalence-c3694d11ed24, accessed 29 January 2020.

Shaffer, R. (1979) 'Women and the Communist Party U.S.A. 1930–1940', *Socialist Review*, 9:3, 73–118.

Shalmy, S. (2018) 'Solidarity forever', *Red Pepper*, Winter, 16–21.

Siddiqui, H. (2000) 'Black Women's Activism: Coming of Age?', *Feminist Review*, 64, 83–96.

Sisters Uncut (2018) *Feministo*. www.sistersuncut.org/feministo/, accessed 2 January 2020.

Skilbrei, M and C. Holmström, (2013) 'The "Nordic model" of prostitution law is a myth', 16 December. *The Conversation*, https://theconversation.com/the-nordic-model-of-prostitution-law-is-a-myth-21351, accessed 19 April 20.

Snyder, R.C. (2008) 'What Is Third-Wave Feminism? A New Directions Essay', *Signs*, 34:1, 175–96.

Sodha, S. (2017) 'Old and vulnerable people and financial whiz-kids don't mix', *Observer*, 17 December.

Solnit, R. (2014) *Men Explain Things to Me* (London: Granta Publications).

Solnit, R. (2017) *The Mother of All Questions* (London: Granta Publications).

Spelman, E. (1988) *Inessential Woman: Problems of Exclusion in Feminist Thought* (Boston: Beacon Press).

Spratt, V. (2016) 'How Sisters Uncut Are Changing The Way Politics Is Done'. *Grazia*, https://graziadaily.co.uk/life/real-life/sisters-uncut, accessed 2 January 2020.

Squires, J. (1999) *Gender in Political Theory* (Cambridge: Polity Press).

Squires, J. (2007) *The New Politics of Gender Equality* (Basingstoke: Palgrave Macmillan).

Steel, H. (2017) *My Statement on Events at London Anarchist Bookfair 2017*, 23 November. https://helensteel12.wordpress.com.

Stites. R. (1978) *The Women's Liberation Movement in Russia: Feminism, Nihilism and Bolshevism 1860–1930* (Princeton, NJ: Princeton University Press).

Stone, S. (1987/1992) 'The Empire Strikes Back. A Posttranssexual Manifesto', *Camera Obscura*, 10:2, 150–7. https://read.dukeupress.edu/camera-obscura/article-abstract/10/2%20(29)/150/31158/The-Empire-Strikes-Back-A-, accessed 9 July 2020.

Stonewall and nfpSynergy (2018) *Supporting Trans Women in Domestic and Sexual Violence Services. Interviews with Professionals in the Sector.* www.stonewall.org.uk/system/files/stonewall_and_nfpsynergy_report.pdf, accessed 6 January 2020.

Swinson, J. (2019) *Equal Power: Gender Equality and How to Achieve It* (London: Atlantic Books).

Teekah, A., M. Friedman, A. O'Reilly and J. Scholz (eds) (2015) *This Is What a Feminist Slut Looks Like: Perspectives on the SlutWalk Movement* (Bradford, Ont: Demeter Press).

Thatcher, M. (1954) Article in *Onward*, a Conservative Party publication, April. Reprinted in *Guardian*, 21 March 1990.

Thompson, W. (1824/1983) *Appeal of One Half of the Human Race, Women, Against the Pretensions of the Other Half, Men, to Retain Them in Political and Thence Civil and Domestic Slavery* (London: Virago).

Tobias, S. (1997) *Faces of Feminism. An Activist's Reflections on the Women's Movement* (Boulder, Colo.: Westview Press).

References

Toksvig, S. (2019) 'The idea of Boris Johnson as prime minister terrifies me – that's why I'm saying no to his sexist Brexit', *Independent*, 19 July.

Topping, A. (2013) 'UK urged to follow Nordic model of criminalising prostitution clients', *Guardian*, 11 December.

Topping, A. (2014) 'FGM unit set up to stop practice in UK', *Guardian*, 22 July.

Topping, A. (2018) 'Save the date, but party to mark end of gender pay gap not until 2235', *Guardian*, 10 November.

Tronto, J. (2017) 'There Is an Alternative: *Hominess curans* and the Limits of Neoliberalism', *International Journal of Care and Caring*, 1:1, 27–43.

Trotsky, L. (1924) *Problems of Life*, translated by Z. Venerora, with an introduction by N. Minsky (London: Methuen).

Trump, I. (2017) *Women Who Work* (New York: Portfolio).

TUC (2015) *Gender Pay Gap for UK's Top Earners Hits 55%, Says TUC*, Press release, 9 September. www.tuc.org.uk/news/gender-pay-gap-uk%E2%80%99s-top-earn ers-hits-55-says-tuc, accessed 28 December 2019.

TUC (2016) *Still Just a Bit of Banter?* (Research report). www.tuc.org.uk/research-analysis/reports/still-just-bit-banter, accessed 28 December 2019.

UN News (2018) 'Ending inequality means ending "global pandemic" of violence against women – UN chief', 19 November. news.un.org/en/story/2018/11/1026071, accessed 28 December 2019.

UN Population Fund (UNFPA) (2018) *Safe Birth, Even Here*. www.unfpa.org/safe birth#/en, accessed 28 December 2019.

UN Women (2017) *Women Migrant Workers and Remittances*, Policy Brief No. 3. www. unwomen.org/en/digital-library/publications/2017/7/women-migrant-workers-and-remittances, accessed 7 January 2020.

UN Women (2018) *Putting the Rights of Migrant Women at the Centre of the Global Compact for Migration*. 7 December. www.unwomen.org/en/news/stories/2018/12/news-migrant-women-at-the-centre-of-the-global-compact-for-migration, accessed 28 December 2019.

Varoufakis, Y. (2018) 'How I became an erratic Marxist', *Guardian*, 18 February.

Vogel, L. (1983) *Marxism and the Oppression of Women* (London: Pluto Press).

Vogel, L. (2018) 'Beyond Intersectionality', *Science and Society*, 82:2, 275–87.

Wainwright, H. (2015) 'Why I became a feminist socialist', *Jacobin*, 28 December.

Wakefield, H. (2019) *Triple Whammy: The Impact of Local Government Cuts on Women*, Women's Budget Group. www.wbg.org.uk, accessed 7 January 2020.

Walawalkar, A. (2019) 'Trans women inmates could spend weeks stuck in male prisons', *Human Rights News, Views and Info.*, 24 July. https://rightsinfo.org, accessed 6 January 2020.

Walby, S. (1990) *Theorizing Patriarchy* (Oxford: Basil Blackwell).

Walby, S. (1997) *Gender Transformations* (London: Routledge).

Walby, S. (2011) *The Future of Feminism* (Cambridge: Polity Press).

Walter, N. (1998) *The New Feminism* (London: Little, Brown and Company).

Wang, J. (2019) 'Oprah, Kylie Jenner and the Other Richest Self-Made Women in the World', *Forbes*, 8 March. www.forbes.com/sites/jenniferwang/2019/03/08/oprah-kylie-jenner-and-the-other-richest-self-made-women-in-the-world/#30dc3b4a2683, accessed 7 July 2020.

Waring, M. (1988) *If Women Counted* (New York: Harper and Row).

Watkins, S. (2018) 'Which Feminisms?', *New Left Review*, 109, 5–76.

Watson, E. (2018) *Interview with Reni Eddo-Lodge*. www.youtube.com/watch?v=Jk lR7jZT-zU, accessed 2 January 2020.

Weigland, K. (2001) *Red Feminism: American Communism and the Making of Women's Liberation* (Baltimore and London: The Johns Hopkins University Press).

Wemrell, M., S. Stjernlof, J. Aenishanslin, M. Lila, E. Gracia and A. Ivert (2019) 'Towards Understanding the Nordic Paradox: A Review of Qualitative Interview Studies on Intimate Partner Violence against Women (IPVAW) in Sweden', *Sociology Compass*, 13. Wiley Online Library, https://doi.org/10.1111/soc4.12759, accessed 27 January 2020.

Wiggen, M. (2017) 'Scandinavia: the radical right meets the mainstream', *The Conversation*, 4 August. http://theconversation.com, accessed 26 January, 2020.

Wignaraja, K. and B. Horvath, (2020) 'Universal basic income is the answer to the inequalities exposed by COVID-19', *World Economic Forum*, 17 April. www.weforum.org/agenda/2020/04/covid-19-universal-basic-income-social-inequality, accessed 19 April 2020.

Wild, A. (2019) 'The Cotton Ceiling'. www.objectnow.org/news/2019/3/29/get-the-l-out-the-cotton-ceiling, accessed 6 January 2020.

Wilkinson, R. and K. Pickett (2009) *The Spirit Level: Why More Equal Societies Almost Always Do Better* (New York: Bloomsbury Press).

Wilkinson, R. and K. Pickett (2018) *The Inner Level. How More Equal Societies Reduce Stress, Restore Sanity and Improve Everyone's Well-Being* (London: Penguin).

Williams, J. (2017) *Women versus Feminism: why We All Need Liberating from the Gender Wars* (Bingley: Emerald Publishing Limited).

Wilson, A. (1978/2018) *Finding a Voice. Asian Women in Britain* (Ottawa: Daraja Press).

Wolf, N. (1993) *Fire with Fire: The New Female Power and How It Will Change the 21st Century* (London: Chatto and Windus).

Wolf, N. (2017) 'The voices of Weinstein's accusers have torn the fabric of patriarchy', *Guardian*, 14 October.

Wolfe-Robinson, M. (2019) 'Calls for Boris Johnson to withdraw Geoffrey Boycott's knighthood', *Guardian*, 10 September.

Women and Equalities Select Committee (2016) *Sexual Harassment and Sexual Violence in Schools*. https://publications.parliament.uk/pa/cm201617/cmselect/cmwomeq/91/9105.htm#_idTextAnchor008, accessed 28 December 2019.

Women's Aid (2020) *The Domestic Abuse Report 2020: The Annual Audit* (Bristol: Women's Aid).

Women's Budget Group (2010) *The Impact on Women of the Coalition Spending Review 2010*. wbg.org.uk/budget-analysis/2010-budget-assessment, accessed 7 January 2020.

Women's Budget Group (2016) *A Cumulative Gender Impact Assessment of Ten Years of Austerity Policies 2010–20*, 31 March. wbg.org.uk/analysis/a-cumulative-gender-impact-assessment-of-ten-years-of-austerity-policies, accessed 28 December, 2019.

Women's Budget Group (2020a) *Covid-19: Gender and Other Equality Issues*, 19 March. wbg.org.uk/blog/briefing-covid-19-and-gender-issues, accessed 20 April 2020.

Women's Budget Group (2020b) 'It is women especially low-paid, BAME & migrant women putting their lives on the line to deliver vital care', 31 March. wbg.org.uk/blog/it-is-women-especially-low-paid-bame-migrant-women-putting-their-lives-on-the-line-to-deliver-vital-care, accessed 2 April 2020.

Women's Budget Group and Runnymede Trust (2017) *Intersecting Inequalities*. wbg.org.uk, accessed 2 January 2020.

World Bank (2018a) *Poverty and Shared Prosperity 2018*. www.worldbank.org/en/research/brief/poverty-and-shared-prosperity-2018-piecing-together-the-poverty-puzzle-frequently-asked-questions, accessed 8 January 2020.

World Bank (2018b) *Inequality and Shared Prosperity*. www.worldbank.org/en/topic/isp/overview, accessed 7 January 2020.

World Economic Forum (2019) *Global Gender Gap Report 2020*. www.weforum.org/reports/gender-gap-2020-report-100-years-pay-equality, accessed 28 December 2019.

World Health Organization (2017) *Violence against Women*. www.who.int/newsroom/fact-sheets/detail/violence-against-women, accessed 10 July 2018.

Wren, A. (2018) 'Intersectionality: what is it and why does it matter for employers?', Blog, 4 October. www.farrer.co.uk/news-and-insights/blogs/intersectionality-what-is-it-and-why-does-it-matter-for-employers, accessed 2 January 2020.

Yeandle, S., Y. Chou, M. Fine, M. Larkin and A. Milne (2017) 'Care And Caring:

Interdisciplinary Perspectives on a Societal Issue of Global Significance', *International Journal of Care and Caring*, 1:1, 3–25.

Yuval-Davis, N. (1998) 'Beyond Differences: Women, Power and Coalition Politics', in N. Charles and and H. Hintjens (eds), *Gender, Ethnicity and Political Ideologies* (London: Routledge).

Yuval-Davis, N. (2006) 'Intersectionality and Feminist Politics', *European Journal of Women's Studies*, 13:3, 193–209.

Zuboff, S. (2019) *The Age of Surveillance Capitalism* (London: Profile Books).

Index

Index

EU authorised representative for GPSR:
Easy Access System Europe, Mustamäe tee 50,
10621 Tallinn, Estonia
gpsr.requests@easproject.com

www.ingramcontent.com/pod-product-compliance
Lightning Source LLC
Chambersburg PA
CBHW020242290326
41929CB00045B/1487

9 781526 138514